Starting a Tech Business

Starting a Tech Business

A Practical Guide for Anyone Creating or Designing Applications or Software

Alex Cowan

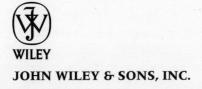

WILEY

JOHN WILEY & SONS, INC.

Published by John Wiley & Sons, Inc., Hoboken, New Jersey.
Published simultaneously in Canada.

For general information on our other products and services or for technical support, please contact our Customer Care Department within the United States at (800) 762-2974, outside the United States at (317) 572-3993 or fax (317) 572-4002.

Wiley publishes in a variety of print and electronic formats and by print-on-demand. Some material included with standard print versions of this book may not be included in e-books or in print-on-demand. If this book refers to media such as a CD or DVD that is not included in the version you purchased, you may download this material at http://booksupport.wiley.com. For more information about Wiley products, visit www.wiley.com.

Library of Congress Cataloging-in-Publication Data:
Cowan, Alex, 1975–
  Starting a tech business : a practical guide for anyone creating or designing applications or software / Alex Cowan.
    p. cm.
  Includes index.
   ISBN 978-1-118-20555-6 (pbk); ISBN 978-1-118-22853-1 (ebk); ISBN 978-1-118-24077-9 (ebk); ISBN 978-1-118-26568-0 (ebk)
   1. Computer software industry—Management. 2. Computer software—Development. 3. Business—Computer programs. 4. Computer industry—Management. 5. New business enterprises. I. Title.
  HD9696.63.A2S73 2012
  005.068'1—dc23
                                                                                                2011047545

Printed in the United States of America

10 9 8 7 6 5 4 3 2 1

To Sarah

Contents

Chapter 3

The Product: Pin the Butterfly of Incoherence   **63**

Chapter 4

The Architecture: Unravel the Python of Monolithic Architecture   **99**

Chapter 5
The Team: Dodge the Magpie of Discord

Chapter 6
Getting to Beta: Discipline the Chihuahua of Unruly Development

Chapter 7
Beta! Slaying the Hydra of Operational Readiness

Chapter 8

Acknowledgments

I'd like to thank my reviewers for their help in improving the book: James Brewer, Neil Brewster, Matt Chagan, JoAnn Christiansen, Bruce Cowan, Michael Elisofon, Howard Freidman, Lii Ling Khoo, Jessica Miller, Lee Miller, Madison Mount, Kathleen Hayes Onieal, David Rosenthal, and Nick Vermeer. I'd also like to thank the team at Wiley for their insight, hard work, and patience.

Finally, I'd like to thank everyone else who made the book possible. You know who you are.

Introduction

Abdulrahman Al-zanki, a 14-year-old Kuwaiti boy, is on his way to a million downloads of his iPhone application "Doodle Destroy." Abdulrahman used ready-made game-authoring software and sold his product through the iTunes store to a prequalified audience of millions. His first version took "about two weeks."[1] Though Abdulrahman is not your average 14-year-old, the point is that he didn't need access to vast development and distribution resources to achieve success in a tech business. The opportunities are real, and they are available to you now.

Who Should Read This? Why?

The fact that you've picked up this book means that you likely have an interest in starting a technology-enabled business, which may mean launching a new company or reengineering your existing company. The point is that you have an idea, you wonder whether you should pursue it, and, if you do, how you'll go about it.

This book's premise is the following:

1. Anyone can start a technology-enabled business.
2. Now is one of the best times in recent history to start a technology-enabled business.
3. Succeeding in technology-enabled businesses requires a certain amount and kind of preparation.

This book provides that preparation.

It's been obvious for years that technology is transforming existing businesses and creating new ones. Technology-enabled businesses offer one of the today's best available ways to create wealth, and the ability to apply technology is what separates an industry's winners from its losers. The exciting part is that while a decade ago the barriers to creating a technology-enabled business required a pole vault, they've now lowered to where a determined step in the right direction is enough to get started.

The key for a businessperson is to know what you want and be able to describe it. The technology required for your particular business may be as simple as an iPhone application or as complex as a web

---

[1] www.p0ach.com/2010/07/02/abdullah-interviews-abdulrahman-al-zanki-7amaniii/.

of interconnected subsystems. Regardless, successful execution follows a set of established patterns requiring the following:

- Rigorous but adaptive business planning
- Careful product formulation
- Well-articulated design
- Economic use of systems
- Adaptive management of technical resources
- Empathic deployment to customers

Starting a Tech Business provides these tools to any businessperson.

Building a technology system and delivering it to the customer is cheaper and easier than ever. While creating a technology system meant grinding out a massive (and expensive) code base in years past, nowadays it's more about assembling the right components and the most important component is simply a good idea. If you've read this far, you probably have that or know where to get it. Innovations in software delivery have simplified distribution for new technology. Platforms like the iPhone and Salesforce.com[2] provide ready access to qualified buyers while eliminating the complexity previously associated with installation of new software components. Where systems development was once the domain of dedicated techies and companies with deep pockets, it has become accessible to the well-prepared entrepreneur with a good idea.

Computer technology has completed a kind of arc over the past 50 years, returning to a place that makes it accessible to the untrained tinkerer. There were many novices in computing's early days; and though experts dealt with the specialized hardware, the lines between user and developer blurred. As a result, many individuals tinkered with these new machines. Over the next few decades, the computer business grew and deep subspecializations emerged. Specialization has been the norm up until recently; however, the underlying power of available computing resources has allowed software/systems developers to operate at increasingly higher levels of abstraction. This means that it's less important to

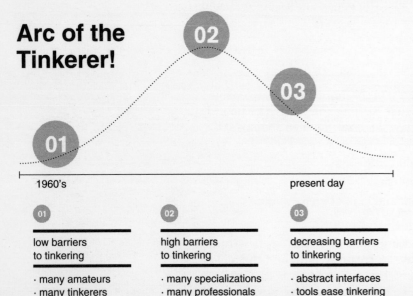

Arc of the Tinkerer!

1960's   present day

01
low barriers
to tinkering

· many amateurs
· many tinkerers

02
high barriers
to tinkering

· many specializations
· many professionals

03
decreasing barriers
to tinkering

· abstract interfaces
· tools ease tinkering

---

[2]Salesforce.com started out as an online (cloud) "customer relationship management" system and has morphed into a dominant platform for business applications in general.

understand the lower-level details of the system. Instead, the casual tinkerer can use fairly intuitive tools to prototype and build new technologies. The chapters that follow provide several examples of this.

Of course, this doesn't mean you *have* to tinker to be successful with your tech business; it's still common to leave the details to specialists. If there's one thing I hope this book helps you do, it's to start a successful technology business. But if it can help you do two things, I hope the second is to release your inner tinkerer. If you're intimidated, keep in mind that Steve Jobs did not have an engineering degree, and going back a bit further, neither did Eli Whitney, who revolutionized agriculture with his cotton gin.

If you have an idea for a technology-enabled business, you should read this book to prepare yourself and then you should go for it. Success is probably not nearly as distant or as difficult or as you think.

What Is a Technology System?

Technology systems have five primary layers: (1) hardware, (2) operating system, (3) application, (4) application add-in, and (5) cloud. Hardware is the equipment you can touch and hold: your laptop, your phone, or a server sitting in a data center somewhere. Operating systems are installed on top of hardware and provide a foundation to run applications. Operating systems you might use every day are Microsoft Windows on your laptop, Apple iOS on your iPhone, or the Linux operating system (popular on servers). Applications do something useful (or interesting) for the user: Microsoft Outlook on your laptop, Angry Birds (a game) on your iPhone, and Facebook on the web are all applications. On top of applications are application add-ins, which run on top of other applications. For example, I have a Norton Antivirus add-in running on top of Microsoft Outlook to protect against e-mail spam. Facebook created an entire industry around its application add-ins: The game "Farmville," for instance, allows groups of users to tend a farm together. The following table summarizes the first four layers for these examples.

Application Add-In's

Application

Operating System

Hardware

Cloud

Layer	MS Outlook	Angry Birds	Facebook
Application Add-In	Norton Antivirus	n/a	Farmville
Application	Outlook	Angry Birds	Facebook[3]
Operating System	MS Windows	iOS	Linux
Hardware	laptop	iPhone	industrial servers

[3] Facebook is actually a system of interrelated applications. For more information, see www.facebook.com/Engineering.

If you are in the high-technology industry, you've likely heard a lot about cloud computing and Software-as-a-Service (SaaS). In terms of the layers above, a cloud application is just an application in which a third party manages the hardware, OS, application, and (optionally) application add-in layers instead of you as a user installing and maintaining them yourself. Though cloud/SaaS applications have recently increased in significance, they're certainly not new. Hotmail (est. 1996) was an early cloud/SaaS application. So were the Yahoo! and Google search engines, as well as the mail services they later offered. If this is clear as day, skip to the next paragraph. If not, here's a more specific example: SugarCRM is an open-source customer relationship management (CRM) application, a tool businesses use to organize their sales and customer service operations. SugarCRM is available on both a cloud/SaaS and non-SaaS basis. If you buy the SaaS version, you go to sugarcrm.com, create an account, pay, and off you go. Pull up a web browser, direct it to sugarcrm.com, and you can log in from anywhere in the world. You can also use SugarCRM on a non-SaaS basis and install it on your own server(s). If you were to do this, you'd buy a server,[4] install the Linux operating system on it, download the install media for SugarCRM from sugarcrm.com, and run the install routine on your server. Then you point your browser to your server's Internet Protocol (IP) address or domain name and you can log into your own instance of SugarCRM.

The underlying question is this: What kind of a technology system makes sense for your particular business? To get to your idea to market as quickly and inexpensively as possible, you want to build as little original technology as possible. Companies that create hardware or operating systems require tremendous scale. Just a few large ones dominate the industry. If your business requires that you do so, you'll want to make sure you have a strong understanding of the costs and adequate financing. Even if you're planning to build an application, you should consider whether it wouldn't be better executed as an add-on to an existing application. For example, many entrepreneurs have succeeded by building add-on applications to platforms like Facebook and Salesforce.com,[5] an approach that requires less upfront investment. This is particularly true if your business's goal is to leverage a technology system to improve on an existing business, since you'll be spreading the cost of the technology across just one customer (yourself). An example of such an improvement would be allowing your customers to order and/or track orders online. Naturally, the fastest and least expensive means to a technology-enabled business is to build no new technology at all. Entrepreneurs and managers have created huge amounts of value for their companies by applying existing technology to a new business opportunity.

---

[4]Dell has a simple ordering system at www.dell.com if you're looking for a place to go.
[5]Salesforce.com is another CRM application.

Leveraging Industry Shifts

But why all these new rules about how to leverage technology? And why now? The short answer is this: Changes in the way users access software are driving changes in the way companies develop software. In the dawn of computing, a tremendously expensive computer the size of an auditorium could barely add two numbers. A small cohort of students and scientists had access to operate or develop software. In 1961, my father would wake up at 2 a.m. just to run simple arithmetic operations on his university's supercomputer. Two decades later, the personal computer (PC) was a big leap in terms of accessibility, yet most software was still written from scratch at great expense. This is why developing computer software has remained the domain of specialists until recently. Over the past few years, the cost of developing software has dropped by as much as an order of magnitude (10x): An application that would have cost $2 million to build a few years ago might cost $200,000 to build today. A critical part of these reduced costs are interrelated forces that make software easier to access and cheaper to develop.

One key driver is the availability of interchangeable software "parts." During the Industrial Revolution 1.0, the availability of interchangeable parts drove down the cost of manufacturing and led to increasing specialization and diversity. For example, whereas pre-Industrial Revolution rifle makers would go out and chop their own timber, mill their own stocks, cast their own barrels, and assemble the whole package, specialists in stocks, barrels, assembly, and so on, emerged over the course of the Industrial Revolution. Software is undergoing the same transition. The typical software development process today is much more about evaluating building blocks and assembling them than starting from a blank sheet of paper: We might even call it "Industrial Revolution 2.0." The great thing about this transformation for the businessperson is that it is changing the focus of successful technology-enabled ventures, making them more about having a great idea than being one of the few firms with the resources and money to build a piece of software. Industrial Revolution 2.0 means that you can view technology as a means to your end, now more than ever.

	Pre	Post
Industrial Revolution 1.0	custom goods built one by one	standard goods built from interchangeable parts
Industrial Revolution 2.0	monolithic software custom built from the ground up	purpose-built software created from best practice/off the shelf components

Another large industry shift is the evolution from an environment where most applications run locally on a user's PC to one where most applications run in the cloud with users accessing them through a browser or on a mobile device. For example, you can access spreadsheet applications that resemble Microsoft Excel online using Google Apps. Users spend hours per month using applications they download onto their mobile phones with a few simple clicks. What this means for the businesspeople is they no longer have to get a prospective customer to grab their application off a shelf, pay for it, and install it on their PC to have them try it. They can try it with just a few clicks while browsing online. This substantially lowers the barrier to entry and cost of customer acquisition for new applications.

The rest of this book will show you how to identify your ends and understand the means technology systems offer.

What Will I Get out of These Chapters?

Over the course of your venture, you'll need to confront eight trials that commonly snag entrepreneurs:

1. Crystallizing your idea
2. Defining your strategy
3. Designing your product
4. Defining your architecture
5. Assembling your team
6. Executing your development
7. Having a successful beta
8. Scaling the business

Since it helps to visualize these challenges along with their resolutions, I've created a series of adversaries as focal points for the eight trials.

We'll see how to succeed in these trials using the case of a fictional company called Enable Quiz,[6] which provides online skills assessment quizzes for engineers. The following subsections describe the book's chapters. All of these chapters will help you if you're a starting a technology-enabled venture. However, you might find some chapters more immediately relevant than others depending on your background.

---

[6]Enable Quiz is a real idea but a fictional entity. That said, I am not an expert in e-learning, and other than the Google statistics you'll find, the results of their work is hypothetical. The purpose of Enable Quiz as an example is to illustrate what a startup process might look like, rather than specifically testing the market for a new e-learning product.

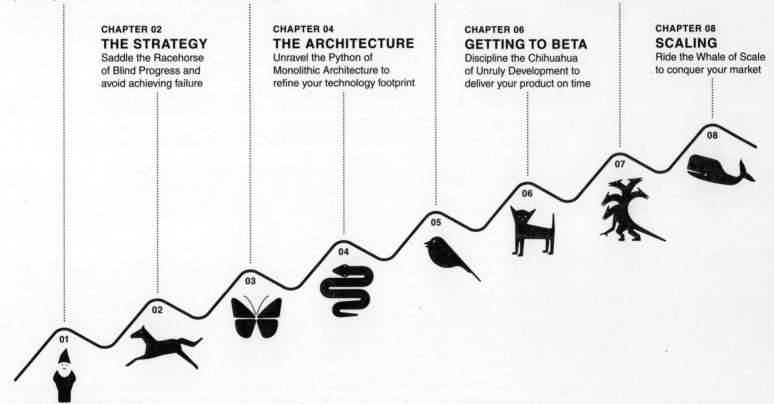

Chapter 1: The Idea

Confront the Lawn Gnome of Indolence to crystallize your idea

Even when you have an idea that's been percolating, making the decision to go after it isn't easy. You have your regular job, your family, your personal life. Doing nothing is easier. The Lawn Gnome of Indolence stands in the same place every day because he prefers to do nothing. Your first step is to confront the critical question of whether you want to look back in twenty years at an idea that likely could have been successful, knowing you did nothing.

To crystallize your idea, you'll need to get outside your comfort zone and take the leap of faith that you have an idea worth pursuing. It is unnecessary, however, to upend your whole life just on faith.

This chapter describes techniques to formulate and then quickly and effectively reality test a new product idea. We perform several reality tests on Enable Quiz, identifying assumptions that are critical to its success, and determining what it will take to support those assumptions with proven facts. We review platforms you can use in starting the business and start thinking about what to look for in early customers.

This chapter answers the following six questions:

1. How do you identify a good idea?
2. How do you reality test a good idea?
3. How do you define your idea's footprint?
4. What platforms are available for launching your tech business?
5. What are the pros and cons of moonlighters? How do you manage them?
6. What should you look for in an early beta customer?

Chapter 2: The Strategy

Saddle the Racehorse of Blind Progress and avoid achieving failure.

Next, you have to saddle the Racehorse of Blind Progress. The Racehorse of Blind Progress charges ahead in the face of evidence it's headed in the wrong direction. There's some equine in all of us, and there's something comforting about fixing on a goal and just charging towards it. But in a startup tech business, hard work and traditional business planning methods aren't enough. You're operating in an environment of uncertainty. You must lay out the business assumptions you need to test and methodically work toward validating them or (and this is the critical part) you must quickly change course if they're proving invalid.

This chapter lays out frameworks you can use to structure and reality test your strategy, including practical ways to organize and track your business planning.

This chapter answers the following seven questions:

1. What is a strategy?
2. How do you organize your marketing mix?
3. How do you reality test your company strategy?
4. How do catalysts drive change in high-tech, and how do you identify the ones that are relevant to your venture?
5. How can you use iterative management techniques to manage through uncertainty?
6. How do you understand and organize around your key profit drivers?
7. How do you bundle all this into a complete but useable plan?

Chapter 3: The Product

How do you describe an airplane to someone who's never seen one? Even a simple product has hundreds if not thousands of facets. The Butterfly of Incoherence flits from one thing to another, failing to provide a coherent product description to the implementation team. The good news is that a reliable formula exists for creating a good product design.  Pin the Butterfly of Incoherence to nail your product design

In this chapter, we review the key steps involved in creating a great product design, and explain what such a design should include. We also step through the Model-View-Controller (MVC) framework, which will provide you an important set of shared concepts you can use in working with your development team.

This chapter answers the following nine questions:

1. What are the best ways to contain product development costs?
2. What does it mean to be a designer?
3. Where does good design come from?
4. How can simple stories become the basis for a great design?
5. What is the MVC framework, and what do you need to know about it?
6. How do you organize the design of a Model?
7. How do you organize the design of a View?
8. How do you organize the design of a Controller?
9. How does the practice of good design dovetail with lean, iterative management?

Since this chapter offers more technical depth than the previous ones, don't be put off if you find yourself needing to reread sections of it. Also, don't hesitate to move on to the rest of the material since it's unnecessary to understand all of the chapter's details to grasp what follows.

Chapter 4: The Architecture

Unravel the Python of Monolithic Architecture to refine your technology footprint

Once you've designed your product, you need to figure out how to build it. The Python of Monolithic Architecture is a dangerous creature, strangling businesses with overly complex and expensive product implementations. More than ever, successful high-tech products are pack animals. They leverage complementary products to build their own company's product, rather than constructing the whole thing from scratch. If you build a social game as a stand-alone product on your own website and your competitor builds a similar game on Facebook, who do you think will win more users? The keys here are identifying how you can leverage the best of what your technology ecosystem has to offer, incorporating standard piece parts, and using your expertise to add value on top of them.

Working from the product design we created in the last chapter, we'll walk through a best practice architecture using the Enable Quiz example. Most web technologies you use (Facebook, Google) are a set of interconnected software applications forming a software system, rather than a single, discrete application. The trick to formulating a winning product architecture is to build as few of the necessary building blocks as possible. We'll define the requirements for Enable Quiz's major building blocks. Then, toward selecting the right pieces, we'll walk through criteria for evaluating off-the-shelf components. We'll also cover the pros and cons of open-source components.

Once you've defined your architecture, you're often left with a few options on technology tool sets. We'll review drivers for various technologies in terms of three key factors: fit with the customer environment, availability of compatible components and tools, and the availability of experienced developers. Then we'll walk through several of the most common software development technologies.

This chapter answers the following eight questions:

1. What is Industrial Revolution 2.0, and why does it matter?
2. How do you identify the functional blocks in your architecture?
3. What are the options for integrating those functional blocks?
4. How does all this apply to Enable Quiz, our example web application?

5. What criteria should you use in selecting piece parts for your architecture?
6. What is open source, and why isn't it a free lunch?
7. What's a programming language, and what are its pros and cons?
8. What are the pros and cons of the following:
    * Java
    * PHP
    * Ruby
    * .NET

Like Chapter 3 (the product chapter), Chapter 4 has a fair amount of detail. If your technology system is discrete, you may not need to understand all the detail in this chapter.

Chapter 5: The Team

Once we know what we want to build and how to build it, the most critical item is identifying and aligning the human resources we need. When your team is put together incorrectly, it's impossible to ignore constant squawking from the Magpie of Discord. You can avoid the Magpie of Discord by defining roles, including their skill sets and interdependencies, and building and managing your team accordingly.

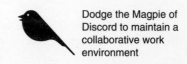

Dodge the Magpie of Discord to maintain a collaborative work environment

We'll discuss differences in background, perspective, and personality between engineers and business-people. We'll go through key job roles that Enable Quiz (and most any tech business) needs to fill. As preparation for interviewing potential new hires, we'll review different personality types common among engineers and how to identify them in an interviewee using selected interview questions. Instead of hiring individual employees or contractors, you may also be considering third-party firms to take on parts of the project. We'll cover an evaluation framework for third-party development firms. The chapter closes with an overview of the pros and cons of offshoring, and whether offshoring is the right thing for your company.

This chapter answers the following seven questions:

1. What are stereotypical disconnects between engineers and businesspeople? How can you avoid them?
2. What key roles and required skill sets are common to most tech businesses?
3. What are some of the most prevalent personality types among engineers, and how do they function in a team?
4. How do you evaluate new technical hires?

5. How do you evaluate third-party firms or contractors?
6. How do you motivate the technical team?
7. What are the pros and cons of offshoring? How do you determine if and when it's a good fit?

Chapter 6: Getting to Beta

Discipline the Chihuahua of Unruly Development to deliver your product on time

Now that we're ready to build our technology system, we have to confront the Chihuahua of Unruly Development. The Chihuahua runs to and fro, spends a few moments on whatever catches its eye, then moves on. The mythology of high-tech has a genius nerd staying up all night drinking Coca-Cola and the next morning launching a new website to wild acclaim and instant success. The reality of delivering high-tech systems is more like regular life: To succeed with any kind of reliability, you need realistic, methodical planning and discipline.

We'll review common software development methodologies, which runs a spectrum of "predictive" to "adaptive." Enable Quiz will be developing its system in adaptive, four-week "iterations," and we'll review the content of each iteration, including key dependencies and success factors. We'll also review successful approaches in critical areas like documentation, systems administration, and quality assurance.

This chapter answers the following seven questions:

1. What is agile development?
2. What is the difference between predictive and adaptive development methodologies?
3. How do you know which of these methodologies to apply, and how?
4. How do you know if it's working?
5. How do you organize your system development into discrete iterations?
6. What are the critical success factors for getting your system to beta?
7. What are the critical success factors to go from beta to release?

Chapter 7: Beta!

Slay the Hydra of Operational Readiness to get your product online

Beta is a controlled release of your product to a select set of customers. At this point, you confront an adversary that's done in more than one technology-enabled business: The Hydra of Operational Readiness. Slice off one head from the Hydra and two appear in its place. Without a formulaic approach to slaying the Hydra, your hard work is unlikely to deliver much in the way of results. With many high-tech businesses, running a strong operation is as important as having great technology. Strong operations start with processes that link the company's strategic objectives to employees' daily work.

We'll describe how to link your strategic objectives to processes you can apply across the organization. Only bad process design is incompatible with creativity, dynamism, and learning. Good process design will free your organization from lots of wasted time and frustration.

Once you get serious about support, it's important to classify customer complaints for better early warning on widespread issues. The chapter closes with guidelines on how to categorize and handle customer requests for new features and functionality.

This chapter answers the following four questions:

1. What is business process design, and how should you use it?
2. How do you define a process?
3. How do you create a process inventory?
4. How do you prepare for rapid response and learning during beta?

Chapter 8: Scaling the Business

Your final trial is riding the Whale of Scale to conquer your market. To date, your organization has been small and dynamic. Every customer win was a cause for celebration. Riding the Whale of Scale means determining what works and preparing to replicate it on a large scale. You'll need to master the currents of your market and point the company in a direction it can pursue without lots of rapid twists and turns.

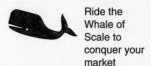

Ride the Whale of Scale to conquer your market

The first step here is understanding your customer "funnel" and finding ways to identify what's successful and replicate it. We'll look at how to dissect the key components of the funnel along the lines of a tried and true sales framework that's over 100 years old. We'll look at the role of partnerships, and how you can use them to scale the business. Your existing customer segments may not be what will propel you into the mainstream to achieve the "hockey stick" sales curve tech startups covet. We'll look at the technology adoption lifecycle and how to understand your customer acquisition in that context. Then, we'll look at how to evaluate customers' requests for product enhancements. We'll close with a few litmus tests you can use to assess how well you've positioned the company to scale.

This chapter answers the following nine questions:

1. How do you know if your launch is succeeding?
2. How do you make it succeed?

3. How do you identify worthwhile partnerships and make them successful?
4. Why is focus important, and what does that mean?
5. How will your customer profiles change as you move into the mainstream market, and what does that mean for your operation?
6. What is a "whole product," and how do you define yours?
7. How do you monitor customer input and issues?
8. What are post-mortems, and how do you use them effectively?
9. What are common pitfalls founders encounter as they scale the business?

Who Is the Author?

I've been starting and growing technology businesses for over 17 years. My first endeavor involved fixing broken computers in Santa Barbara, California, for a few dollars an hour. Even then, working as a computer mechanic, the need to couple what the technology could do with what people wanted stood out as a huge opportunity. Since then, I've worked with electrical engineers from Motorola and Sharp, software developers from Pixo[7] and Symantec, product designers from IDEO and Tommy Hilfiger, advertising giants from Wieden & Kennedy, and bankers from Goldman Sachs. Speaking Chinese, Japanese, and Spanish gave me the opportunity to work with customers, engineers, and managers on six continents. As a contemporary of many of the dot-com pioneers at Stanford University in the late 1990s (and later in Silicon Valley), I experienced the full force of the dot-com period, its aftermath, and later its commercial evolution. I started Leonid Systems, in 2007, to help communications service providers (phone companies and cable companies) launch and scale next-generation services, like voice and video over IP (VoIP). Leonid currently works with some of the world's largest service providers creating scalable technology systems to manage their operations.

I've always had one foot in the business world and the other in the technical world. Growing as a businessperson and an engineer gave me the perspective I've applied here, one that will help readers sort through the plethora of available technology to arrive at an effective implementation of their idea.

I've personally made every mistake this book cautions you to avoid. The good news is that they're all avoidable, and this book will help you avoid mistakes and implement most of today's high-tech best practices. In short, this is the book I wish someone had handed me when I started.

---

[7] Apple used the Pixo OS in the first iPods.

The Idea

Confront the Lawn Gnome of Indolence

1

Chapter

The biggest barrier to starting a tech business is taking your own ideas seriously. The Lawn Gnome of Indolence sits in the same place every day, which is opposite of what you need to do to launch your idea. In this chapter, we'll walk through techniques to create ideas, reality test them, and identify the key assumptions whose validation is most critical to your success.

Conception

It all starts with a simple need or desire. Facebook creator Mark Zuckerberg wanted a way to meet girls. Google co-founders Sergey Brin and Larry Page envisioned a better way to find things on the Internet. In the same way that the investment advisor Charles Schwab wisely advised us to invest in what we know—and years before that, our high school English teacher told us to write about what we know—your runaway success may be right under your nose. To conceive the next great technology-enabled business, you need to look for something you or your immediate friends and family want or would want but don't have.[1]

Although big successes like Facebook and Google are the ones we hear about, it's so easy to deliver high-tech products today that countless smaller successes exist. Though you'll never read about these in *Fortune* magazine,

---

[1]The corollary to this is "seek to know more." The most active entrepreneurs are voracious learners.

they have been a genuine success for their creators and their users. They can come in any size: They might be something you do within your current company, or they might be the reason for you to start a new company. The following scenarios illustrate a few possibilities:

- You're a trucker who wants an iPhone app that tells you how long you have until you reach the next qualified service station.
- You're a soccer parent whose spouse and kids are on Facebook, and you want a Facebook app to help organize household activities and shopping lists.
- You operate a chain of dry cleaning stores, and your customers have been asking if they could arrange pickup and check the status of their items online.
- Your company does dinner cruises on a set of boats you own. You'd like to improve your ability to take reservations and book company events online, as well as getting customers on an e-mail list.

Introducing Enable Quiz

Enable Quiz is a fictional company we'll use as a central example to apply the material that follows. Enable Quiz is another result of necessity spurring invention. Andrew, its soon-to-be-founder, is a program manager at an insurance company. As is the case with so many companies today, many of his key projects have to do with information technology (IT). He's constantly pitching for IT resources but getting less than what he needs. His company's IT director seems to spend a lot of time deciding whether a given employee or contractor is suitable for a job. Can the employee develop in the programming language PHP? Java? What about doing development on top of the company's customer relationship management (CRM) platform, Salesforce.com? Since Andrew's been in the insurance industry, which is essentially about measuring and pricing risk, he has wondered why there isn't a more straightforward means to measure IT engineers' ability in a given area.

As a result of his musings, Andrew conceives the idea for Enable Quiz, a service that allows managers to create and administer technical quizzes in specific areas of interest. For example, if a manager wanted to see how qualified a job candidate is to develop applications in the programming language Java on top of the Linux operating system, he or she could select ready-to-use questions from the Enable Quiz question bank and formulate a quiz that includes questions on Java and Linux. The manager could give candidates this quiz during their interview to assess their ability in Java and Linux.

Reality Testing

Why and How?

Though it's important to reality test your idea, I recommend against doing it too early. If you're thinking about your idea a lot, spend at least a week expanding on it. Make lists or keep a journal. Different things work for different people, but I recommend keeping some kind of written record since most people remember less than they think. If you think about your idea occasionally, wait longer. Reality testing it too soon increases the risk that you may find something that initially appears to be an obstacle but isn't one once you've articulated your idea more.

The first question in your reality test should be this: Is my idea out in the market to a degree that makes a new entry unattractive? However, being the first mover and building a "platform" was more important when the Internet was in its Wild West phase in the late 1990s/early 2000s. People adopted a kind of gold rush mentality then: They *had* to be the first to offer e-mail online, deliver dog food online, sell books online before someone else claimed the space. In fairness, many successful companies began this way. The Internet was a wide-open prairie, but now it's full of cities, suburbs, freeways, and rest stops. Developing high-tech products these days is a lot like the developing anything else: You don't have to be the only player in your category as long as you're serving a market that justifies the amount of your investment. An important corollary to this is that the required investment to execute for a high-tech endeavor has fallen dramatically.

Examples

Let's revisit one of the examples from our list in the previous section on conception: a Facebook application to organize household activities. A quick Google search on "household calendar online" shows us a significant player exists in the area called Cozi (http://www.cozi.com/), which has a stand-alone application (not a Facebook add-in). The website and press tie-ins look fairly credible. More searches and tech articles from reliable sources such as Tech Crunch and *Wall Street Journal*'s "All Things Digital" reveal that a company, Astrid (http://astrid.com/), offers a "social to-do list." So, we know we have a player in our product category that operates as a stand-alone application (vs. an add-in on Facebook) and a player that offers a technology product similar to one of our functions (shared to-do list). However, our search in the Facebook app store doesn't uncover a household calendaring and to-do list application.[2] Would such an application targeted at

---

[2]As of August 2011, at least.

households pull in enough users to justify the investment? Maybe, maybe not. The point is that you shouldn't abandon your idea because someone out there has done something similar. After all, if a plumber works in your town, is there room for another plumber? The answer depends on whether you live in a one-plumber town, a 1,000-plumber town, or something in between. Another crucial element of methodically considering the market has to do with geography and nationality. Think about creating a domestic clone for successful endeavors you encounter abroad. This isn't the kind of blue sky inventing that's popularized in the annals of high-tech history, but it's made many individuals wealthy. For example, the Samwer brothers, in Germany, have profited to the tune of tens of millions of dollars by launching domestic technology-enabled businesses that were inspired by existing successes in other countries.[3]

Early Reality Testing and Enable Quiz

Let's return to Enable Quiz. Andrew starts his reality testing by conducting an Internet search. Though he finds companies that allow users to create quizzes online and some that offer high-end technical exams, he doesn't come across one that focuses specifically on simple quizzes targeted for IT engineers. Based on his findings, Andrew feels he has enough of a niche to press forward. He talks to an engineer to see if anything else is out there he's unaware of: Is there a standard test or quiz engineers can take to certify their abilities? He gets the response he expects: Real engineers don't need a silly quiz to prove they know what they're doing. Well, fine, but managers do need such a quiz. He does a more systematic review of how companies solve the problem of evaluating technical talent for hire/contracting. He believes HR managers, software development managers, and operations managers whose business has a large technical component are all potential customers for Enable Quiz. The five key questions Andrew wants to answer are the following:

1. Does a significant population of potential buyers exist?
2. What are the "hot buttons" that would make them buy this product?
3. Are they reachable? How would they purchase such a service?
4. Would they purchase it from Enable Quiz?
5. How much would they pay for it?

Andrew makes the rounds with a few contacts and receives encouraging results. For example, he learns that managers with an engineering background still struggle to assess whether new hires are up on the latest

---

[3]"Attack of the Clones," *The Economist*, August 6, 2011.

technologies and systems. After two weeks of interviews, he has a set of eager beta customers.[4] Dreams of being a dot-com millionaire dance through his head.

Iterative Reality Testing

Iteration means repeating a process toward reaching some final goal. By contrast, classical management involves long-term planning, extrapolating forward to a set of results from a set of assumptions, and sticking to that plan come what may. Managing a startup requires an equal degree of rigor, but you have to apply it differently. Startups operate in an environment of flux and uncertainty. Lean management and adaptive (or agile) development are the most popular management frameworks in the startup domain, and they involve frequent but structured review of the business' key assumptions and plans.[5]

Iterative reality testing means testing your assumptions against reality, revising them, and retesting them. Think of your idea as a set of assumptions. Ask yourself whether these assumptions are supported by existing data and practice or if they require a bit of intuition and faith. If the latter is your answer, how can you remove that requirement? One way is to use the scientific method to prove your key assumptions, and this is a facet of leading theories on how to succeed in a startup.

You may remember from science class that this process begins with a hypothesis, an idea that you need to prove based on experimental results. So, let's say you have a hypothesis: Deer find pineapples irresistible. You might design an experiment where you place food accepted to be favored by deer (alfalfa) next to a set of pineapples then record how the deer approach each. If you repeat this across a few deer populations and the deer consistently eat the alfalfa and pass on the pineapple, you could reasonably consider at least a universal version of your hypothesis disproven. Proving or disproving assumptions in this fashion is the basic principle behind the scientific method. Practicing the method in a startup means designing quick and inexpensive experiments to confirm your critical assumptions. This practice will serve your venture much better than the most elaborate long-term planning.

---

[4]Beta is release of software planned for evaluation by outside parties, usually customers; following beta, companies take various steps culminating in general availability (GA) of the software.

[5]The idea of lean management was introduced by Jim Womack in his work on successful manufacturing techniques at Toyota, formalized in *Lean Management*. Adaptive or agile development reappeared in the mid-1990s and was substantially formalized in the *Manifesto for Agile Software Development* in 2001. More recently, the principles have been applied to startups in the Customer Development framework, pioneered in Steven Banks' *Four Steps to the Epiphany*, and recently expanded upon and married to agile development by Eric Ries in *The Lean Startup*.

Figure 1.1

**Scientific
Method**

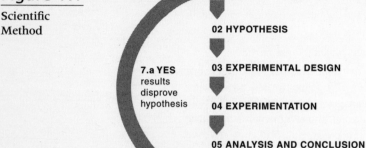

01 IDEA!

02 HYPOTHESIS

7.a YES
results
disprove
hypothesis

03 EXPERIMENTAL DESIGN

04 EXPERIMENTATION

05 ANALYSIS AND CONCLUSION

06 REVISE?

7.b NO
we appear to
have a valid
hypothesis

Figure 1.1 describes the process in more detail.

1. First, you have your idea.
2. Then you need to identify the key assumptions (hypotheses) you must prove to make your idea a successful business. (The next chapter will cover that in more detail.) Don't mistake an important hypothesis for one that needs to be proven. They are different. For example, your venture might assume working mothers use Facebook. Plenty of data can prove that fact, and most people will believe the statement.
3. Once you've stated the hypotheses, you need to design experiments to prove or disprove them. You don't need anything fancy. In fact, think of the simplest experiments possible. The minimum requirement is that the experimental result is a definitive yes/no or a/b/c type of result.
4. You must conduct your experiments as expediently as you can since the idea is to find out if you're barking up the right tree.
5. Ensure your analysis is clear and links clearly back to your hypothesis. The more vivid and understandable your results, the more definitive they'll be for you and the more convincing they'll be for your other audiences. You may find your experimental design didn't give you the results you need. Don't worry if this happens. Just trek back to step three (designing the experiments), revise, and proceed.
6. Honesty is the best policy during this step. If the experiment disproves your key assumptions about the idea, you may need to go back to the drawing board. Don't kick yourself though. Instead, congratulate yourself. You just saved a lot of time and money and have another shot at success.

Iterative Reality Testing and Enable Quiz

Let's take a look at Enable Quiz's key assumptions: whether they need proving and how we might design an experiment to do so. Enable Quiz will offer simple, cheap, ready-to-use technical quizzes to businesses that need structured assessments of technical talent. Table 1.1 summarizes the key assumptions they need to validate. They generally go from the general to the particular.

Note: Many assumptions are listed; feel free to skip the balance of the table if you feel you've got the idea.

#	Key Assumption	Needs Proving?	Experimentation
1	Businesses want structured assessments of technical talent.	The general form of the assumption is supported and does not need proving. In IP networking and systems administration, certifications are popular. They're less popular in software development, but that doesn't disprove the general form of the assumption.	not required
2	Businesses want structured assessments of technical talent via simple online quizzes.	Yes, this one needs proving. It's crucial because it's Enable Quiz's unique niche.	1. The quickest experiment would be to investigate the popularity of relevant Google search terms. We'll go through a few examples in the next section. 2. Another easy experiment would be to identify Google AdWords[6] and set up a placeholder site with a signup link. Measuring the portion of users who click through and who sign up for an e-mail notice will provide one good, empirical gauge of interest that's easy to explain. 3. Creating a prototype and sitting down to conduct demos with target customers would yield a smaller data sample but a much richer context. Prototyping tools like Google Sites (nontechnical) and Balsamiq (a little more involved) have simplified the process. This experiment should help Enable Quiz paint a picture of their subject and the customers' reaction to the product. Such a prototype would help Enable Quiz test the more specific cases below. Having a prototype is not a prerequisite to talking to a few customers. In general, you should feel free to start with that if it seems applicable.

(continued)

[6]These are advertisements available throughout Google, but most principally on pages with search results users receive from a Google search. The advertiser is able to buy ads against specific keyword searches, making AdWords a very powerful tool for reaching a target audience in a target context. AdWords is Google's main advertising product.

Table 1.1

Key Assumptions: Enable Quiz

Table 1.1

(continued)

#	Key Assumption	Needs Proving?	Experimentation
3	Businesses want structured assessments via a quiz of talent in IP networking.	Though this one is less questionable than some of the others below, it would benefit from validation. There is an established market for technical certifications in this area (most of them from Cisco). Is there a role for quizzes, perhaps for those that aren't certified? Does a quiz exist for those who are, whose managers want to check that they know about a specialty topic?	This is a variation on the item in #2. Enable Quiz would use more focused AdWords than in experiment one and two and perhaps more specific examples in their prototype.
4	Businesses want structured assessments of talent via a quiz in Unix or Linux system administration.	There are active certifications in this area, but they are less prevalent than those in IP networking. This will be an interesting middle case between disciplines where certifications are prevalent and those where they are not.	(see #3)
5	Businesses want structured assessments of talent via a quiz in Microsoft server system administration.	This variation is similar to the Unix and Linux items though certifications are more common in Microsoft community.	(see #3)
6	Businesses want structured assessments of talent via a quiz in website development.	Official certifications are almost entirely absent here as they are in most of the cases below. This is the first test case that involves a broadly applied technical skill without any professional certifications of note.	(see #3)
7	Businesses want structured assessments of talent via a quiz for Java, PHP, Ruby, or .NET programming.	This item is similar to the website topic above in that there are few official certifications. Ruby is a hot, new topic, and rates for Ruby developers have soared in the last couple of years. Ruby might be a good subtopic for an initial test.	(see #3)
8	Businesses want structured assessments of talent via a quiz in quality assurance testing.	(see above)	(see #3)

<u>Table 1.1</u>

(*continued*)

#	Key Assumption	Needs Proving?	Experimentation
9	Businesses want structured assessments of talent via a quiz in development management.	(see above)	(see #3)
10	Businesses would use a hosted system for testing and learning management.	This assumption is supported, since there are many SaaS offerings in the area of training and learning management.	not required
11	Businesses would want a lightweight system for administering technical quizzes to existing employees for learning and skills management.	This is a variation on #2, but the focal questions around existing employees vs. job candidates is material in how Enable Quiz sizes, segments, and approaches the market.	The sign-up/pre-launch webpage could present options specific to "learning management for your team" vs. "interview questions." Another option, more attractive if a substantial split appears, is to buy separate AdWords and put up separate sites for both propositions.
12	Businesses would want a lightweight system for administering technical quizzes to job candidates.	(see above)	(see above)
13	Companies that offer learning management systems would promote a company like Enable Quiz if the references went both ways.	Yes, this needs proving. Working with a larger partner in the Learning Management System (LMS) space could provide Enable Quiz with a ready-made source of sales leads and possibly financing and eventually exit.	Enable Quiz needs to approach this carefully because it could incite a competitor. But the competitive risk probably isn't as great as Enable Quiz may think. If the LMS firms don't show an interest in training, they're probably doing all they can to execute on their existing business.
14	The target customer will primarily learn about Enable Quiz online and buy directly from Enable Quiz through their online store.	This needs proving. Enable Quiz is somewhere between resegmenting the online learning market and creating a new market for lightweight online technical quizzes. A more hands-on approach may be required to introduce the product to its target buyer.	The best way to measure this will be the AdWords testing and the landing pages.

Always reach for the largest, lowest hanging fruit first when you're reality testing. Andrew's identified this priority list for his initial reality testing:

1. Search Terms
   Checking out the prevalence of existing search terms is quick and easy. We'll review a few caveats and tips on approach in the following subsection.
2. Customer Interviews
   There's nothing wrong with going out and talking to a few prospective customers. This will help Andrew figure out where to focus and what to expect.
3. AdWords Trials
   This involves buying AdWords and linking it to prototype landing pages on your site. Though it sounds like a lot of work, it isn't.
4. Prototype Demos
   This requires you return to those prospective customers and show them a basic prototype. Though this is likely to be the most time-consuming test, prototyping tools remove much of the grunt work and you'll probably learn a few things you can feed into your product design process.

While you're reality testing, keep in mind that if you are introducing a new product category, you shouldn't necessarily expect to find lots of existing searches for your new product. Along the same lines, avoid the common fallacy of asking customers if they want what you're developing and expect them to respond with an instant ''Eureka, I need that!'' The Walkman and Facebook are good examples of products where we didn't know how much we'd love them until we met them in person. The key is to think like an anthropologist, not a salesperson. You're there to learn about your target buyer, not instruct, judge, or sell.

Testing Search Terms at Enable Quiz

Every individual on Earth has direct access to Google's data on who's searching for what. I've found Google Insights to be the most effective tool: www.google.com/insights/search/. It's easy to get carried away with the data so I recommend structuring your questions first.

Our first key assumption for Enable Quiz was ''Businesses want structured assessments of technical talent via simple online quizzes.'' Andrew will start with the most direct test: Are users searching for such quizzes? Figure 1.2 shows Insights' results for the search phrase ''technical quiz online.''

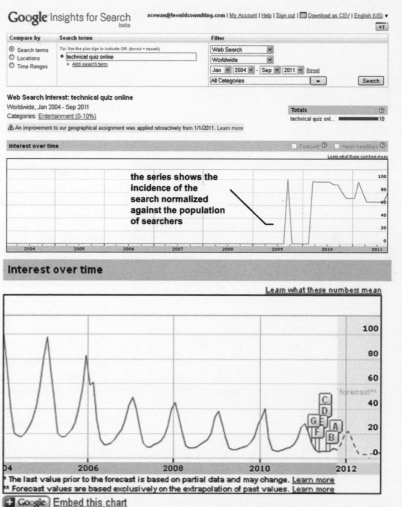

This data from Google Insights are scaled and normalized on a scale from 0 to 100 by the relative incidence of the search. In other words, every term will have a point on the time series that is 100, and every other point is scaled against that. Let's take a look at something more predictable, such as searches for the term "skiing" (Figure 1.3). What the graph tells us is that users search for skiing during the winter and to a decreasing degree over time, probably because they're doing more specific searches. Back to the previous data: What does the information tell Enable Quiz about searches for "technical quiz online"? First, it looks a little funky. What's with the wild peaks and valleys? It looks as if either some major events in the world of online quizzes occurred (unlikely) or that we're looking at a small sample size where a few searches wildly change the index (likely). These data don't describe absolute number of searches, but there are some clues.

Figure 1.4 shows additional data on searches by geography and related searches, and lo and behold, all the panes say "Not enough search volume to show results." In fact, I had to expand the search from "US-only" to "worldwide" to get any results at all. This tells us there isn't much activity for the search term.

Searches for similar terms look roughly the same. So what? What does this tell Enable Quiz about its key assumption, which was "Businesses want structured assessments of technical talent via simple online quizzes"? It shows that people aren't currently

Figure 1.2

Google Insights Search for "Technical Quiz Online"

Figure 1.3

Google Insights Search for "Skiing"

Figure 1.4

Supplementary
Information
for Google
Insights
Search on
"Technical
Quiz Online"

Figure 1.5

Windows
Admin

Figure 1.6

Network
Admin

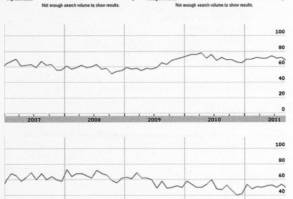

Figure 1.7

Sysadmin
(Linux, etc.)

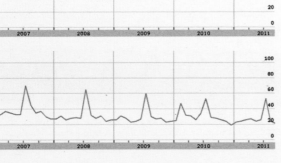

searching for online technical quizzes per se. Bad news? No, not really. In a way, it's good news. One of Enable Quiz's assumptions is that they will be a first mover in this niche, and this result is a reasonable (though not definitive) indication they will be.

We still want to see what we can learn about demand. Let's take a step back and think about the fundamental needs that Enable Quiz believes its product fills and see if Google Insights can prove interest exists. Enable Quiz targets two related use cases: technical assessments for job interviews and skills audits of existing employees. Enable Quiz has broken this down by technical subtopic: Linux, Windows, Java, QA, and so on. Do employers want to hire and employ people with the skill sets Enable Quiz has identified? Finding this out wouldn't entirely validate the key hypotheses, but it would show a strong fundamental basis for the assumption that prospective employers want a way to validate these technical skill sets. Figures 1.5 to 1.15 show search results from Insights for the job descriptions in the Enable Quiz assumptions in Table 1.1.[7] Take a look at these results. What do you think they say?

I think they tell us these job roles have a steady demand, and that's a good sign that Enable Quiz can assume there's solid hiring in these key areas. Most show a decrease then stabilization. No one likes to see lines going south. Why is that? In most cases, areas like system administration (sysadmin) and web developer have become more specialized over time, and more specialized sub-searches are probably taking up more share. The fact that for the most part the "Top searches" and "Rising searches" suggestions below the results show more specialized searches within the area further supports this.

[7] As of 10/2/11, searching in the United States only.

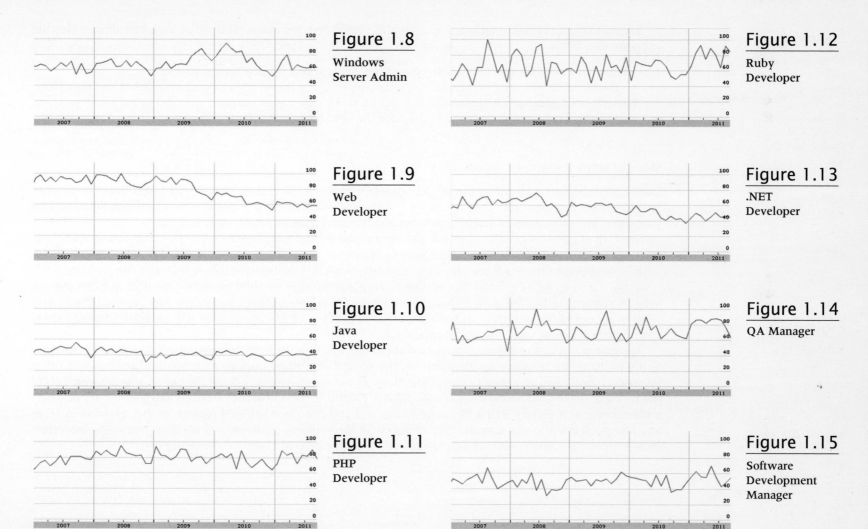

Figure 1.8
Windows
Server Admin

Figure 1.12
Ruby
Developer

Figure 1.9
Web
Developer

Figure 1.13
.NET
Developer

Figure 1.10
Java
Developer

Figure 1.14
QA Manager

Figure 1.11
PHP
Developer

Figure 1.15
Software
Development
Manager

I wouldn't call the following conclusions entirely validated, but they will serve as useful focal points for the exercises that follow.

1. Enable Quiz's buyers don't currently possess the concept of an online technical quiz.
   - Enable Quiz will need to create the category by reaching them through related searches and inquiries.
2. There is strong and steady demand in the technical skills they plan to target with the initial set of quizzes.
   - The related keywords are useful inputs for the next tests Enable Quiz will run.

Testing with Customer Interviews

Done right, customer interviews can be your quickest means to pivotal insights on the target buyer. Customer interviews are not sales calls, they're not statistical collection, and they're not simple questionnaires. Think of yourself as an anthropologist wanting to learn about these target buyers in their natural environment. There's no fixed list of questions that will get you the right answers. You won't get to every person involved with your product, so it's important to understand how to craft your proposition so that it will naturally resonate with your target buyers (or users if the project is internal). Don't sell, instruct, or judge; just try to understand.

Table 1.2 describes a general line of questioning and its various objectives. The areas of questioning are roughly sequential, but the most important preparation is taking an inventory of the fundamental things you want to get out of the interview and establishing a rapport with the subjects (you'll likely want to talk to them again), rather than being thorough or consistent.

If you don't have a prototype, you may want to visit again to see how that changes the customer's reaction. You'll probably have follow up questions on the second visit that you forgot or accumulated in your other interviews. Don't feel you need to repeat questions if you're consistently getting the exact same answer: You're not trying to make your data statistically significant. Finally, if you think your subjects will go for it, try bringing a video camera. A picture tells a thousand words and you can show selected footage to the rest of your team and investors. If you're not sure how it will play with the subjects, try it out and see if you think the interview feels different. It's also something you can introduce on the second visit if you're doing that.

Objective	Example Questions and Techniques
Understand the Buyer Like You Understand Your Best Friend This might seem superfluous and a little too touchy feely, but it isn't. You'll be surprised at how the most seemingly insignificant insights about your buyers help you design your product, describe them to your implementation team, and craft your message and promotion. Additionally, these questions and those in the next row will give you important context in considering the variation you get on your more specific questions around the product/market fit.	Always start the interview by being clear and open about who you are and what you're doing. However, avoid describing your product. It's fine to explain it in general terms as a solution in their area but emphasize you're in the learning phase. Don't be too coy—most people won't open up much if they feel you're being secretive or aloof. Ask the customers about their job. If you have a consumer product, ask them, "What's a typical day like?" You'll probably get a vague and general answer, which is not what you want. You want specifics. Most people perceive things to be the same even though they differ in important ways. Ask the subjects to describe what they did yesterday without being too nosy. Ask for more detail about things that come up that seem particularly interesting or relevant. Ask them about what's on their A-List, that is, what's top of mind lately. What problems would they most like to solve or like to do better?
Understand the Buyer's Operating Environment This might be companies or households. You want to understand what they do, how, why, and how they feel about it.	Find out about people and systems that the subject interacts with and to what end. Why? Which do they find difficult vs. easy? Pleasant vs. unpleasant?
Understand the Buyer's Learning Environment Find out where they go to find out about new things in your general area. You need to understand what kind of promotion is going to reach the target buyer and be credible.	This might be publications, websites, friends, colleagues, professional networks, or trade shows.
Understand the Buyer's Perception of the Problem or Need You're Addressing Do the buyers think this problem exists? How important is it to them, and what terms do they use to describe it? This will serve as an important reality test of your product idea, its price, and its promotion.	You've probably talked about the general area in which your proposed problem exists. For Enable Quiz, it would be the hiring process and skills management for existing technical staff. Ask the customers in as general terms as possible about the problem area. How much prompting do they need to know what you're talking about? How do they describe it? Do they think it's important? Who else has this problem: colleagues inside the company, peers elsewhere?

Table 1.2

Customer Interview Questions

(continued)

Table 1.2

(continued)

Objective	Example Questions and Techniques
Understand How the Buyer Is Solving the Problem Today How are your customers solving the problem today? Their current solution is effectively your competition. You want to understand how satisfied they are with their current solution and how much it costs. Pricing is essentially about measuring value. This means your price is proportional to the value of the problem you're solving, net of any additional costs for your buyers to deploy it and the premium they place on trying out something new. See the Pricing section under the Four Ps in Chapter 2 for more detail.	If this is a business setting, you should be cautious and considerate about asking the subjects to talk about their company's "inside baseball." That said, gleaning this information is important. Investigate a bit, but allow the customer to pull back if they don't want to talk about specific figures. They may not know or have not framed the issue in the terms you have. If that's the case, get as many data points as you can about how much the problem is worth. Don't take it as a bad sign if you find that the customers have something they've developed themselves internally, because this may actually be a good sign. It shows your assumption that a problem does exist is correct. If the product is internally developed, that means it's highly likely another buyer in the segment hasn't done anything or has done something different. Basically, you're looking at a nascent opportunity, which is perfect. Additionally, you may be able to solve the problem much better with something you develop that is standard and thought through end to end by experts, leveraging the industry or user segment's needs and best practices.
Present Your Solution You want to be careful here: You're not selling. You're describing in an attempt to see how the customers react to the proposition without your prompting. Do they squint quizzically or react with delight and desire?	Describe the solution in general terms. If that doesn't work, articulate it more specifically. Keep in mind that the more you have to explain, the more you'll have to do to educate the market. If you think they understand but don't seem to care, don't push them. You have your answer: This reality test doesn't pass. The worst thing that can happen is that the buyer tells you your idea is great when they don't think it is. Their reluctance to hurt your feelings will only result in creation of a product that's not truly viable. If you get this kind of reaction consistently, it's time to step back and see if you need to vary your approach or go back to the drawing board. Hey, it's better than spending time and money on something that's not going to take with the buyers.

Enable Quiz and Customer Interviews

Andrew arranges interviews for Enable Quiz through friends, professional contacts, and some folks he got online who signed up with the landing page testing. His target subjects are the Human Resources (HR) and functional managers responsible for technical staff. His understanding of the buyers and their operating environment improves greatly. His questions about process relate to the hiring of technical talent and how the company invests in its technical talent to improve it organically. He asks how things are going in the area and what they'd like to do better, about the cost of a bad hire and how much the company thinks it could increase output from existing staff with more skills development. He asks about the résumé screening process and interview process, and about how the company proactively encourages technical skills development. Finally, he explains Enable Quiz in three sentences for ten seconds. If the customer doesn't get the concept or has more questions, he shows them a few paper mockups. Andrew learns 15 actionable things:

1. Functional Managers Want Better Screening from HR

    Functional managers would love better screening of the "junk" résumés they feel HR sends them. Most acknowledge that recruiting consistently gets pushed downward by their daily jobs, even though it should be at the top of their list. Getting more qualified résumés would reduce the time they have to spend on reviewing them and, most importantly, on conducting interviews.

    Andrew knows that HR not functional managers would be doing the buying in most cases, but this suggests that Enable Quiz may need to promote to functional managers and get them to ask HR for the service. It tells Andrew that one good promotional message is "cut the number of interviews you do by half while increasing the quality of candidates" or something along those lines.

2. HR Managers Would Like to Do Better Screening

    Several of the HR managers independently mentioned that they would like help screening technical resumes. They find it difficult to sort out all the specific jargon to find the signals of a promising vs. nonpromising candidate. That said, this pain isn't as big as that of the functional managers.

    This tells Andrew he's going to have a responsive audience in the HR manager, though the economic buyer looks like it will usually be the functional manager.

3. Larger Companies Have a Training Department

    Larger firms, roughly 100 employees or greater, often have a training department. Andrew talked to a few people in the role. They were interested, but tended to want bigger solutions, like complete learning management solutions.

    Enable Quiz can learn from these managers, but it still looks like the HR manager and functional manager are the target buyer for the kind of casual quizzing Enable Quiz offers.

4. HR Managers and Trainers Read Certain Publications

    These buyers read a small set of publications.

    While buying space in the print section of these magazines is likely outside of Enable Quiz's budget, it may be possible to do some advertising on their websites and guest editorial if Andrew can craft something interesting, possibly a case study written with a customer.

5. Functional Managers Read a Variety of Publications

    The various functional managers read a variety of publications, depending on their industry and specialty.

    The variety is too big to do worthwhile promotion, at least directly. So, Andrew must find another way to grab these individuals' attention.

6. You Can Buy Ads on Monster.com

    Two of the HR managers mentioned that it's possible to buy advertising on Monster.com and similar sites. It may be possible to buy targeted ads as well.

    This is a promising possibility for promotion, depending on the price and ability to target by types of technical jobs. However, Andrew sees two drawbacks here: The functional managers are the real demand driver, and in all but small companies, the HR managers are the ones on Monster.com, and so on. They usually download and send selected résumés to the functional managers.

7. HR Would Like to Improve Technical Hiring

    HR knows that making good technical hires is crucial to the company's success. Succeeding in this area is one of the most important parts of HR's job.

    This is promising in that messaging around improving technical recruitment will resonate with the HR managers, who are much easier to target as a segment than the functional managers. One promotion technique Andrew will test is whether the message can be promoted in a way that will prompt the HR managers to put it in front of the functional managers.

8. All Managers Recognize the Financial and Emotional Cost of a Bad Hire

    This is the single largest pain point: It costs money and takes a huge emotional toll on the employee, hiring manager, and HR manager, and the functional managers admit they end up with bad hires all the time. It takes three to five months for the whole thing to wind down at an average cost of 10,000USD/month. There's the opportunity cost of not having fully qualified staff in the position for this period, as well as the time it takes to replace them and train someone else (another three to six months). If the hire is just ordinary and the hiring manager was hoping for more, all parties end up in a crummy, unproductive working environment.

Andrew is sure this is the key message for their promotion activities: "What is the cost of a bad hire? We can help." This finding is good fodder for a white paper, possibly in the form of a blog post on the Enable Quiz site.

9. Measuring Offshore Talent Is Hard

Many of the firms Andrew interviewed use some amount of offshore resources. Issues like language barriers and cultural differences make it difficult to evaluate these hires. Additionally, there are other subtle cues hiring managers would normally use in the United States that they cannot apply in these new operating environments.

This is a potentially interesting sub-segment for Enable Quiz to pursue. Andrew will make it a priority to include a few such companies in the beta to observe usage and relevance.

10. Functional Managers Feel Testing New Recruits Would Raise Morale

The functional managers know that morale among engineers grows when they feel they're working with a highly qualified team. Engineers want to work for "smart" companies. This is one of the many negative side effects of a bad hire: a weak link on the team lowers morale throughout.

The hiring managers themselves like the idea of having their technical talent vetted and validated through something like this quiz. They'd then like to create "level 1, level 2, etc." exams to keep raising the bar.

11. Some Functional Managers Quiz but Not Many

A few of the functional managers have their own ad hoc quizzing they do. That said, these managers were the most receptive to an off-the-shelf solution.

This helps validate some of the key product/market fit assumptions.

12. Skills Management Is Usually Ad Hoc

Few of the companies had a systematic approach to skills management and wish they did. They pay for employees to undertake whatever professional education and certification they like, but managers don't drive this in any systematic way.

Andrew recognizes that part of their promotion strategy needs to involve educating the market on the idea of systematic skills management. White papers will help drive traffic to the site, and Andrew needs to find partners to provide a recommended "whole product" around the follow-up training since Enable Quiz just handles diagnosis.

13. The Solution Makes Sense, but Not by Name

In general, HR and hiring managers reacted positively and intuitively to the solution. However, no one had a standard lexicon that really fit. The term "technical quiz" made sense to the subjects once Andrew had explained it, but not on first glance.

Andrew will need to find oblique terms to get at the idea of technical quizzing while building up and establishing ownership over the category.

14. The Whole Product Is Small

None of the managers identified anything in particular that they'd need to do to start using the solution. They were comfortable with SaaS solutions and felt they could take it out of the box and start using it.

While establishing a learning management ecosystem would help promote the use of Enable Quiz for skills management, customers should be able to be onboard and start using the solution for basic applications quickly. Having partners that offer follow-up training for skills assessments will be nice, but it doesn't look like a barrier to purchase and implementation.

15. The Spend Can Come Out of Operational versus Capital Dollars

Managers claimed that it was easier for them to get approval to spend operational dollars vs. capital dollars. The Enable Quiz solution would come out of operational dollars since it's not a purchase of hardware or licenses.

This makes the buying process simple since Enable Quiz's price point is below what most managers are allowed to spend without any or much approval.

Based on learning about the customer, Andrew sketched out the following "with vs. without" diagram for Enable Quiz (see Figures 1.16 and 1.17).

This diagram will serve as fodder for the website, presentations, and white papers.

The e-learning industry has a number of trade shows, and Andrew attends a few of these to look for competition, partners, and customers. He finds a number of potential partners and though there's functional overlap with what Enable Quiz does, there are no competitors with the same specific focus.

X: The job description goes to HR with few or no measureable criteria.

the hiring manager passes the job description to HR

X: Many candidates that should have been screened out reach the hiring manager.

screened candidates go to hiring manager

X: Without measureable criteria, the risk of a bad hire is needlessly high. Unraveling a bad hire is the absolute worst thing that can happen to a manager and an employee.

if a bad hire, hiring manager works with HR to unravel

Hiring Manager

The hiring manager writes up a job description.

HR Manager

The HR manager interprets job description, posts, and screens candidates

Hiring Manager

For valid candidates, the hiring manager conducts interviews (30–60 minutes/each). A candidate is hired.

X: The hiring manager invests hours of time interviewing candidates who turn out not to be qualified.

HR Manager

HR manager deals with unpleasant (for everyone) process of figuring out what to do with the hire and re-starting the process.

X: How does the team avoid making the same mistake again without measureable criteria?

Figure 1.16   Hiring Process Before Enable Quiz

✔ **The job description goes to HR with measureable criteria.**

the hiring manager passes the job description to HR with specific quizzes and minimum scores

✔ **All candidates that go to the hiring manager have at least the basic required technical skill sets.**

screened candidates go to hiring manager

✔ **With measureable criteria, the risk of a bad hire is greatly reduced.**

if a bad hire, hiring manager works with HR to unravel

Hiring Manager

The hiring manager writes up a job description.

HR Manager

The HR manager interprets job description, posts, and screens candidates with quizzes

Hiring Manager

For valid candidates, the hiring manager conducts interviews (30–60 minutes/each). A candidate is hired.

✔ **The hiring manager only interviews candidates with the basic technical qualifications.**

HR Manager

HR manager deals with unpleasant (for everyone) process of figuring out what to do with the hire and re-starting the process.

✔ **If a mistake happens, the team has specific criteria to help look at where the process went wrong.**

Figure 1.17 Hiring Process After Enable Quiz

Testing with an AdWord Trial

This step involves testing key AdWords with a set of landing pages, including a call to sign up for promotions and updates. What you're doing here is matching the landing page with the hook you posted in the AdWords. One thing you *do not* want to do is use a variety of AdWords and direct everyone to the same generic home page. Guiding each method of outreach and each topic to a unique landing page will improve your conversion rates and make your website analytics (progress "funnels") simpler to analyze. The difference between a landing page and a home page is that you use a landing page to orient users who are arriving at your site from a specific message. The generic form of such a landing page looks something like Figure 1.18.

Figure 1.18

Landing Page

You want to present the user with a refined, simple message on the landing page. A popular way to gauge the effectiveness of your message is to conduct the five-second test. Present a prototype page to people in your general target for five seconds, take the page away, and ask them to describe the page. Did they get it? If not, revise.

The second element in the landing page is an area to subscribe to updates (a newsletter, etc.). This usually includes a hook and a related call to action to see if the users are interested to get more involved and buy something. The call to action has to be compelling. For example, let's say that you got the users to come to your site from an ad, and the site is not up and operational. You'll probably need to show something more persuasive than just asking them to "Sign up here to find out when we're really operational." For example, you might limit the offer to three months free to people who sign up, or you might limit the offer to the first 500. The final element is a link to the home page (if you have one) for users that want to learn more about your company.

If you're thin on site design and implementation resources, the number one thing to remember is to keep things simple. Stay away from items where it's easy to go off track: use of colors, complex graphics, multiple site elements. A number of website prototyping tools as well as a few sample landing pages from Enable Quiz are available at Alexandercowan.com/landingpages.

AdWords Testing at Enable Quiz

Enable Quiz runs a series of AdWords, most of them around specific technical topics. If they run an ad about testing your Ruby developers, they don't want to direct these users to a general page on technical quizzes. It's all right to have the users check out the site at large, but if they come to the page wondering about quizzing developers on Ruby, tell them about that and see if they respond to the "call to action" (CTA). The CTA, in their case, is to sign up for a free beta trial. Enable Quiz created a template landing page and from there formulated AdWord-specific landing pages for each specific proposition. Though a moonlighter completes the actual pages, Andrew brings out his inner tinkerer and roughs out a few ideas to help prepare.

Enable Quiz sees particularly strong conversions on the Windows, Ruby, network, and PHP-related AdWords. The strength of the response on network and Windows AdWords was a bit of a surprise, suggesting more focus there than Andrew had originally planned.

Testing with a Prototype

After you've gathered the information you need from the previous steps, you may want to create a mock prototype to show to your target buyers. This is an easy way to get a genuine reaction, especially if your category is somewhat new to your target buyers. We talk more about product design in the next chapter, but the general idea behind your prototype is to think through the basic story of how you see your target buyer using the product.

A number of great prototyping tools are out there, Balsamiq (balsamiq.com) being one of the most effective and approachable in my experience. That said, no tool is inherently better than another. If you're working with partners who have an environment they want to use for the prototyping, that's fine. It's ultimately about what medium makes high-quality output easiest.

Prototyping at Enable Quiz

Andrew creates a Balsamiq prototype and follows up with his interview subjects. In cases where he had already described the product, he was surprised by some of the questions. He thought they understood the product when he described it in the last meeting. Clearly, the mockup is effective in making Enable Quiz's intent clear. Andrew doesn't encounter any major revelations. Most of the questions cover areas he'd considered for himself conceptually, like how the customers can add their own questions to supplement the precanned "banks" of questions Enable Quiz offers. You can download the Balsamiq prototype at Alexandercowan.com/prototype.

A final note on reality testing: Even if you're using your results internally, if you think you may *ever* present to investors, maintain all your findings in good order. They are likely to be highly compelling to investors or any outside party who you want to convince about the validity of your product and model.

Footprint

Step Lightly

Once you've completed basic reality testing on your idea and before you dive into its design (which we do in Chapter 3), it's time to consider your application's footprint. This is the niche that you'll occupy in the larger ecosystem of your customers and partners. You want to avoid the Python of Monolithic Architecture. Most high-tech successes these days are pack animals that leverage complementary technology systems. Here are a few questions you should be able to answer about your footprint:

- What are all the product functions and services my customer needs to solve the target problem or need? (This is often referred to as the whole product or extended product.)
- Which ones are consistent with my company's competitive advantage and focus?
- Where will the rest come from? Are they generally in place at the customer or not?
- How will we work with partners to deliver the additional products and services required to make our solution work for the customer?

Footprint at Enable Quiz

Andrew is clearly not operating in a vacuum in the case of Enable Quiz. Their target customers do a number of things under the general rubric of managing technical skill sets. They hire third parties to come in and do training. There are industry-standard training and certification programs in key disciplines like IP networking and Linux administration. Some use an elaborate LMS for tracking employee skills and training. A few functional managers use free sites like Survey Monkey or write their own simple applications to quiz their staff.

Andrew wants Enable Quiz to solve the problem of easily screening new technical hires and doing simple skills audits with existing staff. Andrew believes Enable Quiz's particular niche is in a stand-alone system that administers simple quizzes in relevant technical topics. It's easy to use right out of the box and requires little setup.

Andrew knows that Enable Quiz should have reports that allow an administrator to see what quizzes students have taken and how they scored. How elaborate should this reporting be? For example, an entire category of products called LMS's help companies assess and manage their employees' skill sets. It's a big space where people are spending lots of money. Should Andrew build an LMS into Enable Quiz? The upside to this is that he would have a more complete product and potentially more revenue. The disadvantage is that he'd turn the existing players who are focused on LMS from potential partners to competitors. Therefore, Andrew should almost certainly avoid an LMS, particularly in the 1.0 version. First, he's going to have to work hard to get the resources he needs to execute the current footprint of Enable Quiz. Second, several large LMS companies are in the market and establishing a strategic partnership with one of them could be pivotal to Enable Quiz's success. For example, once Andrew gets the 1.0 version of Enable Quiz off the ground, he can approach the leading LMS companies and find out how they might be willing to help Enable Quiz if Andrew were to integrate Enable Quiz with their LMS product.

Platforms

You have five primary platforms to get your idea off the ground, and they're not mutually exclusive. You may well start with one and transition to another as you get rolling.

1. Do It in Your Existing Company

    If your goal is to upgrade your current company's IT infrastructure, this is the obvious and only option. Even if it isn't, it's an option you should consider. As a manager, I run across at least one article every week about "fostering innovation inside your organization." Companies are increasingly recognizing that recruiting, retaining, and putting innovators in an environment where they can perform is critical to their long-term success. If you're an employee, building your technology-enabled business inside your existing company may not provide the upside of going it alone; however, it will reduce your risk and probably your time to market substantially. And you'll be appropriately rewarded if your company values innovators. If not, you'll have the experience under your belt. Additionally, if you at least offer to build your new technology-enabled business inside your existing company, you're likely to remain on better terms with your management if you do go it alone. Finally, have a look at the employment agreement you signed when you started the job and make sure it allows you to do what you have planned. Otherwise, it may put you at risk for trouble later. If in doubt, consult an attorney.

If you're a manager, your job is to put your employees in a position to innovate on your behalf and the first step is to buy them all a copy of this book.[8] For example, Google is a coveted place to work for engineers. When I ask people why they're so eager to work at Google, they almost all mention the fact that Google has a "20 percent program" where employees are allowed to spend 20 percent of their time on special projects unrelated to their standard workload. Likewise, many top MBA programs work with their university's engineering schools to run classes where business and engineer students work together to conceive, design, and execute a technology-enabled business. What's to stop you from doing the same within your organization?

2. MacGyver/Garage Style

    This is the classical startup story: An engineer in his or her garage creates the next great technology franchise. This is an option if you have an engineering background or are willing to acquire the necessary skills. The key consideration here is how much of your time this will take and how it measures up against your other options. Anyone who's written a piece of software knows that it almost never takes as little time as you originally estimated. That said, getting a prototype online will go a long way with potential investors or partners.

3. Bootstrap

    If you're not an engineer or don't want to invest the time to build the technology yourself, bootstrapping is another option. The general notion here is that you're going to use a relatively small amount of your own money, possibly supplemented by money from your family and friends, to start the venture. The considerations here are similar to Garage Style: You need to be conservative in your estimation of how much time it will take you to reach your key milestones, which are raising money from an outside source or achieving profitability.

4. Bootstrap with Consulting

    An additional variation on bootstrapping is to start your business with a heavy mix of consulting vs. product sales. This allows you to bring in revenue in a more reliable, short-term fashion while taking on much less risk. It allows you to get your feet wet in the marketplace. Be careful how you license your intellectual property in these arrangements, or you may encounter difficulty later when you try to productize the fruits of your labor. This option is increasingly popular as Industrial Revolution 2.0 makes solutions more about leveraging existing technology components (which requires consulting) rather than building lots of brand new software.

---

[8]Kidding! . . . kind of.

5. Raise Capital

This is a fairly common next step from the second and third options above. Entire books have been written on the process of raising capital, so we cover just a few key points here. First, don't limit yourself to traditional high-tech venture capitalists. Though you're apt to see elite high-tech venture capital firms like Kleiner Perkins Caufield & Byers behind lots of successful technology firms, these investors are looking for a team with an established history and an idea with gigantic upside (and capital requirements). Though you may have a great idea, it might not be a fit for this type of investor.

Other avenues to consider are strategic investors, who might be customers or suppliers, and wealthy individuals. One of the LMS companies we reviewed above would be a good candidate for Enable Quiz. Frequently, wealthy individuals with a background in the entrepreneurial area of endeavor are behind the early investing at technology-enabled businesses and are referred to as angel investors. Geography-independent websites like www.raisecapital.com seek to provide an open market for raising capital, but these are in their infancy. Venture investors tend to invest in local companies they can visit in person and in industries they know. Finally, even if you have solid inroads with an institutional venture capitalist, the institutional conservatism of the finance industry, coupled with the legal paperwork required, means this is almost never a quick process. Raising venture capital in three months, for example, is considered lightning fast, particularly for a first-time entrepreneur.

Engaging Moonlighters

When the Moon Hits Your Eyes

When you're in the early stages of launching your technology-enabled business and don't have the resources to go whole hog, working with moonlighters is a popular way to go. We'll define moonlighters as people who are working on your project outside their primary job. They might have a day job and work for you at night (hence the term) or they might be an internal resource at your company who have been assigned to help you get your project off the ground but still have other primary responsibilities.

Taking this approach has several virtues: It costs less than a dedicated full-time resource, and both parties get to see how things go before they commit fully. Of course, it has downsides. If you're the primary force behind the business, remember that you're probably third on the moonlighter's list: Their main job is first, their social life/family is second, and your project follows (the first and second may well be flipped, but the point is that your project is almost always third). If their dog needs to go to the vet, that time is almost certainly coming out of the time they'd set aside for your project.

If you're hiring a moonlighter (engineer) on contract, you can expect to pay between $50–$120/hour in the United States. Shorter projects with more specialized expertise and seniority will run on the higher end of the scale. If you manage to find someone offshore (in Eastern Europe or India, for example), you'll likely pay $20–$50/hour with the same drivers on the range. One approach, which is great if you can do it, is to pay the moonlighters in whole or in part with equity. If you do this, do not make the mistake of vaguely promising them a piece of the action. You'll likely end up with a mismatched set of expectations on both your parts at just the wrong time. Even though it's hard to do for an early-stage company, you'll need to establish a value for your venture and for the moonlighters' services and then agree on how the moonlighter's interest in the company accrues.

A final note on moonlighters: You may start out with one contractor that's quick, easy, and inexpensive and fill out your team later. Don't be too surprised if a lot of the product needs to be rewritten. Though there's a tendency among engineers to want to build everything from scratch, early code that's written for demos usually includes lots of unpredictable changes at the last minute, often ends up squirrelly, and needs to be redone.

Moonlighters and Enable Quiz

Let's say Andrew has identified a contractor, Rajeev, who's interested in working on the project. Andrew's interested in proposing that Rajeev be compensated in sweat equity, at least in part. He has estimated that a prototype will take 320 hours to build. Andrew knows that Rajeev's usual rate is $80/hour, but he'll probably have to pay him more since it's a small project and Andrew's proposing he be paid in equity. After looking at public companies and startup valuations, Andrew has established that Enable Quiz is worth $1,000,000. Based on all this, he formulates the table shown in Figure 1.19.

Rajeev would receive a 3.2 percent stake in the company for doing the prototype. Good deal? It depends on Rajeev's perspective. Unless he is highly invested in the project and wants to become a full-time employee once things get off the ground, he'll almost definitely want at least part of his compensation in cash. But, hey, if Andrew is bootstrapping, it's certainly worth a try. Regardless of how Rajeev is compensated, Andrew knows Enable Quiz will be third on Rajeev's list.

Weeks of Labor	320	a
Rate/hour	100	b
Dev. Spend	**$32,000**	c = a * b
Valuation	1,000,000	d
Equity Stake for Rajeev	3.20%	e = c / d

Figure 1.19

Valuation and Equity Stake for Contractor

note: the "*" symbol means multiplication, like the

The other aspect of the contract with Rajeev is timeliness: Andrew will work out a specific schedule with Rajeev that includes weekly milestones. This is a good exercise in general since it pushes the developers to think through the project in a step-by-step fashion if they haven't already. The question for these kinds of arrangements is "What happens if you're late?" called the "remedy" in legal parlance. If this happens for a big project, a contract developer might agree to discounts. However, that's unlikely because even then customers frequently change their requirements. At the time of this writing, there is an abundance of software development projects and a shortage of good engineers. The best you'll probably do with the schedule is to establish a set of expectations. If the engineers are systematically late because they're unable (time-wise or skills-wise) to work on your project, the best you can do is pay them for their work to date and part ways.

Beta Customers

We've reviewed options on financing the venture. Every financier will tell you that the best money you can acquire as a new venture is a customer's money. You may hear stories from the late 1990s and early 2000s in which a large company gave a startup a million dollars to solve a big problem for it. Though that kind of situation is rare now, many customers commonly commission a small company to build a piece of software on a custom basis. In those situations, the company (seller) sometimes arranges in its contract to provide the software on a royalty-free, nonexclusive basis. Basically, this means that once you provide the software to your buyers, they can do with it whatever they want and so can you.

On the surface, the customer may have a reaction such as "We're paying for this. Why should you own it?" The answer has a couple of facets. First, if you've won this business as a small company and it's strategic to your growth, you probably have some specialty expertise. This expertise in the customers' industry allows you to build better software at a much lower cost than a generalist the customer would hire off the street. Second, your retaining ownership means that you may take what you've done and create a product out of it. Your creating a product out of your custom software delivery almost always accrues to your customer's benefit. If you deliver them a one-off piece of software, they will have to pay you for every change and bug fix (after any warranty period). However, if you decide to make a product out of it, they can elect for a support and maintenance contract. This contract will provide your customers with ongoing bug fixes and improvements for 10 to 20 percent of the purchase price, much less than they would have to pay someone on a one-off basis to implement fixes and enhancements (not to mention documentation and other ancillary benefits of having an actual product).

Finally, consider offering a discount if you're close to such a deal but not there with the customer: "Hey, we'll give you 20 percent off plus the possibility of incremental support and maintenance if you allow us to retain the rights.'' Alternatively, and this is probably a better option if you expect a lot of hand holding, offer to throw in more consulting hours rather than discounting the deliverable.

In any case, having a successful beta is your pivot point into a successful launch to the market at large. The following are four characteristics of ideal beta candidates:

1. Aligned with Your Product Direction

   You may find exciting beta customers (willing to pay, friendly) who aren't aligned with your direction for the product. They're trying to fit a square peg into a round hole. Is this a deal killer? Not necessarily, no. It's good to be pragmatic in the early stages of your venture (and often there's no choice). You'll need to balance the money and intellectual property you receive from the deal against its cost to you and the degree of intangible distraction from your core mission.

2. Willingness to Pay

   If your product is for businesses, good beta customers will pay. Aside from the obvious benefit of the cash, a willingness to pay shows the customers are serious. You might think companies will be grateful and work to return the favor if you give them something for free. They may, and your particular customer contact is likely to feel a sense of obligation. But when it comes down to a difficult decision on priorities, which product do you think your prospective customers are going to take to make sure they implement properly: your free stuff or something for which management paid a lot of money?

3. Friendliness

   What I mean here is that customers have a genuine interest in being friends of your company. Friends make a commitment to each other based on a set of shared values, interests, and general affinity. Don't discount this aspect of your relationship with beta customers, and remember that the higher up in their organization the friendship goes, the more significant (economically) it will be.

4. High Regard

   One crucial aspect of your beta relationships is that they're referenceable. If the beta is successful, you should have a specific arrangement in place to use the customers as a reference (by way of a press release, quote on your website, case study, and so on). Your ideal beta customers are well-regarded thought leaders in their industry, something that will greatly enhance their value as a reference.

Your obligation to your beta customers is to deliver what they expect, on time. In the next few chapters, we review how to further refine your strategy, design your product, and deliver it in a timely fashion.

Once you have an idea and a basic understanding of how to go implement it, you need to figure out your company's strategy. In the next chapter, we work on company strategy.

Chapter 1 Summary

1. Find Your Pony

   The most powerful ideas come from direct personal experience with a problem or desire. That said, it's a good idea to do some reality testing with other potential users to ensure you're on to something. For target users who get the idea, it should be like a kid who's been told they're getting a pony.

2. Reality Test

   Think of your idea as an experiment. Presuppose whatever you want, but identify the key assumptions that need to be true for you to succeed. Then design experiments to validate your assumptions, moving from the quickest, most valuable experiments to those that take more time and investment.

3. Survey the Landscape, Stake Your Claim

   A good software concept needs careful assessment as to what it does and doesn't do. While determining the scope of your product, make sure you know how it fits in with your user's related business processes or activities. Also, consider potential partners and how what you're doing fits in with their business. They may become important as sales channels or investors.

4. Consider Your Platform

   There isn't just one way to launch a tech business. In addition to the possibility of starting the business in your garage and later raising venture capital, don't discount the possibility of launching the business inside your existing company or supporting the venture with relevant consulting to fund your development.

5. Beware Moonlighters

   Moonlighters may be your only option, but remember that you won't be #1 on their priority list and it may swing your timelines. Also, don't play fast and loose with equity—if you want to pay the moonlighter in equity, agree on specific parameters in advance.

6. Groom Your Beta Customers

   Getting beta customers is great, but you want to make sure they're aligned with your direction, willing to pay (if applicable), and will serve as a good relationship and reference if you're successful.

Checklist

At the end of each chapter, we'll review a checklist. Naturally, you don't need to be able to answer each of these questions to read on, but having thought through these will help you move on to the next chapter.

Can you answer each of the following five questions for your technology-enabled business?

1. What is my product and why does my buyer (user) want it?
2. User Profile: Do you have a detailed, empathic description of your buyers/users? Write as much as you can about your audiences and how you foresee them using your product. Who are they? Where does your product fit into their job? What's important to them? What training/perspective will they have when they sit down to use it? Samples for these items are available on Alexandercowan.com/busplan.
3. What are the key assumptions I need to prove so I know this product is commercially viable? How will I prove it quickly and cheaply?
4. What does my product do versus not do? What are the adjacent products and systems and how does my product fit in with those? How do I need to work with those partners to deliver a comprehensive solution to my target customer?
5. How do I plan to launch this technology-enabled business? Is it a project within my existing company? Will I be building it myself, bootstrapping it, and so forth?
6. If you're using moonlighters, do you have a structured set of deal parameters and expectations?
7. Who are some potential beta customers? Who are the *best* potential beta customers?

You'll find Enable Quiz's work on ideation and reality testing on Alexandercowan.com/realitytest.

Specialty Reading by Topic

This section appears at the end of every chapter and offers further reading if you want more depth on any of the topics mentioned in the chapter. You do not need to read these books to go ahead with your venture, let alone proceed to the next chapter. However, they provide more detail on some of the topics that we might only discuss briefly within the chapters themselves.

If you want to know more about …	… then read
Iterative Customer Development	*The Four Steps to the Epiphany*, by Steven Gary Blank
	This seminal work details the process of characterizing your customer and your market and systematically progressing to a successful outcome.
Adaptive Product Development and Management for Startups	*The Lean Startup*, by Eric Ries
	Eric Ries is a successful entrepreneur and frequent speaker. In this book, he marries lean management techniques and agile methods to excellent guidance for any company operating against uncertainty.
Leveraging the Internet with Low-Tech Business Models	*Get Rich Click*, by Marc Ostrofsky
	Marc Ostrofsky describes himself as an "Internet wildcatter" and has a long history of identifying opportunities online to make money with low-tech approaches.
Website Tools	Alexandercowan.com/sitetools

The Strategy

Saddle the Racehorse of Blind Progress

2

Chapter

Once you have your product idea, you need a sharp strategy organized around a set of key assumptions and criteria for measuring your progress against those assumptions. Plan ahead for the ability to change course if your assumptions prove wrong, and keep in mind that many successful ventures have changed course over their lifetime. It's tempting to throw yourself into the work and hope your hard work pays off. Unfortunately, you have to work hard *and* smart. In this chapter, we'll walk through a set of strategy formulation frameworks and metrics that will help you determine periodically if you need to press ahead or change course.

What Strategy?

You can think about a technology-enabled company as having three components: a product, a system that supports the product, and a business model by which the product produces earnings for the business (Figure 2.1). The product is the experience you provide to the customer. The system is the infrastructure that supports the product. The business model is the way you produce earnings with the product.

The relationship between these may be one to one (one product, one system, one business model), or you may have multiples of one or more of the components. For example, you could have a single product and system that you sell in multiple ways to derive earnings (multiple business models). The system may be the centerpiece of your company and product,

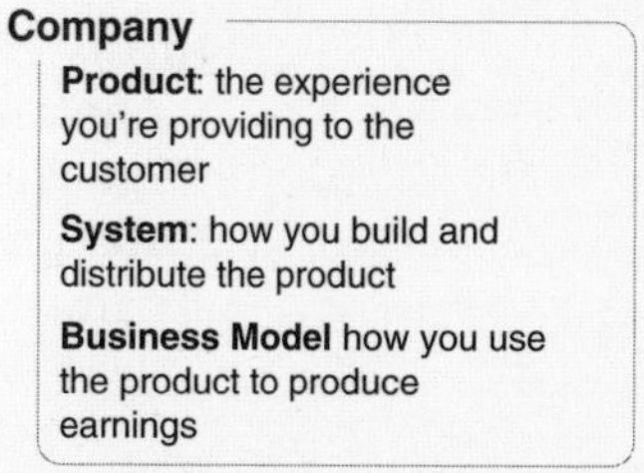

Company
  Product: the experience you're providing to the customer
  System: how you build and distribute the product
  Business Model how you use the product to produce earnings

Figure 2.1

Product—
System—
Business
Model

or it may be an enabler that makes your company more competitive. One currently relevant example is the revenue models for mobile applications on smart phones like the iPhone or the various phones that support Google's Android operating system. You can often download a free version of the application that shows ads and/or has limited functionality and then choose to upgrade to a paid version (this is called the "freemium" model, in case you want to talk the talk). Other applications are available only on an ad-supported basis, others are available for purchase at a standard price. These choices have nothing to do with the product itself: They're choices the respective companies made on business model.

The reason I mention all this is that you may need to decompose these components as you're testing and refining your approach. You may want to divide and conquer if you're working in a team. Next, we'll review two established frameworks that will help you organize your approach: the "Four Ps," which is primarily applicable to your product and business model, and Porter's Five Forces, which is primarily applicable to company strategy.

Squaring the Four Ps

The Four Ps, known by many in the world of marketing, are product, place, price, promotion.[1] While there are many similar frameworks, the Four Ps have been in use for over 50 years and provide a simple, relatively complete checklist for evaluating the business model you apply to your product. The Four Ps come into play in somewhat different ways across enterprise and consumer products. Let's take a minute to explore that distinction.

Most high-tech products break down into one of the following three categories:

1. Infrastructure
2. Enterprise
3. Consumer

> **Infrastructure** means the product is sold to support another product that the end user touches. Examples of infrastructure products are routers, servers, data storage, and software that optimizes any of those to make them more efficient. We won't spend much time here discussing the infrastructure category.
>
> **Enterprise** means that the product is sold to businesses. Examples of products in this category are customer relationship management (CRM) systems, accounting systems, and software that allows employees to collaborate in the workplace. Enable Quiz is an enterprise product since it's sold to businesses.

[1] See http://en.wikipedia.org/wiki/Marketing_mix for an overview.

Consumer means that the product is sold to individuals, and generally used in a personal capacity. Examples of consumer products include games, the iPod, and media services like Hulu. Though some products span both categories, most fall into one of these buckets and when they don't, their companies usually have different approaches to the Four Ps for the different segments.

Product

I defined the term *product* above as the experience you provide to the customer. Though that might sound a little abstract, many high-tech Products aren't things you can touch and hold. In the most reduced terms, the Product is whatever you're selling to your buyer. You may have two tiers of buyers, and it's common to neglect one or the other depending on your perspective. For example, any advertising-driven Product on the web (Google, Facebook, Hulu) has advertisers as the immediate buyer and users as the secondary/indirect buyer.

Mastering an enterprise Product versus a consumer Product takes a somewhat different skill set. To qualify an enterprise Product's potential success, you need to identify how it fits in with and improves your customer's existing business processes. For example, enterprise software is a huge category that broadly includes all the different types of software that companies use to operate. The titans of enterprise software know everything about how companies run and how to leverage technology toward those operations. These experts frequently have backgrounds in operational consulting for businesses, where they help businesses optimize their processes to increase efficiency.

Then we have the other side of the coin: the consumer. Something like an iPhone application is usually in the consumer domain, and assessing Product fit is more intuitive. You need to have an instinctive grasp of whether the Product is interesting and useful, almost as you would when assessing a movie or a TV show. I wouldn't have guessed an iPhone application that mimics fart sounds would see over 10,000 purchases a day on the iTunes store. But there's a guy out there who is part of the fart-sound-making demographic and he grasped the idea and acted on it. For a while, he was netting over $10,000 a day. If you have an intuitive grasp of the buyer, consumer Products can be a goldmine.

Place

The second P is Place, also known as access or distribution. The distribution of high-tech products, particularly software and media, has undergone a lot of changes in the past five years. Online marketplaces and the use of Internet-based software are the primary drivers. Online stores, like iTunes, create a Place for applications that are pre-integrated to a particular platform, like the iPhone. Users access Internet-based applications, like Salesforce.com, exclusively in an online Place. This is a long way from the days of popping a CD into your computer and seeing what happens. Place also includes how you'll contract with and bill your customer, which is also simplified by online stores and online subscription in general.

Price

The third P is Price, the question how much you can charge, and for what. It's fairly clinical with enterprise since you're working to assess how much the problem you're solving is worth to the buyers. You should be able to collect data on how much they're spending on the problem or process that your product improves or solves and be able to demonstrate that you're saving them money, enabling them to make more money, or, ideally, both.

The Price of your "whole product" (license, subscription, installation, training, and anything else additional the buyers have to do/buy to use your product) will be equal to how much the problem/need is worth to the buyers today, net of whatever premium they ascribe to taking a chance on your product and going through the trouble of doing something new. Consider the following product elements:

y = your product pricing
x = how much the problem/need is worth to the buyer today
w = the additional cost of the "whole product" beyond what you're selling
p = the premium the buyer ascribes to trying something new

In this context your Price would be the following:

$$y = x - w - p$$

If you have direct competitors or substitutes, it will be easier to obtain data on value since you can just compare Prices. If you have a consumer product without direct competitors, you'll usually be looking for comparable products as well as Price points.

Promotion

Finally, we have Promotion: How is your customer going to find out your product exists and decide to buy it? Marketing and advertising have changed over the last decade as buyers increasingly move online to acquire information and buy. Nevertheless, the most important factor in developing profitable Promotion will never change: You need to put yourself in your customer's shoes for an entire day. What do they do? What do they see? What do they stop and pay attention to? In what frame of mind are they at those times? A recent advent in most Promotions is the role of social networks (like Facebook) in pushing organic word of mouth Promotion. Buying ad media on social media sites like LinkedIn and Facebook can be economical if you have a highly targeted audience. These sites allow you to hone in on buyers within industries of interest with the job functions, such as HR manager, for example, who you think will be your target buyers. The most powerful use of social media, however, is for organic Promotion. We'll review a few examples of organic Promotion in the case of Enable Quiz.

Figure 2.2 summarizes a few key points around the Four Ps.

PRODUCT (Solution)	How do you stack up against competitors? Substitutes?
	Enterprise - How do you fit in to the customer's existing business processes?
	Consumer - More intangible, except for areas like household finances: Would you buy it? Would your friends? How would you use it?
PRICE (Value)	Price of substitutes?
	Enterprise - How valuable is the problem?
	Consumer - What would you pay?
PLACE (Access/Distribution)	How will you identify customers? How will they access/download your software? If they have to install, what's required? Upgrades?
	How will you contract? Bill?
	Should you make your software an add-on to something the customer already has?
PROMOTION (Information)	What's the daily life of your customer? Where do they normally seek or encounter information about the kind of thing you're looking to sell?

Figure 2.2

The Four Ps

The Four Ps and Enable Quiz

Andrew uses the Four Ps as an initial checklist for his strategy formulation, including the formulation of his key business assumptions. We covered his assessment of Product in Chapter 1, and we touched on Price in Chapter 1 as well. Andrew has an idea of how much the problem of avoiding bad hires is worth. He's still learning about the value companies ascribe to skills management, and he can't see a way to differentiate the two, so he'll probably have to go to the lowest common denominator or choose to focus on the hiring use case and see how it goes. He'll be testing different price points and promotions. In Chapter 1, when discussing Place, we identified the key question of whether customers would successfully locate, purchase, and on-board the service online. If not, Andrew will aggressively seek partners who service the same customer base to measure the incremental success of higher touch sales/on-boarding. With promotion, Andrew identified promotional targets, channels, and messages during his customer interviews. He'll be testing the effectiveness of those more extensively at launch. One item he's working on now is a series of posts for Enablequiz.com about how the lightweight quizzing they offer improves the technical recruiting process and improves employee skills management. For this, he's leveraging what he learned in customer interviews. Andrew's goal is to leverage the posts for organic Promotion on search engines and social media.

Company Strategy

Porter's Five Forces[2] is one of the most popular frameworks for rigorous evaluation of company strategy. We'll use it here to highlight a few key business drivers common to most tech businesses (see Figure 2.3).

Figure 2.3

Porter's Five
Forces

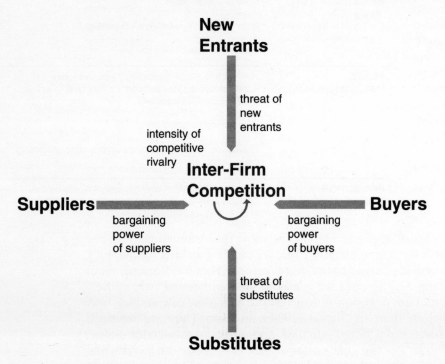

---

[2]See http://en.wikipedia.org/wiki/Porter_five_forces_analysis for a quick review or read Michael Porter's seminal work *Competitive Strategy*.

Bargaining Power of Suppliers

First we have the bargaining power of suppliers. A company with an enterprise product, like Enable Quiz, will have suppliers in two major areas: systems development and software subcomponents (sublicenses) for software piece parts used in the application. The rise of offshoring has made the market for development engineers more competitive. But there's a catch: It's hard to manage an offshore team. The physical distance and language barrier exacerbates any weakness in your ability to articulate your product design or manage developers. One of the most important things you can do to help yourself is to ensure you're not relying on your engineering team to be your product design team, and the best way to avoid that is to start with a well-articulated design. Without a strong product design, you'll be dependent on finding that one developer out of 20 who has the training, experience, natural ability, and desire to design your product as well as execute your software implementation. If you do find and can afford such an individual, use him or her to the greatest degree possible. But I wouldn't bank on discovering such a person. If you want to minimize development costs, you need to write an excellent product design and work with your development lead to maintain dialogue with your developers on the implementation. We'll step through how to do that in Chapters 5 and 6.

The second significant area of spending for a company like Enable Quiz is on sublicenses, meaning software or subsystems you'll use to operate your overall system. Companies that execute technology systems use these components to avoid re-inventing the wheel and to save huge amounts of money. Over the years, an increasingly larger portion of a typical system has been comprised of these off-the-shelf subcomponents. Twenty years ago, it was typical to start from the proverbial blank sheet of paper. Now it's a matter of assembling the right set of piece parts and then developing new software code on top of them.

The good news is that as the market for these piece parts has grown, it's gotten more competitive, which means you can get higher quality software piece parts for less money. Better open source software components have kept prices down, though open source does not mean free. I'll explain more about what I mean when we cover architecture in Chapter 4.

What separates the winners from the losers today is the ability to formulate an architecture that's smart about how it uses complementary software and systems. A lot of companies blow huge amounts of money because their technologists want to build things, since that's what technologists tend to like to do. This is, however, the wrong tactic. Instead, you want to let your audience drive your design, and let your design drive your architecture. The best approach to take in terms of managing suppliers is to start with a solid product design and then get with a technologist who knows how to leverage subcomponents in implementing the design.

Bargaining Power of Buyers

Next we have the bargaining power of buyers, which depends on your particular market. In the "old days," you generally needed a sales force and/or bricks and mortar retail distribution to get a technology product to market. The rise of online application stores and Internet-based applications (Software-as-a-Service or SaaS) has affected a broad swath of companies in consumer and enterprise software by making the market more open and competitive. For example, anyone who purchases a new mobile phone these days hears hype about the duelling Apple iPhone and Google Android platforms. A lot of this discussion is about the quality and quantity of third-party applications that are available to the user in those companies' respective app stores.

On the enterprise side, Salesforce.com has succeeded in creating a robust marketplace for third parties to sell add-ons to their popular CRM[3] suite. Though these marketplaces solve many substantial problems for sellers, they put companies side by side with their competitors. The key with marketplaces is to ensure you have a well-identified buyer and you're doing a good job with your overall solution.

Threat of New Entrants

New entrants crowd a market and drive down prices. New entrants get into a market when it looks attractive, which usually means there's no established leader or the leader has somehow faltered. In the world of software, the accepted rule is to be a first mover. In practice, the point is to emerge a leader in a new market, which may or may not mean being a first mover is the best thing, but more on that later. Because of the low incremental cost of selling software and technology systems, steep returns to scale exist in technology-enabled businesses, a situation that tends to create a long-term competitive environment with fewer players. Also, many high-tech products have some kind of network effect where the more people have a product, the more valuable the product is to everyone. The classic example of this is the telephone: Though it's not useful if one person has it, it's great when everyone does.

Startups almost never enter a market with an established leader—the amount of money they'd have to spend to take customers away from the leader prohibits it. Most frequently, startups are creating a new market or resegmenting an existing market, doing a better job in a particular niche. Their goal is to emerge as a leader in their segment to subsequently discourage new entrants.

---

[3]Customer Relationship Management (CRM) software allows companies to streamline management of their customers.

Let's say that you've done your research and you're a first mover in your niche. The trick is to get your product to market quickly and decisively so you emerge on top. The same basic rules apply to businesses whose industries are changing due to technology. Just look at all the retail businesses that have moved online. Service businesses like insurance and tax preparation are probably not far behind.

Threat of Substitutes

Our next and final topic is the threat of substitutes. Substitutes keep this business interesting, and are the reason you have so many young people starting and running companies. One innovation paves the way for substitution in another related area, and the ongoing, overlapping churn keeps the industry dynamic. For example, Google used to have the lock on online advertising. Banner advertising was discredited and search advertising grew to be a bigger piece of where companies spent money for online advertising. For a while, it looked like Google had nowhere to go but up. Then along came Facebook and other social networking sites. Now people find information through searches and their social networks as well. Google doesn't have a serious play in the space, and Facebook is the dominant first mover. Social networking is being substituted into a larger percentage of ad budgets over spending on search-related advertising. What will happen next?[4] That's the question that kind keeps high-tech business interesting.

Let's look at another type of enterprise software: trouble-ticketing systems. Any business that receives requests from internal or external customers to "do" or "fix" something has a trouble-ticketing system. Such a system deals with creating, categorizing, assigning, and monitoring the task to completion as well as reporting on it. Twenty years ago, this segment had lots of big players. If you had a good product early in the game, got integrators on board who knew how to install it and set it up across industries, paid attention to how users were using the product, and did a good job with help and documentation, you probably had a terrific business. But there was a catalyst that was threatening to kill the business: the emergence of SaaS applications and the emergence of Salesforce.com as the dominant player in that space. General purpose CRM software was becoming increasingly cheap and popular, and then Salesforce.com came along.

Companies started substituting the trouble-ticket module in Salesforce.com for stand-alone trouble-ticketing systems. The majority of companies with whom I work nowadays have some kind of CRM system, and they

---

[4]If I knew, I'd tell you.

don't want one general-purpose CRM and one ticketing system. They want a single system that knows everything about their customers. Salesforce.com offers its product on an SaaS basis so you don't install it locally. Instead, you log in to the application online through your web browser. Customers like that because it reduces their IT administration costs with no servers to deal with, no upgrades, and so forth. And they've been substituting integrated SaaS CRM's for stand-alone trouble ticketing-systems accordingly.

Companies that offer a trouble-ticketing system that customers have to license and install on their own servers are sitting on the wrong side of two major catalysts: a move toward singular, general-purpose CRM systems; and a move toward SaaS-based product distribution models. If I was running a company that offered a trouble-ticketing system, the first thing I would do is develop a version of the software for Salesforce.com. The old guard might not like it: They might believe that success requires having the software sitting on dedicated servers at the customer's office. Being an application add-on instead of an application might seem like a step down somehow. However, a stand-alone application is not what most of their customers want. They may like the product, and in fact, they probably do if they're still using it. But they want to buy it on an SaaS basis and they want it integrated with their general purpose CRM.

The upside of such a company developing an add-on to Salesforce.com is that Salesforce.com has a marketplace for third-party developers, which drives down the cost to acquire and deploy a new customer. You may not see nearly the price points you saw as a stand-alone application, but if you play your cards right, you'll get many more customers.

So, what's the key to managing the threat of substitutes? Stay on the right side of the catalysts.

Intensity of Competitive Rivalry

This has to do with direct competition between firms. If the firms each have a competitive niche and are innovating in their respective areas, this force tends to be relatively stable. If, however, one firm believes that it needs to buy share in the market, raising overall customer acquisition costs, or to lower prices to where the business isn't profitable, this force can be highly destructive.

Figure 2.4 summarizes a few key points around the Five Forces for high tech.

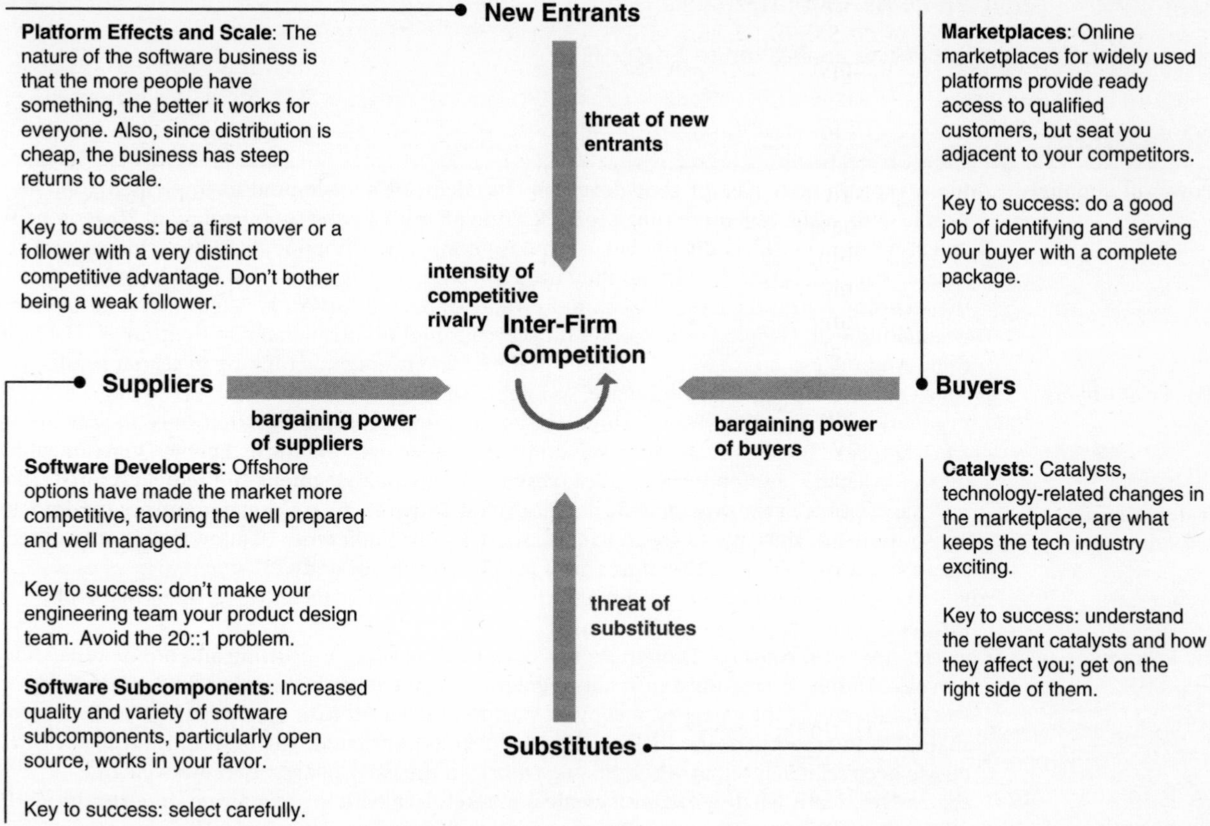

Figure 2.4

Five Forces in
High Tech

New Entrants

Platform Effects and Scale: The nature of the software business is that the more people have something, the better it works for everyone. Also, since distribution is cheap, the business has steep returns to scale.

Key to success: be a first mover or a follower with a very distinct competitive advantage. Don't bother being a weak follower.

threat of new entrants

intensity of competitive rivalry **Inter-Firm Competition**

Marketplaces: Online marketplaces for widely used platforms provide ready access to qualified customers, but seat you adjacent to your competitors.

Key to success: do a good job of identifying and serving your buyer with a complete package.

Suppliers

bargaining power of suppliers

Buyers

bargaining power of buyers

Software Developers: Offshore options have made the market more competitive, favoring the well prepared and well managed.

Key to success: don't make your engineering team your product design team. Avoid the 20::1 problem.

Software Subcomponents: Increased quality and variety of software subcomponents, particularly open source, works in your favor.

Key to success: select carefully.

threat of substitutes

Catalysts: Catalysts, technology-related changes in the marketplace, are what keeps the tech industry exciting.

Key to success: understand the relevant catalysts and how they affect you; get on the right side of them.

Substitutes

Porter's Five Forces and Enable Quiz

Table 2.1 describes the Five Forces application to Enable Quiz.

Table 2.1

Five Forces at Enable Quiz

Force	Notes
Bargaining Power of Suppliers	Andrew is prepared to pay for good development talent. He's made product implementation at Enable Quiz easier and more fungible by starting off with a good product design. The company will also leverage widely distributed, inexpensive software components in its architecture. One notable supplier is Google. Should they use AdWords, one danger is that Enable Quiz invents the technical quiz category and bids up the value of related AdWords. There isn't a lot to do on negotiating with Google as the market for search is highly consolidated in their favor. The best thing Andrew can do is promote his site, and increase his organic ranking in search results.
Bargaining Power of Buyers	Enable Quiz is not a big-ticket purchase, so Enable Quiz is unlikely to be subject to intense negotiations. They are, however, subject to competition. Andrew feels that since they're not in a marketplace, the downward pressure on prices will be light as long as Enable Quiz can evolve into a leadership position in the "quick, easy technical quiz" segment and remain a small ticket purchase. Consider the web hosting company GoDaddy. There are cheaper options for domain registration, but since it's so cheap to start, there's only a difference of a few dollars and other sites are less well known. Therefore, most people opt for GoDaddy.
	Additionally, if Andrew can create a marketplace for third-party technical quizzes, that will further cement his position in the market.
Threat of New Entrants	Copycats are a real concern. Though there's nothing new about e-learning and online tests and surveys, Andrew is creating a new sub-segment. A real danger is that after he does the hard work of inventing the category, a copycat startup or adjacent firm swoops in and steals a lot of share. For the most part, the first mover advantage is overstated. The best things Andrew can do are keep relatively silent while Enable Quiz is in the early phases, execute well and aggressively learn what works, and create a marketplace with lots of partner opportunities.
Threat of Substitutes	Possible substitutes are companies that opt to create their own quizzes manually or use an existing survey or Q&A service like Survey Monkey to build their own quizzes. Andrew is confident that Enable Quiz's execution will render these substitutes less worthwhile to customers.
Inter-Firm Competition	No firms directly compete in the space, so this isn't applicable yet.

More on Catalysts

Industry veterans will tell you that their success was due to spotting catalysts and riding them out. Though they may phrase it in various ways, that's what they mean. As long as the high-tech industry has existed, it's perpetuated a fairly aggressive growth-death cycle driven by the kind of catalysts I mentioned. A big one early on was the semiconductor, which created a new industry in mini computers (they wouldn't look mini to anyone today). These allowed users to run something resembling modern software. Dramatic price/performance reductions in subcomponents arose, which led to the emergence of the PC and cheaper computers that companies used. This set the stage for modern operating systems like Windows and Mac OS.

I'm sure you know that story: It's high-tech's Coke vs. Pepsi. But it had a clear economic winner in the PC space: Windows. (Apple's resurgence has been in the current "post-PC era.") The Internet was not as widespread in the last 15 years or so, and the average user did most things on the PC itself. Before the widespread availability of Internet and cloud-based applications, the operating system on your computer really constrained what you could do with your applications. Microsoft focused on compatibility and partnerships, and Mac focused on product quality through integrated design, arguably falling prey to the Python of Monolithic Architecture in trying to do too much. Though I prefer the Mac myself, the company was on the wrong side of the key catalyst at the time. Since the PC's price point drove greater ubiquity, it created more volume for application developers. Apple, therefore, ended with a set of competitors that had more applications on less expensive hardware. The numbers tell the rest of the story.

The most recent catalysts are the continuing move of applications online to the "cloud" and the advent of application marketplaces. The increased use of mobile devices is a big deal as well and is generating massive amounts of new opportunities for entrepreneurs.

Catalysts and Enable Quiz

Since Enable Quiz is an SaaS application, it is on the right side of that catalyst. I don't see a play for Enable Quizzing on top of an existing marketplace. There is no dominant platform for learning applications, at least not to the extent it would make sense for Enable Quiz. But Enable Quiz has a possible future play as a place for third parties to create and sell their own quizzes, which provides additional upside potential to the business.

Iterative Management

What? How?

Iterative strategy management means applying the scientific method to your company strategy. You look at your business not in terms of a three-year plan where you clench your teeth and hope you're right, but as a series of discrete experiments. *The Lean Startup* author Eric Ries describes the conclusion of these experiments as a "pivot or persevere" moment. Do the results tell you that your approach is on the money, or are they telling you something else? If you're essentially on the right track, then persevere; if not, figure out what the results are telling you and pivot.

   This kind of adaptive approach to strategy management benefits startups in two ways. First, it will help you plan your resources more effectively. You should organize your resources so you have at least one pivot. If you have runway for only one pivot, you're effectively foreclosing on the chance to implement anything you've learned. Making room for the pivot might mean raising more money up front, keeping your first iteration smaller, spending more time on ancillary consulting activities that raise revenue organically, or cutting resources more aggressively on your pivot (avoid this last option if at all possible). Second, it will help keep you and your staff focused on the reality of your business instead of feeling the need to defend your beliefs. Traditional planning and management often compels companies to create a long-term plan around a set of beliefs. The mythology of business teaches us that a person of integrity will defend these convictions until the end (happy or sad). Startups would do better to focus on empirically and objectively learning what's happening with the business. Years ago, I had an effective manager who settled any disagreement (usually between him and me) with this preface: "The only difference between what you think and what I think is a difference in assumptions. Let's start by laying those out." This tells the other parties that you consider them to be your equal, and that their point of view isn't necessarily wrong but is based on different assumptions. Iterative management allows you to lay out the most crucial assumptions for your whole team and use those as a foundation for discussion.

Iterative Management and Enable Quiz

Enable Quiz completed the initial reality testing of its product idea. The overall execution strategy, Enable Quiz 1.0 we'll call it, could be characterized as follows:

"Enable Quiz's vision is to be the leader in casual assessments of technical talent. Its first iteration involves building a minimum viable product and testing useability and uptake with a hand-picked set of beta customers. If the product or business model requires significant revision, Enable Quiz will pivot and revise it. If not, it will proceed with a customer acquisition campaign online and through a partner network. It will watch the metrics and if they're good, scale; if not, pivot on the business model."

This statement involves two possible pivots, one after the other: Is it all right, and doesn't "iterative" mean one at a time? While being iterative does mean executing one version at a time, it doesn't mean you shouldn't think through your success scenario even if that means breaking it into multiple iterations. It does mean, however, that you shouldn't devote a lot of resources to provisional iterations, but it's probably manageable to think through your high-level business plan.

The Reality Test section laid out the key hypotheses about the product that Enable Quiz will validate in the first iteration. Beyond these, Enable Quiz will detail and expand their user stories, with assumptions about how the user will utilize the product (see next chapter). What is the experimental design and how will Enable Quiz evaluate the results? Andrew has a rough picture of most of the beta customers: IT service providers who operate IT infrastructure (servers, etc.), firms that provide IT outsourcing for other companies, and software developers. One other firm does training and skills management, Minucci Brothers, and Andrew's looking forward to their experience with the product. Though the beta customers like the idea of using Enable Quiz for new hires, Andrew knows these results will come slowly as they go through the hiring process. The beta customers are all prepared to do internal skills audits, and that's where Andrew is hoping to get some quick initial results. Along with anecdotal feedback to get the real texture of how the beta goes, Andrew's formulated the following four metrics for structured comparison and coming to a final decision on the pivot:

1. Used as Designed?

    How closely did the customer use the product as designed on a scale of 1 to 10? Andrew plans to have the customer respond to this in addition to making his own assessment. This is a proxy for all the qualitative data Andrew collects on the customers.

2. Ease of Setup

    Andrew wants to work with the participants directly to help them get online with the product. However, he won't be onsite with the customers. He plans to make an appointment with them and use GoToMeeting (a screen sharing service) to watch the customers as they set up the service. He'll be able to answer questions and help out where needed. This format will allow Andrew to see how far customers get on setting up the service by themselves while being available to see where things go wrong and help out where needed to keep things moving.

3. Percentage Responses

    At the end of the beta, Andrew will look at what portion of the participants the manager invited took some kind of quiz.

4. Conversion

    The beta is free and participants will have the option to convert to a paid subscription.

5. Net Promoter Score[5]

    This is a simple, powerful metric that essentially asks, "How likely are you to recommend the product?"

Andrew doesn't have an exact fixed answer as to what he'd consider a successful result since it depends somewhat on the interaction between the answers and experience of the beta. He does have a rough idea though. He'd like to see an average of seven or better on the "Used as Designed" metric to decide whether the product design needs tweaking versus rethinking. He'd like to see 70 percent of the customers set themselves up on the system with "minimal" intervention. He'd like to see around 75 percent on Percentage Responses, though he will probably exclude participating companies that had less than 25 percent since that means they didn't meaningfully engage in the beta. On conversion, he'd like to see at least 50 percent. This would be outrageously high out on the public Internet, but these participants have been picked and pre-qualified by Andrew. He would like to see an 80 percent or better on Net Promoter score.

So, what happens if the results of the beta are positive and there's no pivot on the product/market fit? Andrew still needs to make sure he's aligning the other key aspects of his business with one another. While he's not going to invest his time in elaborate planning until he verifies the product, iterative management doesn't mean short-sighted management. Figure 2.5 maps out the next set of profit drivers and metrics to test Enable Quiz's operational strategy: Tables 2.2 and 2.3 describes the drivers in more detail.

Assuming its basic ideas about the product/market fit are correct, the critical success factor for Enable Quiz is building a great product. That's the subject of our next chapter.

---

[5]Net Promoter Score is a registered trademark of Fred Reichheld, Bain & Company, and Satmetrix.

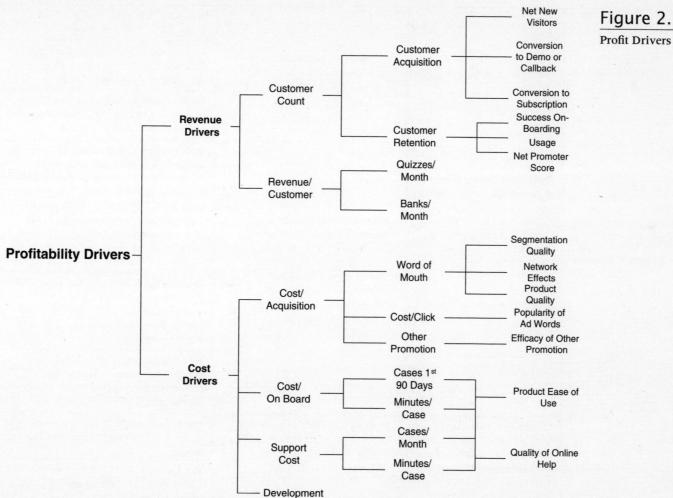

Figure 2.5

Profit Drivers

Table 2.2

Revenue Drivers

Revenue Drivers	**Customer Count:** This is the subscriber base—the total number of customers Enable Quiz has under contract in any given period.	**Customer Acquisition:** Enable Quiz's ability to bring on new customers.	**Net New Visitors:** This is the total gross number of new visitors.
			Conversion to Demo or Callback: This is the portion of new visitors who opt to browse and learn more.
			Conversion to Subscription: This is the portion of new visitors who opt for a paid subscription.
		Customer Retention/ Churn: Enable Quiz's ability to keep the customers they have. Churn is the portion of the customer base that cancels service (per month), so 1/churn rate is the average lifetime of the customer.	**Success in On-Boarding:** This is tightly linked to the success of the on-boarding process in an SaaS model, described below as a cost. You make your service an indispensible part of your customer's everyday life or you lose customers. We look more at how to monitor the on-boarding process in the chapter on scaling.
			Usage: This is generally the top predictor of renewals (unless you have major competition). Enable Quiz will keep a close eye on this and intervene where usage drops.
			Net Promoter Score[6]: This is the portion of customers that would recommend the service and a good predictor of satisfaction and renewal.
		Revenue/Customer: Enable Quiz charges a base fee and then they pay a variable fee based on the number of quizzes a customer uses and the number of quiz banks (the banks are sets of prewritten questions in a given topic, like Linux, that the customer wants to have available).	**Quizzes/Month:** This is the number of quizzes the customer consumes per month.
			Banks/Month: This is the number of question banks the customer is paying to have access to.

[6]Net Promoter, NPS, and Net Promoter Score are trademarks of Satmetrix Systems, Inc., Bain & Company, and Fred Reichheld.

Cost Drivers	**Cost per Acquisition:** Some of these costs are variable (cost/click), and others are fixed (like the money you spend on promotional pieces online). It's a good idea when measuring cost/acquisition to disaggregate the fixed and variable portions. The fixed portions are a question of getting business to the minimum efficient scale, and the variable ones are an ongoing question of unit economics.	**Word of Mouth**	**Segmentation Quality:** This covers the segment's consistency. How easily can you identify prospective customers in the segment? How actively do they reference each other? What percentage of customers claim to have found the service via word of mouth?
			Network Effects: When one person has the product, does his or her peers need it to keep interacting? This is not a strong area for Enable Quiz. (It is a big deal for something like Facebook or Skype.) The best way to measure this is a survey on how a customer found the service.
			Product Quality: How great is the product? Do customers like it? Would they tell each other, measured by the Net Promoter score? Ditto above on metrics. We look at how you can set yourself up for good product quality in the next chapter.
		Cost/Click	**Popularity of AdWords:** You can measure this by the cost of the AdWords.

Table 2.3

Cost Drivers

(continued)

Table 2.3

(*continued*)

		Other Promotion	**Efficacy of Other Promotion:** This includes all other promotion items that result in direct visits and an increase in hits on organic search (vs. paid links), with things like content generation on the site to interest users, e-mail marketing, and other public outreach.
	Cost to On-Board and Support Cost	**Cases/[Period] and Minutes/Case**	**Product Ease of Use:** How often do users get confused and need help? You can measure this by the post-mortems on your cases.
			Quality of Online Help: How well do you help the users find answers for themselves? You can measure this on case (trouble-ticket) post-mortems. We look at how to organize your thinking on help in the next chapter.
	Development: Networks' effects and economies of scale are the classic drivers for high-tech businesses. An important qualifier, driven home in the dot-com bust, is that the unit economics need to make sense.		

Working the Numbers

Financial diligence is not something you hear about in the mythology of any famous tech business—because it's not interesting, not because it's not important. The first internal pep talk I heard from a professional CEO ended with him saying he would make sure we didn't run out of money because then it would be "game over." (Epilogue: The company ran out of money four days later, but it wasn't his fault. He'd been on the job for about as many days.) The reality is that having a well-defined financial plan will keep you from worrying about your finances on a daily basis. Plan the work, work the plan. You'll need a structured financial model, and there's an example on Alexandercowan.com/finplan.

You can easily avoid a few common mistakes in this area. First, especially for your first pivot while you're learning about the product/market fit, you want to discount all revenue 100 percent unless you're certain about its arrival. That doesn't mean you shouldn't include it in your model. It means you should do your cash planning around a revenue-less version of your organization to avoid cash shortages. Revenue tends to push out, while expenses tend to pull in. If you have a VP of Sales and a CFO, don't make the mistake of blaming either unduly. If the VP of Sales wasn't an optimist, he or she wouldn't be able to get out of bed in the morning. If the CFO wasn't a hard-nosed realist, he or she would be guilty of negligence. If you're doing both of those jobs, don't blame yourself for your conflicting points of view; however, you must be sure to manage them.

You can waste tremendous amounts of time and obfuscate the visibility of your financial situation if you're maintaining your financial model in a way that doesn't match with how you're keeping your books. Whether you're using a shoebox, QuickBooks, or something fancier, you must ensure you match your General Ledger (GL) codes to your totals on the model. GL codes are defined "buckets" where you allocate items from an accounting perspective. As long as these match the various totals in your model, it's easy to reconcile the two. Like a lot of things, good planning and design at the outset will pay for itself many times over down the road. The model mentioned in the paragraph above has some examples of how to do this.

Finally, in the early days you should keep a close eye on your unit economies, meaning the amount of revenue you get from a unit of sale vs. its direct cost. If you were selling pizzas, this would be the selling price of a pizza net of the materials and labor to produce that one pizza (as opposed to the cost of leasing a storefront, etc.). One popular metric if you are an SaaS company is lifetime value (LTV). This is the net present value of the free cash generated by an individual customer account. This useful metric can be difficult to measure, particularly when your operation is not at scale. The most important thing you want to watch for is that you're not paying more variable cost (that you don't expect to decrease) to acquire a customer than you are earning. This is a sure sign you need to revise your customer acquisition strategy, with possible ramifications for the rest of the business.

You can find examples of all these metrics for Enable Quiz on Alexandercowan.com/finplan.

Bringing It All Together

What Do I Need?

The exact materials you need to prepare to execute your strategy depend on your objectives and audience. Various facets of the lean management movement have challenged the importance of a traditional business plan. These more agile management philosophies point out that too much time and hope is invested in long-range business plans when the reality of the operating environment is uncertain. That said, you'll need something that resembles a traditional business plan if you're dealing with investors or bankers. The key is not wasting time trying to predict to the nth degree. For example, let's say someone asked you to predict tomorrow's average temperature. You could go online, look at average temperatures for the season in your area, and make a good guess. What if you were asked to predict it to the third significant digit, e.g., will it be 70.001 degrees or 70.0002 degrees? You would probably have to guess.

Unless your business is lightweight, it's probably a good idea to write a traditional business plan. It will help you think through the business and it's nice to have on hand if you find you need to pitch investors or strategic partners. The key thing is not to overinvest in its preparation, not to expect it to come true just because you wrote it down, and to acknowledge that many parts of it are likely to change, even in the short term.

Table 2.4 describes the major sections in a typical business plan and the questions you should be answering in each.

An example of such a plan is on Alexandercowan.com/busplan. The last item, Financials, will come from the financial model we discussed in the previous section and a sample is available on Alexandercowan.com/finplan.

Topic	Key Questions
Executive Summary	What is this company, and why is it of interest to me?
	What is it looking to do, and what is crucial to its execution?
	(You may want to save this for the end.)
Customer	Who is the buyer? What do they do all day? What do they care about? (Paint as vivid a picture as possible—leverage specific interviews and figures if you have them.)
	What unmet need is the company fulfilling for this customer?
	How much is that need worth to the customer?
	What is the customer's buying process?
	How will the company reach this buyer?
	Into what market segment does this customer fit?
	Will the company be addressing a new market or an existing one?
	If new, how will the company create the market?
	If existing, what is the company's competitive advantage?
	Who are the company's chief competitors?
Product(s)	What is this company selling?
	To whom? (Save details on the customer for next section.)
	Why will the potential customers buy this product or service from this company?
	What are the key assumptions for this product to be successful?
	How has the company reality tested those assumptions or do they plan to reality test them?
Strategy	What is the company's long-term competitive advantage? (This is a good place to deploy your Five Forces analysis.)
	How will the company reach, sell, and service the buyer?
	How will the product be priced? (These last two questions are a good area to deploy your Four Ps.)
Competition	What is the set of competitive products and companies?
	How does it compare to the proposed product and company?
	What about substitutes and alternatives? Why is this preferable?
Management	What is the organizational structure for the company, and why is it appropriate to the company's operating model? (You'll want an organization chart here. It's all right to repeat people in different positions.)
Financials	How much cash is required for the company to reach key milestones (pivots)?
	What are the most likely set of scenarios for the company? (It's all right to have more than one.)
	When is the cash flow breakeven in each scenario?
	What are the most critical metrics, and how will they be measured?

Table 2.4

Components of a Traditional Business Plan

A new approach to business planning is the business model canvas, introduced by Alexander Osterwalder. This canvas is popular in the lean management community since it allows for thorough but quick and visible business model planning. An example from Osterwalder's site is shown in Figure 2.6.

One nice thing about the canvas is that you can spend 10 to 15 minutes walking through your key assumptions and initiatives without trudging through your whole business plan. An online tool for canvas generation is available via Alexandercowan.com/canvastool.

Figure 2.6

Business
Canvas

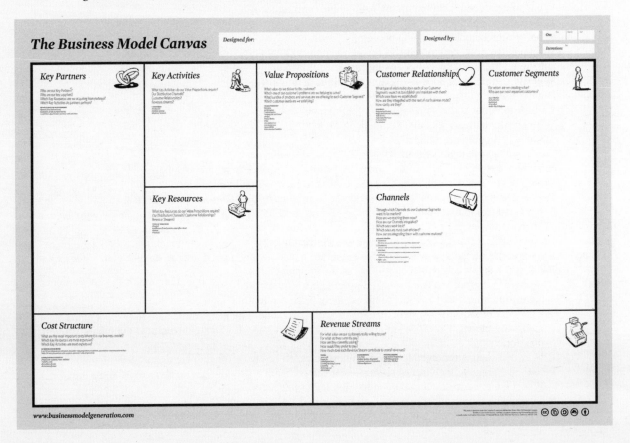

In practice, you'll probably find yourself visiting your sales tracking tool, financial model, and perhaps the business model canvas most often. Your sales tracking tool might be a CRM (like Salesforce.com) or internal tools. You'll want to reconcile your financial model periodically with your actuals. The business model canvas you may find useful for a quick but systematic view of the business.

Most of the best tech strategies start with a great product. In the next chapter, we look at how to prepare yourself to deliver a great product.

Chapter 2 Summary

1. Mind the Four Ps

    The Four Ps (product, place, price, promotion) are a quick and useful checklist for validating the business aspects of your product.

2. Mind the Five Forces

    The Five Forces are: bargaining power of suppliers, bargaining power of buyers, threat of new entrants, threat of substitutes, and inter-firm competition. For suppliers, put yourself in a position to make development easy by doing a good design. For buyers, consider your market type and the degree to which you're differentiated. For entrants, consider how long it will take you to reach the mainstream market and the strength of potential entrants. For substitutes, think about why your way is compelling, what you're assuming to make that the case, and what catalysts are driving change and product substitution in your area. For competitive rivalry, make sure your competitors have a coherent strategy that won't decrease the quality of the segment overall.

3. Don't Mistake Developers for Designers

    Very few development engineers are equipped to double as product designers. Don't expect your average developer to be able to take your high-level product concept and turn it into a piece of software. Completing a well-articulated product design document is the first and best way to control costs, quality, and timeframes.

4. Build Less Software and Leverage Subcomponents

    Talk to your software lead (or anyone else you can find) to ensure he or she is thinking about what existing system components you can leverage with your product. Those may be software libraries, application components, or development platforms. Building technology is expensive and it's wasteful to do it from scratch when off-the-shelf alternatives could suffice. (More on this in Chapter 4.)

5. Leverage Marketplaces

If you see an opportunity to build a stand-alone application or build it as an add-on application for an existing marketplace, err on the side of the marketplace. This will help you focus development and reduce distribution costs. Example marketplaces include the following:

- Salesforce.com for enterprise software
- iTunes and Android Market for mobile applications
- Facebook for social networking

Alternatively, if you see a chance to create a marketplace, you may have a powerful opportunity on your hands.

6. Understand Your Profit Drivers

Understand your key profit drivers and make sure you can link them to your key business assumptions. Have a target range for each that validates your model.

7. Organize Around Iterative Management

Think of the business as an experiment—it has a set of key assumptions and a set of events that will prove or disprove its validity. Leave yourself at least one pivot.

8. Plan, but Don't Overplan

You'll definitely want a financial model and probably a traditional plan. Acknowledge that you'll need to revisit these often and they'll probably change.

Checklist

1. Experimental Design

Do you have a specific set of assumptions that you'll validate with specific metrics over a specific timeframe?

2. Business Plan

It doesn't have to be fancy, but you should cover most of the key bases mentioned in the table above.

3. Financial Model

    This is an extension of the business plan, but bears its own mention.

4. Profit Drivers

    Have you identified your key revenue and cost drivers? Have you linked them to your key assumption set? The Enable Quiz examples are available on Alexandercowan.com/drivers.

Specialty Reading by Topic

If you want to know more about …	… then read
The Four Ps	Additional information is available here: Alexandercowan.com/4ps
Corporate Strategy	*Competitive Strategy*, by Michael Porter
	This seminal book on corporate strategy will give you an expanded view of the Five Forces. Michael Porter is a long-standing leader in consulting and academia.
Business Planning for New Ventures	*Technology Ventures: From Idea to Enterprise*, by Thomas Byers, Richard Dorf, and Andrew Nelson
	This textbook is frequently used in classes for engineering students wanting to learn about entrepreneurship. The authors are professors, several with a history in entrepreneurship and/or venture capital.
	The book offers in-depth coverage of managerial items like structuring an opportunity, valuing the opportunity, preparing for presentation to a venture capitalist, legal, HR, and exit strategies.
Writing a Business Plan	A sample business plan for Enable Quiz is on Alexandercowan.com/busplan. This section of the site lists helpful online resources.

The Product

Pin the Butterfly of Incoherence

You have a winning idea, and you need to describe it to your implementation team. The Butterfly of Incoherence flutters from one thing to another in no coherent pattern. Successful development follows systematic patterns, and we'll review those here, applying them to the example of Enable Quiz.

Thinking Like a Designer

Of all the dictionary definitions for "design," the following is my favorite:

> design *verb* \di-ˈzīn\ to assign in thought or intention

The discipline of design remains highly rarefied and largely misunderstood. Chances are that if you were to tell people you were a designer, they'd probably ask you about the color of their drapes, wall paint, and so forth. Identifying yourself as a designer will compel them to expect an immediate answer, like "I see pink over there." However, this is one of the most destructive myths about the practice of design: that it's a wholly artistic and inspirational discipline. The effect of this myth is twofold: It discourages individuals from approaching design tasks, and it prompts them to take any opinions they form personally, which makes the process of brainstorming and revision difficult. Design teachers often lament that though we spend years in school learning written communication, most Americans graduate college without a day of training in how to communicate visually.

The discipline of design is part science, part art. Much of visual communication is easier to objectively measure and qualify than similar types of written communication. Good design is self-evident: the item in question feels right. Author Donald Norman uses the example of sewing scissors in his seminal book, *The Design of Everyday Things*: Your hands just slip into the exact right position when you pick up a set of sewing scissors. You've probably had plenty of experiences in the reverse: products that just always feel awkward, difficult, or unnatural to use. One thing you'll rarely hear good designers do is blame the user. They'll first ask questions about where the user went off track and how the product could have been better assembled to avoid confusion. The next time you think, "I don't get this," ask yourself this: "Did it get me?"

Fortunately, the tide is turning and more people are developing a wider and more inclusive understanding of the nature and value of design. The number of Design MBA programs has exploded in recent years. Books and articles on design thinking are seeing increasingly heavy rotation. (I've listed a few of my favorites at the end of this chapter). The balance of this chapter provides some practical, ready-to-use guidance on how to think like a designer, specifically how to deliver an effective product specification to the engineers who will implement your product. Rouse your inner tinkerer and don't be afraid to experiment with ideas and prototypes.

The Designer as Anthropologist

Good design doesn't happen in a vacuum. It results from an empathic and often highly detailed understanding of your audience. What's right for one person may not be right for another. Back to the example of the "I see pink" misconception, I remember asking a friend of mine who is a professional designer how to furnish my new apartment. He told me to think about what I did in the apartment. What was I looking to do when I first walked into the apartment? What was I looking to do when I walked into the kitchen? What about the living room? Bedroom? His simple but powerful advice was that the definition of a good design would be a function of the natural patterns of my activity.

A close friend of my family's was a senior officer in the CIA after World War II. He always described his job of recruiting CIA assets as helping people do what they wanted to do. Your job as a product designer is to help the users do what they want to do. Your first step is to understand the audience. If your application is complex, you may have several different audiences and segmenting them will be critical to delivering a product that suits everyone well. If you're not sure whether to break out certain types of users as their own type of audience, err on the side of doing so. Providing more detailed description is preferable at this point. In the big leagues, they go out and film their target audience in their natural habitat, Animal Planet style. Though that approach may be too extensive for your purposes, it is good to anchor the description of your audience with specific examples.

Here's a simple starter checklist of questions you should be able to answer about the audiences you identify:

1. Who are these people? Paint a picture that would allow anyone off the street to envision them.
2. What do they want to do with the product? Why?
3. What is their likely frame of reference? How much do they typically know about your product and any relevant background related to it?
    *   For example, if it's a tax application, are your users highly tax savvy or novices?
4. How frequently will they use the product?

These questions are similar to the ones we posed in Chapter 1 around customer interviews, and you'll likely be able to apply a lot of what you learned here.

Audiences at Enable Quiz

Back to Enable Quiz, Andrew has identified several audiences for his application. Table 3.1 that follows is a synopsis.

Though this is a good start, Andrew needs to make sure he covers his internal audiences. Even though the customer-facing aspects of the product are most critical, neglecting the tools you need internally to operate the system can increase operational costs for your technology-enabled business. Continuing, in this vein, Table 3.2 describes Enable Quiz's internal audiences. Keep in mind that audiences in this section are familiar with the application.

Not all of these audiences will require their own special additions to the product, but they might, and it's better to identify them up front.

The best way to gather this kind of information is to spend time with users. Andrew's been doing this from the start. Remember, you're an anthropologist. You're not there to depose the users for requirements or even expect them to tell you what they want. Your job is to understand them, what they do, and build a great product for them (or at least paint a vivid pictures so you can collaborate with the rest of your team on the solution).

If, for whatever reason, you're working on a project where you're not allowed to work with users directly or working with them is impractical, push for shorter cycles and get the most basic possible product in front of the users for feedback as soon as possible.

Table 3.1

External Audiences for Enable Quiz

Audience	Description
HR Manager	The typical HR manager's job in terms of hiring is to help the functional manager write the job description, identify channels for recruitment, and perform initial candidate screening. They usually have minimal domain knowledge, so they're getting the functional manager to give them the detail they need to screen for any specific qualifications. This makes it especially important that we make it easy for the HR manager to forward or otherwise present the functional manager a clear list of technical topics they can choose from for quizzing candidates. Allowing the HR managers to administer the technical quiz as well as perform initial candidate screening will give them the opportunity to increase the value they deliver to the functional manager on screening unqualified candidates. The HR department may or may not be involved in ongoing skills management for existing employees. However, it will almost always be involved in employee assessment tied to anything financial, such as raises or bonuses. If the functional managers use a quiz to determine a raise or bonus (particularly if the HR manager initially created the quiz as an objective criteria), they are likely to be involved in the administration and/or review of the results. The HR manager likely pays the bills for Enable Quiz, especially in a larger company. If Enable Quiz is used for screening candidates, the HR managers may use the system more than the functional manager. If it is used for skills management, they are likely to use it somewhat less than the functional manager.
Functional Manager	The functional managers are responsible for a staff of engineers/technicians in the area of product development, technical operations, or technical field service. Their daily tasks require that they understand, manage, and implement requests from other parts of their organization. Recruiting is the functional manager's last priority even though they know it should be their first. They may or may not be intimate with every technology their staff members need to know. They care about Enable Quiz because it's an easy way for them to get a systematic view of their current or prospective staff's technical capabilities. They need to be able to easily select the right question banks to use, often sending the request back to the HR manager to process and buy. Though the HR managers may use the product at high volumes for candidate screening, the functional managers are the primary consumer of the exam's detailed output. Other than possibly the students, they are the only ones looking at the details of which questions the candidates missed.
Student/Quiz Taker	The students fall into two major categories: recruits and staff. The recruits have little involvement with the product, coming in for an interview or two. The staff are more involved. They will want to keep an eye on how they're doing on various skills improvement. They'll be highly intimate with details since they are the test takers and area experts. Relative to the managers, however, staff will use the system infrequently.

Audience	Description
Quiz Developer	The quiz developers are responsible for generating quiz questions for Enable Quiz in one or more topical areas. They're technical specialists in one or more areas. That said, we want to make it easy for them to create, review, and revise technical questions. These individuals will probably have some post-mortem jobs as well, like comparing the ratio of correct/incorrect responses on questions to see if some of them were perhaps too easy or too difficult. The quiz developers may only update quiz questions a few times a year.
Technical Support	These folks are somewhat technical and highly familiar with the Enable Quiz application. They are responsible for handling product-related questions from customers that customer service can't resolve, and they are on the system every day. They will likely be viewing the same screens as customers, but any summary views showing faults on the system will be useful.
Customer Service	Customer service handles all inbound calls. These will likely be evenly divided among clerical items like password resets, sales inquiries/questions on billing, and product-related questions. Though these people are not engineers, they will be familiar with the application, and will be on the system almost constantly.
Management	This refers to all managerial employees of the company, who will have various questions about product and commercial items. For example, they may want a quick view into current subscriptions by product, cancellations, and customers who have signed up but don't appear to be using the product (often a precursor to cancellation). They will use the system on a periodic basis, some more than others. They will have a mix of backgrounds.
Systems Administrator	The systems administrators are responsible for keeping the system up and running. Though they are not the system developers, they will be engineers and highly familiar with the operation of the system. They will be monitoring and updating the system on a regular basis.

Table 3.2

Internal Audiences for Enable Quiz

User Stories

Tell Me a Story, I'll Make You a Product

You might have heard the terms *marketing requirements document* (MRD) or *product requirements document* (PRD). They just sound long and boring, don't they? Do you think you could get excited about writing them? Few people can. Furthermore, the idea that anyone can anticipate and document everything a product should do, toss said document over the trench to developers, and expect to have a great product a few months later is becoming less popular. A large share of the most modern tech businesses use adaptive development methodologies, often described as agile. These processes favor interaction between the developers and product

Figure 3.1

User Stories

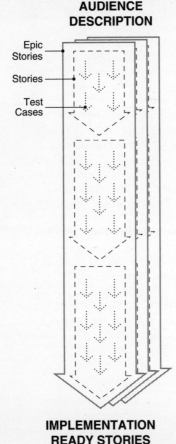

AUDIENCE DESCRIPTION

Epic Stories

Stories

Test Cases

IMPLEMENTATION READY STORIES

designers (owners) over long documents and short cycles with incremental chunks of working software over long development cycles with bigger deliveries.

This doesn't mean you shouldn't sit down and write down as many ideas as soon as you can. Nor does it mean that more extensive documentation isn't ever something you should do before development starts, even with an MRD or PRD. The right amount and type of documentation depends on your project and team, and we review that in Chapter 6. It does mean that developers are likely to find certain structures most consumable, that you shouldn't hold up development while you're writing up said documentation, and that you should avoid being overly prescriptive. This will put you in the best possible position to benefit from the team's wisdom, and the empirical knowledge you'll gain only as the product comes together (see Figure 3.1).

The primary unit of product description in these methodologies is a story. It's nothing more than a simple story about the user written in plain English. The general form of such a story is the following:

As a <user type> I want to <do something> so I can <derive a benefit>.

An example in the case of Enable Quiz would be the following:

As a manager, I want to invite a set of students to take a quiz so I can receive their scores.

These stories range in their level of abstraction and length, and the right size of a story is something you'll work out with your team. Even though good stories are independent, they still can be interrelated. If you discover you have a big story you need to dissect into smaller pieces, you can create an "epic story" with individual stories within. An epic story that might encapsulate the story above is this:

As a manager, I want to administer a quiz so I can assess the skill level of my employees.

In addition to our first story about inviting the students to take a quiz, this epic story would include stories about the manager creating the quiz and loading a list of students, among others.

If you want to add additional detail to an individual story, you can make simple notes around it, but the preferred method is to supplement the story with test cases. A few tests for the above story on inviting students for a quiz might be the following:

User should receive a helpful error message if the list of students is blank.

If the e-mail delivery to a student fails, the manager should receive a notice and the failure should be visible on the portal.

The manager sees the list of students and must confirm before sending.

One popular acronym about the quality of user stories is INVEST[1]:

I: Independent. The stories should function and make sense individually, and should not overlap.

N: Negotiable. The developers and the product owner (probably you) should be able to negotiate the implementation details.

This is important because people start behaving like politicians once you start legislating requirements, with lots of hedging, positioning, finger pointing, and so on.

V: Valuable. The story should be demonstrably important to the end user.

E: Estimable. The story should be readily estimable by the development team. This means designing stories that are the right size for your team, which is something you'll figure out with a little experience and discussion (if in doubt, I usually go smaller).

S: Small. One of the principles of this methodology is that we don't have to wait long to see if something's working, looking right, etc. Stories should be small, and the exact size will vary between teams.

T: Testable. Testability is something you get with any good set of requirements, but it's important here because of the short cycles.

Your ultimate goal here is to paint a vivid portrait of your users and what they want to do with your product. That's why it's useful to do your best to describe the audience for your team. You should be working hard to keep these stories natural and close to the actual user profile, versus arbitrary and disconnected. The classic PRD/MRD approach to systems development, where the business side draws up requirements and hands those to the engineering side, is like establishing a set of rules without explaining the game. In other words, you're not giving the implementer any intuitive sense of what you want and why. The predictable result is that you end up with arbitrary implementations that seem silly to you but seem fine to the developer and are entirely consistent with the requirements. People remember stories. Stories will give you an intuitive blueprint for your requirements, and they will create a framework that's easy to update as you learn more about your users.

[1] Originally published by Bill Wake in his work on Extreme Programming (XP).

Stories at Enable Quiz

Let's continue with Enable Quiz, starting with the most elemental members of the audience: the quiz taker. Why are they taking this quiz? A few possible story lines exist. One is that they've come to the technical part of a job interview, and the hiring manager wants objective data on their ability around key topics. Perhaps they're an employee, and management wants to baseline where they are on one or more technical topics. A variation might be that the company wants to implement an overall skills development program that provides the employees training in areas important to the company. Management wants a gap analysis of the topics it wants everyone to know versus what they do know so it can determine what topics to cover in its training. They're also likely to want a before-and-after comparison to gauge if the training program was effective.

Another possibility is that people want to quiz themselves. This is an interesting case, but it's unclear how it fits into the Enable Quiz business model. Additionally, would more casual users like that be willing to pay for a nonverifiable result—something they couldn't show to their managers to prove they knew something? At this phase, it's better to include items like this and remove them later if they don't fit. For example, maybe this epic story becomes part of the advertising hook to get people to the site: "Do you really know [Linux, PHP, Java, etc]? Click here to see how you stack up." They'll find they're able to take mini-quizzes.

Let's tackle a few stories within the epic story of a company that wants to examine some staff members' skills. How do users find out if they need to take this quiz, and how do they know how to take it? It's likely that managers would call their employees to a conference room and have them take the quiz. But how tightly should they supervise the quiz takers? And how do we avoid cheating?

Let's assume that, based on Andrew's conversations with prospective customers, he discovers their prevailing view: If the quiz takers have enough gumption to figure out the answers to a 25-question quiz on Google, they're capable enough for the job. There are quiz centers that offer certification tests in a controlled environment. However, that's not Enable Quiz's niche. Instead, Enable Quiz is offering more flexible quizzing in a lower pressure environment for more casual use. Any customers it finds later on that wants to avoid this can supervise the quiz (possibly through built in screen-sharing or a third party product like GotoMeeting). Enable Quiz can also impose a time limit that restricts the students' ability to complete the quiz on time if they're researching the answers.

Keep in mind that stories are not necessarily linear and serial: you might have multiple parallel sub-stories within an epic story. Think of it more like one of those "Choose Your Own Adventure" books than a novel with one single plotline, because not everyone in your audience will use the product the same way. For example, some managers might conduct a skills audit of individual staff members in a conference room that they may not supervise. Other managers may be more lenient and send the quizzes out to their staff with the understanding they should respond to them in good faith. After all, this is a quick and easy way to get a baseline, and spending the day in a conference room takes a big chunk out of their schedule. If they aren't going to supervise the quizzes, the manager will probably want to be able to designate a list of students and send out an invitation for the quiz via e-mail.

Let's continue with this example, an e-mail-initiated skills audit for existing staff, and return to the beginning of the story. Managers will need to do a few things. First, they must enter the quiz takers into their account on Enablequiz.com. If there are a lot of quiz takers, managers will probably want a way to do this in bulk. They will likely have some kind of a company phone list in Excel or a similar format. So, let's say the manager has the option to add the quiz takers individually or in bulk by uploading an Excel spreadsheet. Since upload utilities can be a huge pain, we need a way to handle a potential case where they upload a file in the wrong format. That's probably a test case attached to the story of how the managers add students.

Once managers have added their quiz takers to the system, they need to be able to send an e-mail to notify them. They may want to customize the e-mail to explain their particular objectives and guidelines around the quiz to their staff. The quiz takers need a way to record and report the results after they finish since the manager won't be there.

Another useful template for your stories is add/modify/delete: if you're putting data into the system, you'll usually have a need to facilitate all three of these operations and it's useful to keep that in mind as you're organizing your stories.

The following section summarizes the epic story of managers doing a skills audit for their current staff.

Epic Story: Skills Audit

The epic story is this: "As a manager, I want to administer a skills audit so that I can understand the capabilities of my staff." (See Table 3.3.)

Note: Enable Quiz thinks the overall process goes something like this:

A. Make sure the customers have all the questions banks they want (though this might happen after Step C instead of before it).
B. Purchase said quiz banks.
C. Create the quiz.
D. Administer the quiz.
E. View the results.

Table 3.3

Stories at Enable Quiz

Story	Test Cases
As a manager, I want to browse the quiz banks so I can make sure I'm subscribed to all the necessary topics for my skills audit.	The banks are searchable by topic. The user can select a set of quizzes and send an e-mail with a note to the purchasing authority (i.e., "These are the quiz banks we should buy").
As a manager, I want to purchase additional quiz banks so I can add additional technical topics to my quizzes.	The manager is able to purchase additional quiz banks. If the users don't have purchase authority, they see a list of those that do. The charges are correctly prorated against the billing anniversary of the account.
As a manager, I want to create a custom quiz bank so I can add my own questions to the quiz.	The customer is not charged for this bank. The custom bank is invisible to any other accounts on the system.
As a manager, I want to create a quiz so I can use it with my staff.	The administrators can set the length of the quiz in terms of number of questions. The administrators can allocate a set quantity of questions from any of the available quiz banks. The administrators cannot allocate questions from a quiz bank they are not subscribed to. If the administrators try to allocate more questions from a bank than remain against the unallocated total questions in the quiz, they will receive a descriptive error that includes total questions in the quiz, questions from each bank so far.
As a manager, I want to create a list of students from an Excel file so I can invite them to take the quiz.	The system accepts a standard Excel template we provide. The Excel template is downloadable from the page where the users go to create the list of students. If the users upload an invalid file, they receive an error that directs them to the correct template file and warns them not to modify it.
As a manager, I want to create a list of students online.	The users can paste in a comma- or tab-separated list of student e-mails, and the system will identify the individual e-mail addresses. The users can create students individually. The users can specify e-mail addresses and optional names.
As a manager, I want to invite a set of students to take a quiz so I can receive their scores.	The users receive a helpful error message if the list of students is blank. If the e-mail delivery to the students fails, the managers should receive a notice and the failure should be visible on the portal. The managers see the list of students and must confirm before sending.

Table 3.3
(*continued*)

Story	Test Cases
As a manager, I want to see which students have completed the quiz and which have not so I can send them a reminder.	The users can see a list of students who have completed versus not completed the quiz. There is a visual indicator for students whose e-mail invitation failed. The users can customize the body of said e-mail. The e-mail sends in under two minutes.
As a manager, I want to see how the students scored on the test so I can put in place a skills improvement program.	The users can search by student first name and/or last name. The users can see a presentation that shows all the students' scores and the averages. It is impossible to see any reports if you are not an administrator.

Using the MVC Framework for a High-Level Design

The section will give you a high-level view of a few key aspects of application design. The purpose is not for you to become a programmer or an application designer. The purpose is to give you a high-level introduction to a few key concepts that will help you collaborate with your development team on your final design. The adaptive and agile methods most popular today involve a high degree of collaboration. This section will give you additional intuition and concepts helpful in the process.

Once you and your team finish the audience characterization and user stories, you're ready to think about a high-level design for the initial application. Even though it's primarily the job of your implementers to do the software design, you should be neither timid nor presumptuous about participating in the process. The process is collaborative and a product owner unwilling to participate in design is like the businessperson making a vague deal and then leaving all the key points to the lawyers. Everyone should be involved in this part of the process, and I always make sure that I am.

Thinking about your application as having Model, View, and Controller (MVC) components will help you organize your thinking about its implementation. It's certainly not the only way to organize an application, but what's important is having a framework you can use to constructively decompose the application's different facets. The View is the thing the user sees, the collection of screens the system provides for the user to interact. If you follow Figure 3.2, you'll see step one in a typical application is that users supply inputs to the View. The inputs (e.g., a username and password) are handled by the Controller, which implements the application's logic, the processes the application undertakes to do things on behalf of a user. In step two, the Controller checks the username and password. But where does that username and password live? They live in the Model, which is the part of the application that deals with organizing and storing all the application's data. Once the

Figure 3.2

MVC
Framework

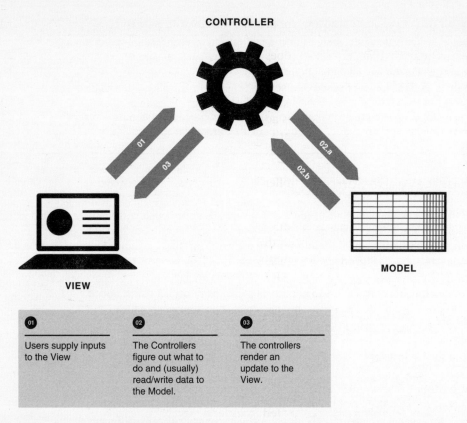

CONTROLLER

VIEW

MODEL

01	02	03
Users supply inputs to the View	The Controllers figure out what to do and (usually) read/write data to the Model.	The controllers render an update to the View.

Controller determines whether you can log in, in step three, the Controller tells the View what to show in response to the user's login request, for example, "invalid password" or rendering the page the users see when they first log in.

A good example for a little more detail here is Facebook. When you go to Facebook.com, you see the login screen, which is part of the View. When you type your username and password into the View, they're passed to a series of logical Controllers, which are the underlying application logic. The Facebook Controllers that deal with you logging in to your account operate something like this:

1. See if the user's username exists.
    • If not, have the View display a message that says "no such account."
2. See if the user's password is valid.
    • If not, have the View display a message that says "invalid password."
3. See if the user has any friend invitations or notices (by checking the data Model).
    • If so, post those in appropriate part of the View after they log in.
4. Have the View put together the user's landing page.
5. Continue these steps until you see the View you're used to when you log in to Facebook.

The technical term for Controller is algorithm, a fancy term you've probably heard used in various contexts. However, it's a simple idea: An algorithm is a fixed set of steps for doing something. Engineers, particularly in software, tend to think in terms of algorithms since they are a legitimate and effective way of approaching this kind of question. The Facebook login algorithm is a fixed set of procedures that figure out how to log you in and then render the right View. (Remember, all this is conceptual: there are probably many different software programs that run when you log in to Facebook.)

The last item is the Model, which deals with the underlying data: How does Facebook store all the different posts and messages you see on Facebook? There's a complex set of structures to manage all that information. Let's take a simple piece of that Model: your profile. You have a Facebook username, which uniquely identifies you versus the other millions of users. When dealing with Models, you must discern what parameter uniquely identifies a record. (In this case, a record is a user account.) Your profile has additional descriptive parameters, such as your city of residence, hometown, gender, and alma mater. That's one small but important piece of Facebook's Model. You have your wall postings, your friends, your privacy settings, your messages, and so forth.

In summary, MVC framework describes a Model, a View, and a Controller, which together constitute the following system.

1. The Model is the set of structures that organize the system's information.
2. The View describes things that a user sees when they're interacting with the application.
3. The Controller consists of algorithms, big and small, that take a set of inputs, and then return outputs.
    - By way of the View, a user passes inputs to the Controller which then return outputs back to the View where they're displayed.

In the following sections, we'll walk through an MVC-based description of Enable Quiz. Though there's no particular correct order in which to cover the M, the V, and the C. I think it would be best to start with the View since it's the most intuitive. Our stories will map most directly and intuitively to View's and what we formulate there will guide us in discussing the Model and Controllers.

We'll cover examples organized around Enable Quiz and Andrew's preparation for engagement with his product implementation team. As is the case with everything we've discussed so far, the world's greatest engineer can't make great software out of an incomplete or poorly articulated product design. The reverse is true as well in that you don't need the world's greatest engineer to make a great product out of a great product design. Walking through the MVC framework will help Andrew think through important aspects of Enable Quiz that are better covered now rather than later.

A final note on the MVC as it's described here: There's lively debate about the "true" and accurate definition of the MVC. There's debate, for example, around whether the real definition should stick to what was said in Trygve Reenskaug's original paper on the subject (1979) and how different technologies do or don't implement true MVC. Unless you're actually using a software programming environment that references the MVC, don't worry about this. As long as your implementation team understands that by Model you mean where the data lives, by View you mean what the user sees, and by Controller you mean application logic, they can interpret and apply your descriptions to whatever frameworks they're using.[2]

The View

See Me, Feel Me[3]

The View is what the users see on the screen.[4] It's probably the most intuitive component since we're all used to looking at applications. You can measure your success on the View component in a simple way by how well you enable the users to do what they want to do. Though the discipline of design pervades every aspect of the product, average people off the street probably think about things like the View when they hear this term. They probably think of the whole thing as an artistic, inspiration-driven process: the ''I see pink'' school of thought. Though the design of the front end View is art and science, it's mostly science.

You can prepare yourself for success. (I've recommended a few books at the end of this chapter on visual communication and human-computer interaction.) One of the most valuable lessons is to clarify your intent. If a silver bullet exists for getting good product out the door, it's making your priorities clear, intuitive, and disciplined. Being disciplined in your priorities means deciding what's important to the users and removing everything else or tucking it away. For example, while Apple allows you to do around 10 things with the iPod, 100 were probably under serious consideration. Bad product and poor design are frequently the result of designing for the 99th percentile of things a user might want to do, throwing in the proverbial kitchen sink on features, making it the user's responsibility to find what they want. Users will avoid this if they have a choice. Instead, they'll simply opt for a product whose designers went to the trouble to narrow their options to what's critical.

Good design at the tactical level is frequently an exercise in reduction against a set of priorities. In one of his most powerful lessons, author Edward Tufte (see Specialty Reading) shows the reader a simple visual explanation, a chart displaying some data. He challenges the reader to keep taking out visual elements until they start removing things that contain meaningful data, which he describes as increasing the ''data-ink ratio.'' Even though this isn't a catchall for improving a visual explanation, it's an easy principle to apply for the layperson. Start with a clear objective and set of priorities for whatever it is you're sketching. Lots of visual communication is thrown together, like a meeting with no agenda, called with some vague sense of need and impulse. Then tinker. I've seen several outstanding designers in action, and each one of them spent a lot of

---

[2]If you want to read about the debate, see http://en.wikipedia.org/wiki/Talk:Model%E2%80%93view%E2%80%93controller.
[3]This is a reference to a song by The Who from their album *Tommy* . . . just so you don't get creeped out.
[4]If you're designing an application without a graphical user interface, like a database or API-only component, the View is also your application program interface, the View to the program that will be calling your program.

time experimenting before they arrived at something they liked. Even if you have no training in design (and I do not), you can evaluate your prototypes against your objectives and your own sense of what feels right. Just remember, it's only a sketch so be ready to toss it and move on. In general, prioritizing what's important in the View should be driven by your knowledge of the audience and assessment of user stories. Implement the View based on the list of things you foresee your users doing weighted against the prevalence and importance of those things.

If building front-ends is not your forte, do not reinvent the wheel. You can get a great sense of what you want by drawing on the experience you have working with front ends you use every day. Consider their relevance to your purpose and how well they perform. Also, many templates are available online. I've referenced a number of resources on Alexandercowan.com/views.

The View at Enable Quiz

Given the scope of what they need to build and their available resources, Andrew plans to hire a professional front-end designer. Given that, Andrew's plan is to put together some preliminary ideas of what might work for Enable Quiz, along with some likes and dislikes to start the dialog with their future front-end designer. Andrew knows that, in the case of Enable Quiz, the View will need two general sections: one for the administrators and another for the students. So, he's looked for sites that have the idea of administrators as well as users.

For purposes of comparing these sites, let's say there are five levels of navigation. The first, super navigation (supernav), is any navigation that takes you to a fundamentally different View, a View that has no navigation elements in common with the page you just left. When building Views, you want to do this sparingly since it confuses the user when you swap between Views that look different. It's like teleportation or waking up after overindulging in drink—it takes time to figure out where you are.

The primary navigation is the first level of navigation that allows the user to start selecting things that will appear on the main screen. The secondary navigation deals with navigating between the next level items, sub-elements of the primary navigation. Tertiary navigation manages the next level down. Sub-navigation is anything below the tertiary navigation. Table 3.4 provides a quick summary.

Navigation Scheme	Notes
Super	Takes you to a different view.
Primary	Selection of first-level elements you want to view.
Secondary	Selection of elements within the view you selected using the primary navigation.
Tertiary	Navigation within an item selected from the secondary navigation.
Sub	Anything within the tertiary navigation.

Table 3.4

Navigation Hierarchy

Figure 3.3

Admin View
on Google
Apps

SUPER
NAVIGATION
These links allow
an admin to pull
up their separate
end user views
for mail,
calendar, etc.

PRIMARY
NAVIGATION
a horizontal scroll
bar with selectable
items

SECONDARY
NAVIGATION
This 'Dashboard'
page provides
shortcuts as a kind of
secondary navigation.
The shortcuts link to
items you can also
reach from the
standard secondary
navigation under the
'Settings' item (see
next example).

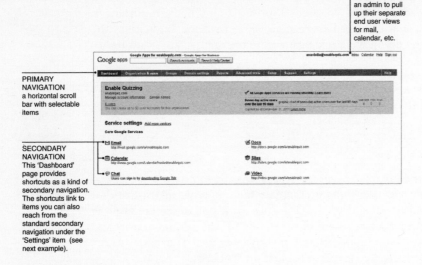

Figure 3.4

Admin View
on Google
Apps II

TERTIARY
NAVIGATION
These links allow
the user to tab
between sub-items
on the page.

We've now selected the
item 'Settings' from the
primary navigation. The
darker shading on that
item indicates the
selection.

SECONDARY
NAVIGATION
Under the Settings
item in the primary
navigation, the left
margin now
presents a list of
services whose
settings we can
choose to
configure.

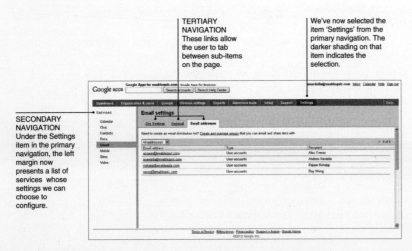

It's key to pick a navigation paradigm and stick with it. It's like the process of organizing your files. Though you may have a number of equally valid ways to do it, being inconsistent is almost always a loser. The navigation scheme typically forms the basis for what's called a site map which lays out the different areas of the site.

First, let's take a look at Google Apps, Google's application suite for businesses (see Figure 3.3). Its site is highly functional for a huge audience, so it's worth looking at. Logging in as an Admin, you're presented a specific admin view. This view allows you to change settings for the application and create new user accounts. They have the primary navigation organized horizontally across the screen. A secondary navigation follows from the primary navigation where they present a drop-down list of items under a primary navigation element. For example, the primary navigation item called Service Settings leads to a secondary navigation where you see a list with Email, Chat, and so forth. The link in the upper right is a super navigation that takes the user to a whole different view, the end user view for that admin's account.

Google threw in a few shortcuts to frequently used items that you can arrive at through the secondary navigation, such as Email, Docs, and so on. If we click on Email, from that shortcut or from the secondary navigation above, we arrive at a screen for managing the company-wide e-mail settings (see Figure 3.4).

This screen provides a tertiary navigation that allows the user to tab between related screens under these e-mail settings.

Let's take a quick look at what happens if we move to the user View by way of the supernav in the upper right (Figure 3.5). If we click on Inbox from the supernav, we arrive at this View of Andrew's individual e-mail account.

The supernav opens the user view in a new tab within the browser, and you don't have a super navigation to go back to the admin level because you cannot return to the admin level, which is common in these situations. The links in the upper left for Calendar and other functions are the primary navigation, allowing the users to move between sub-applications, such as mail and calendar. The left pane is the secondary navigation and allows the users to move between different mail folders.

Let's click over to the Calendar before we head off to another site (Figure 3.6). You can see how that as the primary navigation remains consistent (though it does load a new tab in the browser), the secondary navigation changes for the Calendar application. Though it's desirable to keep the navigation consistent,

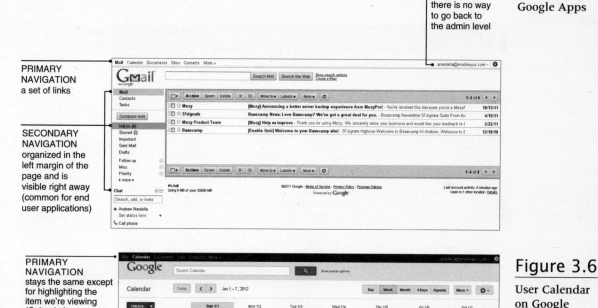

PRIMARY NAVIGATION a set of links

SECONDARY NAVIGATION organized in the left margin of the page and is visible right away (common for end user applications)

the previous super-nav is now gone- from the user View, there is no way to go back to the admin level

Figure 3.5

User Email on Google Apps

PRIMARY NAVIGATION stays the same except for highlighting the item we're viewing (Calendar)

SECONDARY NAVIGATION This part of the navigation changes based on the item we're viewing (mail, calendar, etc.).

Figure 3.6

User Calendar on Google Apps

Figure 3.7

View as a
User (Ray
Wong)

PRIMARY
NAVIGATION
horizontal tabs

Ray Wong is logged
in as a user (vs. an
admin)

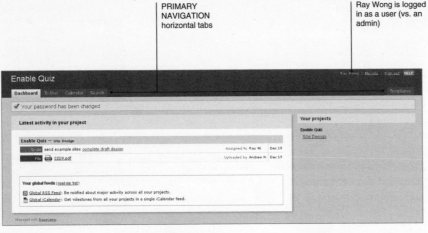

Figure 3.8

Andrew's
View as an
Admin

PRIMARY
NAVIGATION
Andrew's View as an admin
has a few additional items
but is fundamentally the same
as Ray's (user) View.

SUPER
NAVIGATION
Links on the projects list provide
a super navigation scheme that
takes both users and admin's to
a new page.

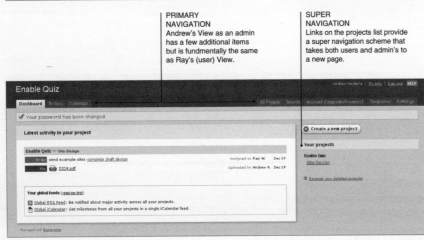

calendaring differs from mail enough that
the difference is warranted.

Let's take a look at the popular Basecamp extranet product, used by many firms
for project management. In Google Apps,
admins log in to complete admin tasks.
They can then transition and act just like
users. The admin and user views are fundamentally different, and Google uses the
supernav to transition between them. Basecamp is different due to the nature of the
application. It's a collaboration application,
so it's vital that all users are seeing and doing
the same things. In Figures 3.7 and 3.8,
"Ray" is a user, and Andrew is an admin.
Do you see how on login Andrew's view
as an admin and Ray's view as a user look
fundamentally the same?

Admins have additional choices to add
companies and users to the system, manage
account options, and configure the account
settings. But their view fundamentally looks
the same. The admin and the user may be
part of a number of projects, and have to-
do lists and milestones associated with those
projects.

Basecamp uses a supernav to transition
between the dashboard view you see when
you log in and a different view for individual

projects. (See Figure 3.9.) If we select the Site Design project from initial dashboard view, we see a whole new view, disconnected from the previous view except for a Back to Dashboard link in the upper left.

The users' view of the project is almost the same, except that the label on the primary navigation allows them to see people on the project and is labelled ''People'' vs. ''People & Permissions'' for an admin. (See Figure 3.10.)

For contrast, let's take a look at Mozy, a hosted backup service (Figure 3.11). From an end user standpoint, the interaction is simple: I have an application from Mozy running on my PC that I use to select the files I want to back up and how often I do so. Admins on the site create user accounts, check which machines are actively backing up files, and ensure they've divvied out enough space. Mozy uses a simple but effective navigation scheme in which the application menu is organized down the left margin of the page with expandable/collapsible

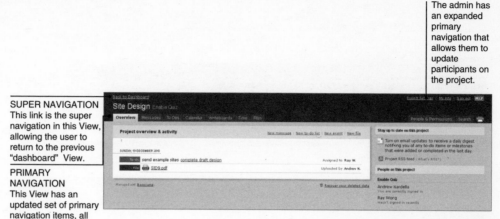

The admin has an expanded primary navigation that allows them to update participants on the project.

Figure 3.9

Project View in Basecamp for an Admin

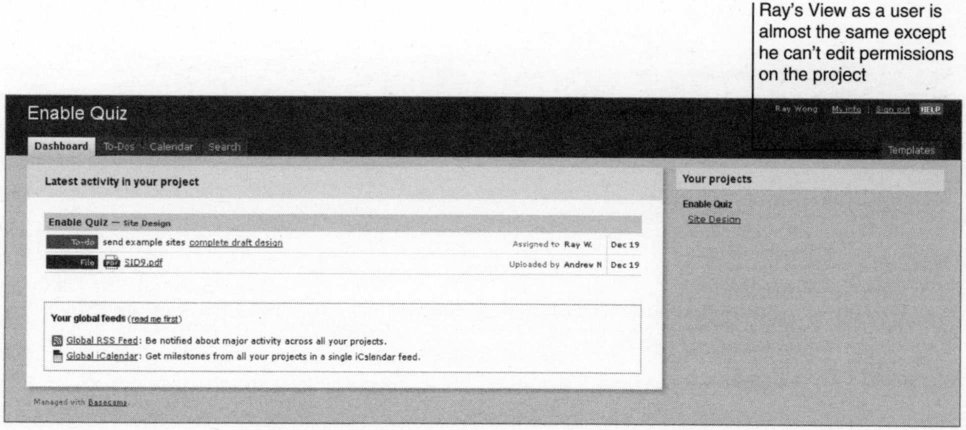

SUPER NAVIGATION
This link is the super navigation in this View, allowing the user to return to the previous "dashboard" View.

PRIMARY NAVIGATION
This View has an updated set of primary navigation items, all relating to the current project ("Site Design").

Ray's View as a user is almost the same except he can't edit permissions on the project

Figure 3.10

Project View in Basecamp for a User

Figure 3.11

**Admin View
on Mozy**

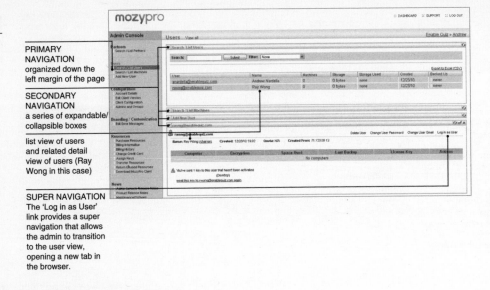

PRIMARY
NAVIGATION
organized down the
left margin of the page

SECONDARY
NAVIGATION
a series of expandable/
collapsible boxes

list view of users
and related detail
view of users (Ray
Wong in this case)

SUPER NAVIGATION
The 'Log in as User'
link provides a super
navigation that allows
the admin to transition
to the user view,
opening a new tab in
the browser.

Figure 3.12

**User View on
Mozy**

Andrew, as admin, is
seeing the user View for
Ray's account

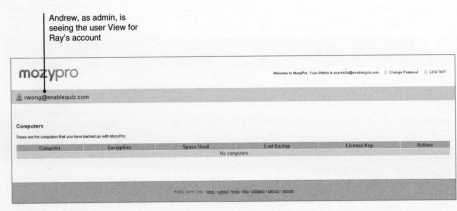

boxes to manage item detail in the secondary navigation.

They use a supernav that allows the admin to see items within a user account (Figure 3.12).

Out of the three, my take is that Mozy most resembles Enable Quiz with a number of options for admins but a simple set of items you need to present to users. The admins using Enable Quiz have a fair amount to do on the site, including purchasing quiz banks, formulating quizzes, creating students, sending the quizzes. The users have a relatively small number of things to do. Something like what is shown in Figure 3.13 might make sense.

Enable Quiz could use a single primary navigation on the left margin, similar to Mozy. Enable Quiz will likely have a larger set of items than Mozy, so the first-level items in the menu could be displayed with a visual cue that shows items under it. The users would click on an item like a plus sign or arrow to unfold the second-level elements. How many items do you think it can accommodate? For example, a medium-sized customer could easily have dozens of quizzes over the course of a year. This is a bit more difficult to discern for the question banks; however, those could be substantial in number since admins can create their own.

The primary navigation probably could not accommodate all that by itself, so Enable Quiz would need to introduce a secondary navigation of some type. The users would select a menu from the primary navigation on the left, and if that menu has lots of items, say quizzes, then this secondary navigation would show a list of those items. The next question is how that secondary navigation should work. On quizzes, for example: Once the user selects Manage Quizzes, how does Enable

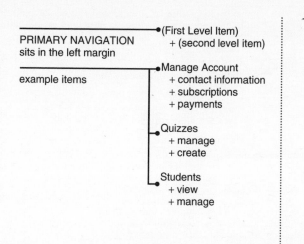

Figure 3.13

Possible Navigation Outline for Enable Quiz

Quiz allow them to find and select the quiz they want? What if they want to browse all the quizzes or a subset of them? Two common choices exist for this: a drop-down control and a list view control.

A drop-down menu-based navigation would display a list quizzes from which to choose after selecting Manage Quizzes (Figure 3.14). Once you select a quiz, you could see its details in the screen area below. If you go back to the drop-down menu and select another quiz, you see that quiz's details.

Figure 3.14

Drop-Down Control

The list view control gives you more information about the items (Figure 3.15). The drawback with the drop-down menu is that you can only look at the quizzes one at a time. So, if users wanted to compare quizzes on some simple piece of information, like which quizzes are using the question bank Basic Unix, they'd have to go through them individually, selecting each from the drop-down menu, viewing its details, and selecting the next quiz from the drop-down menu. Therefore, Enable Quiz might be better off with a list view that shows the source bank list of each quiz for the user story of wanting to see which quizzes are using which question bank. From the list

Quiz	Banks	Students
Unix 1	Basic Unix	30
Unix 2	Basic Unix, Adv. Unix	11
Perl 2	Basic Perl	7

Figure 3.15

List View Control

Figure 3.16

Drop-Down
Concept

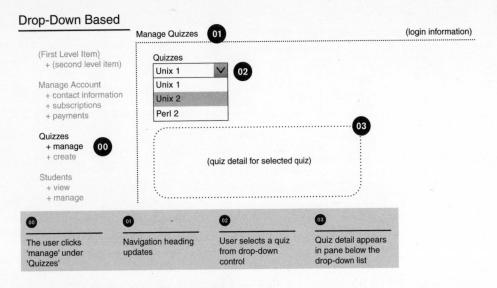

Drop-Down Based

Manage Quizzes **01**   (login information)

(First Level Item)
+ (second level item)

Manage Account
+ contact information
+ subscriptions
+ payments

Quizzes **00**
+ manage
+ create

Students
+ view
+ manage

Quizzes
| Unix 1 | ⌄ | **02** |
| Unix 1 |
| Unix 2 |
| Perl 2 |

03

(quiz detail for selected quiz)

00	**01**	**02**	**03**
The user clicks 'manage' under 'Quizzes'	Navigation heading updates	User selects a quiz from drop-down control	Quiz detail appears in pane below the drop-down list

Figure 3.17

List View
Concept

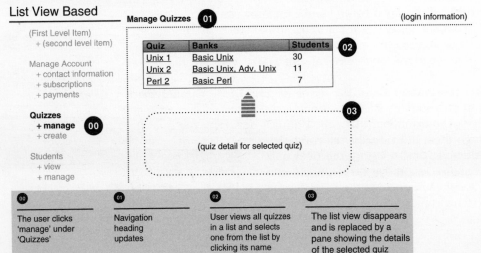

List View Based

Manage Quizzes **01**   (login information)

(First Level Item)
+ (second level item)

Manage Account
+ contact information
+ subscriptions
+ payments

Quizzes **00**
+ manage
+ create

Students
+ view
+ manage

Quiz	Banks	Students	**02**
Unix 1	Basic Unix	30
Unix 2	Basic Unix, Adv. Unix	11
Perl 2	Basic Perl	7

03

(quiz detail for selected quiz)

00	**01**	**02**	**03**
The user clicks 'manage' under 'Quizzes'	Navigation heading updates	User views all quizzes in a list and selects one from the list by clicking its name	The list view disappears and is replaced by a pane showing the details of the selected quiz

view, you'd click on the name of a quiz to see its details. Figures 3.16 and 3.17 compare interactions across the two alternatives for secondary navigation. Figure 3.18 compares the drop-down and list view controls.

If you look back up at Mozy (Figure 3.11), you'll notice that it uses a list view table for the user accounts. The issue with list views is how the users transition between the primary navigation, the list view, and the detail view without losing their way. Once you're seeing the detail view for a quiz in Enable Quiz, you have to again click Manage under Quizzes and select the other quiz you want to see from the list view if you want to go back and see the detail view of a different quiz. Once you click Search/List Users from the primary navigation in Mozy, you will see a list view with users on the main page in one of their expandable/collapsible boxes that make up the secondary navigation scheme. If you click on one of the users, the details appear in another secondary navigation box at the bottom of the screen. Though it works for Mozy, it's a little arbitrary and potentially confusing to users. Why does the detail view box appear at the bottom? Why are there those other boxes, like Add a New User, in between the list view and the detail view boxes?

It's desirable that navigational controls in a View present a clear hierarchy, ideally with a global navigation, to keep the users anchored. Mozy's approach to locating and viewing users makes the detail view conceptually subordinate to the list view since selections from the list view are driving the detail view. The problem is that the list and detail views appear parallel in the visual hierarchy: They're both boxes within the main frame on the page, which is potentially confusing. Unfortunately, I haven't seen a lot of great alternatives. In CRM systems it's common to go into the detail view once you click on an item from a list view. If you want to return to that same list view, you have to reselect it from the primary navigation. You have three steps on the path to find users in most systems: select from the primary navigation, select from the list view, and see the detail view. You have to loop all the way back to first step in the CRM system before you can go back to second step. Some applications I've seen cheat with a kind of supernav to take you back from the detail view to the list view. In that case, you will have yet another navigation control users have to see and understand. Mozy, however, allows you to go back to the second step directly without having to loop through the first step.

For another option, what if Enable Quiz uses the drop-down control to keep the core secondary navigation simple but adds a search button next to it? This button presents a pop-up control that allows users to search, showing the results of the search in a list-view. The primary drop-down menu will update if the users select something in the list view, allowing them to see the detail view free and clear. If they want to see the list view again, they click on the search button. Figure 3.19 describes this approach.

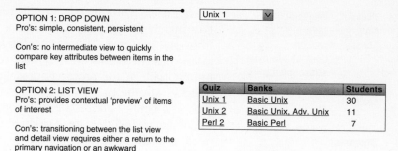

Figure 3.18

Drop-Down vs. List View

OPTION 1: DROP DOWN
Pro's: simple, consistent, persistent

Con's: no intermediate view to quickly compare key attributes between items in the list

OPTION 2: LIST VIEW
Pro's: provides contextual 'preview' of items of interest

Con's: transitioning between the list view and detail view requires either a return to the primary navigation or an awkward super navigation shortcut

Quiz	Banks	Students
Unix 1	Basic Unix	30
Unix 2	Basic Unix, Adv. Unix	11
Perl 2	Basic Perl	7

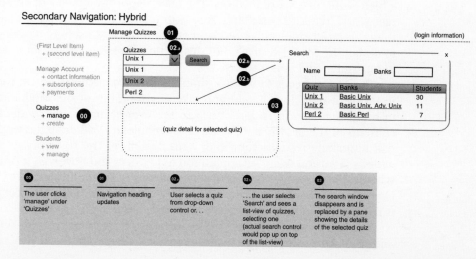

Figure 3.19

Hybrid Concept for Enable Quiz

Figure 3.20

Site Map
Example

Primary Nav.	Seconary Nav.
Manage Account	
	contact information
	subscriptions
	payments
Quizzes	
	manage
	create
Students	
	view
	manage

If Enable Quiz had to decide on an approach right now, I'd recommend the hybrid. Fortunately, it doesn't. This was a brainstorming exercise toward providing inputs to a front-end designer. These notes look rough, but that's all right. Prototypes are sometimes more constructive when they look rough. It keeps people from focusing on details that are unimportant at the prototyping stage. The key inputs Enable Quiz needs to present to the designer are the user stories we discussed earlier, a site map to lay out the desired content, and, as a kind of bonus, a distillation of these brainstorming notes (along with anything else the designers feel they need to do their thing). The site map looks something like Figure 3.20.

You might have some additional notes in the margins. The point of the site map is to keep an inventory of things you think will need to appear on the site, and their relationship to each other. Enable Quiz will collaborate with their front-end designer on the alternatives, arriving at a set of final concepts, and make a final decision for beta.

The Model

Peeling and Slicing the Onion

The Model's job is to organize and store the application's data. That data might be a folder of emails, a document, a high score, or a set of invoices. The most important quality of an application's Model is its conformity to the real-world items it's describing. And your job is to give your team members the real-world insight they need so they can build an intuitive Model that faithfully and usefully describes its real-world analogs. You don't need to design the Model yourself, but this section should give you some insight on how to peel back the proverbial onion and model your data.

The Model needs to balance simplicity and robustness. Again, the easiest way to think about simplicity is in terms of reduction: Could you take anything out of the Model and still get the same functionality? Keep in mind that the users don't need to see everything in the Model because Views deals with displaying the contents of the model. But the Model's complexity will drive development and maintenance cost. Complexity will ultimately restrain your long-term flexibility. The best way to think about robustness is in terms of the various tasks you want the application to perform and how well it can perform them. Is it flexible enough to do whatever you want? You'll probably find you're frequently working to balance robustness and simplicity. For example, you'll often find yourself asking whether the additional complexity that a new feature would require is really justified in terms of the overall user base.

The last thing to consider before we start is two key types of relationships for describing a model: Has-A and Is-A. This terminology just means, for example, a dog Has-A tail and a dog Is-A(n) animal. In a Has-A relationship, a thing "A" (dog) has a subcomponent "B" (tail). In an Is-A is a relationship, a thing "A" (dog) is an example of some general category "Z" (animal). Figure 3.21 summarizes this.

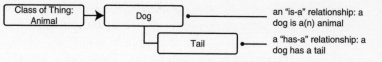

Figure 3.21

Basic Model Constructs

The Model at Enable Quiz

Let's start with the audience types we described at the beginning of the chapter. There was the HR manager, the functional manager, and the quiz taker. This fits a typical pattern where hosted services have admins and users. The HR manager and functional manager would be different types of admins, and the quiz takers would be users. A key question is this: Could the managers be quiz takers?

The answer is probably yes. They might take a dry run of the quizzes in some kind of a trial mode, so they wouldn't need to have a user account for that. It's also possible functional managers would want to quiz themselves and put it on record, just as users would. Given that, we probably want to have an idea of different profiles associated with a single user. A quiz taker would have a Student Profile, and an admin would have an Admin Profile, and a single user could have both profiles. See Figure 3.22.

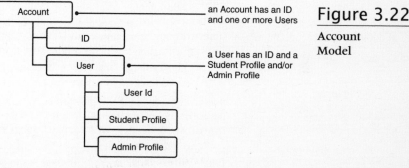

Figure 3.22

Account Model

Let's review all of this using our new lingo. An account represents a company using Enable Quiz and has an Account ID, one or more users, who are uniquely identified by a userID and may have a student profile, as well as an admin profile, or both. The userID could be the user's e-mail address for simplicity. What properties would the student profile need to have?

The students' profiles would be simple. They would have a list of quizzes the student can take or has taken. You'd probably want some kind of indicator as to whether they're supposed to have access to the portal since you don't necessarily want to grant interviewees (non-employees) access to subsequently log in to Enable Quiz. Let's call this item that describes the quizzes they can take a "registration." We'll use curly brackets next to an item to denote that it's a set of items since, for example, you could be registered for more than one quiz. Figure 3.23 summarizes this.

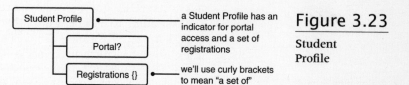

Figure 3.23

Student Profile

Next we have our admin profile. An HR manager and a functional manager are admins (Is-A), so they have admin profiles. What properties would the admin profile need to have? Enable Quiz only wants one billing contact for collections purposes, so there'd have to be a property that designates the billing admin. Enable Quiz will offer short answer questions and someone has to grade those. The customer may not want all the admins to be able to grade, so the admin profile will need something that designates an authorized grader. What about the idea of an account owner? Usually, the owner is the only person who can create new admins. We'll assume the billing contact is the owner for simplicity.

One question Andrew should ask at this point is how hard it would be to change the above design if the billing contact and owner need to be separate. That's a question you want to ask yourself when you make the brave decision to keep things simple: How much more painful will it be if we have to make this more robust later on?

Unless you're doing some of the programming or are working with a development team already, you won't know the answer to this while you're doing your design. But these questions will make great discussion points when you do engage with your implementers since it will help give you a sense of how attuned they are to your design goals. One idea is to mark questionable items as "discuss" in your notes. Remember, this rough document is for the purposes of sharing ideas with our implementers and collaborating on the implementation. It should be clear. It doesn't have to be pretty and it won't be final. A little roughness may help encourage your implementation team members to get in there and make their own notes.

To keep things simple, we'll make the account owner the billing contact.

The next set of items in the account is the set of question banks. Enable Quiz will sell the quiz questions in a series of banks. For example, there would be a Unix Bank with questions about the Unix operating system. As long as the customer has a current subscription to the bank, Enable Quiz will keep updating it with new questions since this will keep students from sharing answers.

The account would have a list of the banks to which it has an active subscription. Keep in mind that the bank differs from a quiz since it's a repository of questions. A quiz is different in that it has a set number of questions that describe additional parameters for what the quiz taker will see. For example, the Unix bank might have 100 questions; however, an administrator might only want to ask 25 questions per quiz. Another configuration would be a quiz that has questions from multiple banks. Such a configuration is likely to be prevalent since customers can create their own banks and they're likely to want to interleave a few of their own questions into a quiz. It's important to keep the Model modular, which means adequately separating elements of the Model which will need to vary independent of other related items.

Figure 3.24 shows the blueprint for user accounts.

Let's move on to the quizzes themselves. For starters, the quiz has a name, an ID, and a total number of questions it should contain. There needs to be a way of making sure that the admin doesn't create a quiz with a quantity of questions greater than what's available in the bank. How would this fit into the Model? That's a trick question: It wouldn't. That's something we'll need to help users avoid by way of the Views we provide and the logical Controllers behind those Views.

Would the quizzes reference the banks directly to get their questions? It seems like something would need to exist between the quiz and the bank that says how many questions the customer admin wants from each bank, since we allow the admin to use multiple banks in creating a quiz. Some customers will want to ensure they give all quiz takers the same questions because they're subject to stringent rules about fairness and consistency. There's the peril of a lot of complexity here to accommodate relatively few customers since Andrew assumes 80 percent of the users will want to create a quiz with a fixed number of questions from a single bank.

The good news about (necessary) data Model complexity is we can work around it when we get to the Views. Remember, not all users have to see everything in the Model, and a good View hides complexity in a way that allows the users who need it to get access to it while allowing everyone else to readily ignore it. It's important to capture this idea of key feature versus a marginal one somewhere in your design notes, probably back in the View section. Remember, your implementation team hasn't had the benefit of sitting with prospective users for dozens of hours. There's no reason why they won't ascribe equal importance to every story and requirement. It's your job to give them the cues around what should be front and center for the 80th percentile of users and what should be a bit more tucked away for the power users.

To address the question of how quizzes know which banks to use and how many questions to take from them, let's say we have the notion of a question source, which references a bank, specifies a number of questions from that bank, and optionally specifies a static list of questions. A quiz could have multiple sources as shown in Figure 3.25.

Let's go into a little more detail about the question banks. Each has an ID and a name. You'd want to know if it was a custom bank that the customer created for themselves since Enable Quiz will not bill for those and it might confuse the billing system if it isn't able to easily tell that a bank is not billable. The bank has a set of questions. We'll need some way to tell whether the customer has a current subscription to the bank. That's something we missed on the account: it needs a list of subscriptions, each with an expiry date

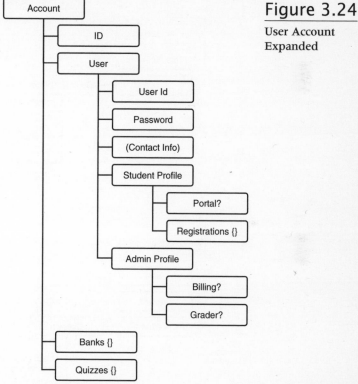

Figure 3.24

User Account Expanded

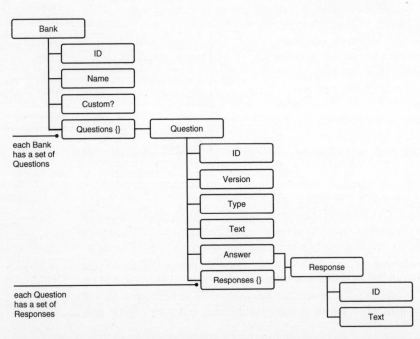

Figure 3.25

Quiz Model

each Quiz has a set of
Question Sources that
reference the desired
question "Banks", and a
declaration of how many
questions to pull from the
specific Bank

the Question Source can
optionally have a Static List
that defines a specific set
of questions to always use

Figure 3.26

Questions
Model

each Bank
has a set of
Questions

each Question
has a set of
Responses

so we know if it's active. I've added that to the master diagram at the end of this section. Another key question is this: What happens if customers don't have a current subscription to a bank? Can they still use the bank? Let's say they can but place restrictions on it, such as they don't get any new questions. That's something for our Controllers to handle. But how will the Controllers determine what's a "new" question for a particular account? We could add a version to each question and keep updating the versions. How do we link that question's version to the expiry date on the account's subscription to the questions bank? Why don't we just make the version a date? We'll do that and our Controllers won't provide access to questions in a bank that have a date more recent than the expiry date on the account's subscription (we'll step through an example in the Controllers section).

Let's cover the questions in more detail. Enable Quiz will offer three types of questions: single choice (multiple-choice questions with a single right answer), multiple choice (multiple-choice questions with possibly more than one right answer), and short answer (descriptive written answer). Each question would have the question text, a set of available responses, and then a designation of what response or responses are correct. The responses should probably be their own type of item since we don't want to present them in a fixed order. Figure 3.26 summarizes both banks and questions.

We've described the user accounts and quizzes. Now here's a real challenge: How do we tie this all together? How do the users get these quizzes, take them, and store their results?

Let's start with the model structure for how students know they should take a quiz. We called this a registration when we went over the user profile. The registration should have an ID, an issue date, a name (which we can make optional), and a state (pending or completed). The registration would then reference a quiz along with a structure for storing the quiz results, which would include an ID, the date the quiz was completed, a grade, the answers students supplied, and whether they were right or wrong. See Figure 3.27.

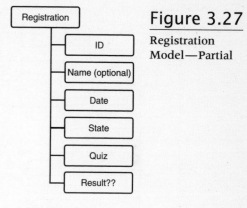

Figure 3.27

Registration Model—Partial

One of our primary design goals in the Model is to avoid repetition, but since the quizzes don't always have the same set of questions, we should probably store the set of questions the students answered in the result along with the answers they submitted. As long as we don't allow the admin to modify a question after it has been created, we could reference the question in its original form in the result, rather than storing a new copy of it every time a student answers it. I'm inclined to think that we should keep admins from modifying the questions they're created since this could create complexity in a number of places. But what if the admin wants to delete a question or they realize there's a typo and want to fix it? It's common in systems like this where you have lots of cross-references to not to allow the users to delete items; instead, they can mark as inactive items they don't want to use anymore. So, if admins want to fix a question, they could make the current version of it inactive and create a new active version. The old version of the question remains. If someone responded to the old version of the question, it's there, but we'll make sure the Controllers stop using it in any future quizzes.

It would look something like Figure 3.28.

Once we clean up a few things, and add the inactive property to the question model, we have an overall draft of the general Model (Figure 3.29).

I added the "subscriptions" items under the Account to designate the banks to which the account has an active subscription. Each subscription has an expiry date and a reference to a bank.

That was a lot of stuff. Are we done? No, we're just getting started! The items above are a draft and their purpose was to exercise our thinking on the Model for Enable Quiz and have some rough ideas to hand our implementation team. From there, the Model will undoubtedly change and improve over the course of the actual implementation.

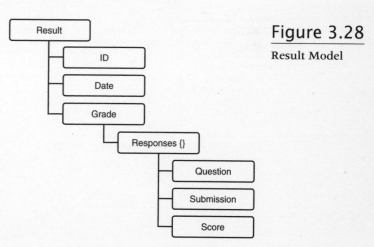

Figure 3.28

Result Model

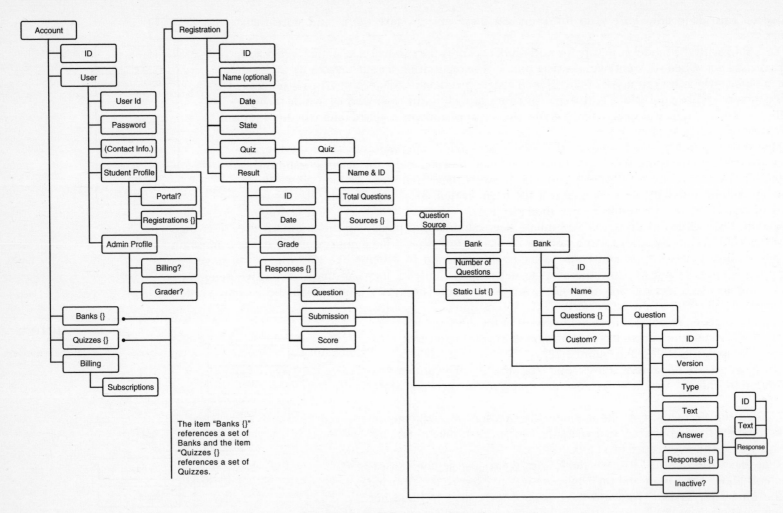

The item "Banks {}" references a set of Banks and the item "Quizzes {}" references a set of Quizzes.

Figure 3.29   Overall Model

The Controller

You're in Control

If you're feeling a little worn out, the good news is that this is our last section in the MVC framework and probably the simplest in the case of Enable Quiz. The Controller is the brains of the application. I guess you'd have to say it's the part of the brain that does the thinking since the brain remembers things, too, and that's the Model's job. The Controller deals with the application's underlying logic or, to use some computer science lingo, algorithms. Obviously, a typical application will implement many algorithms and most of them you can leave entirely up to the software developers. However, there are many more places than you might assume where it's important to give your input on how things should work. Also, when you're troubleshooting an issue or evaluating a useability question, it's useful to have a notion about the Controllers so you can ask the right questions or collect the right specifics for a diagnosis. As such, this section will cover some example controllers for Enable Quiz. Hopefully, this section will give you a sense of how to describe and understand your key Controllers.

The Controller at Enable Quiz

Before we go through the first example Controller for Enable Quiz, we should question and refine a few key assumptions. These are the kind of questions good engineers will ask you as they flesh out your user stories. Recall that when customer administrators create a quiz, they have the option to pull questions from a number of question banks, which serve as sources for questions. The customer admins can indicate whether they want the questions to appear in a random or static (fixed) order. We need to decide whether a quiz can be modified after it's created since this will have implications for what actions the Controllers are allowed to take and how they take them.

One of the most important things about quizzing a group of students is to compare apples to apples. Allowing customer admins to change the quizzes potentially makes the quiz harder or easier for students who take the quiz later, which breaks the ability to compare results among students. That's not best practice, and we want to help our users who may not be experienced doing this kind of testing to keep to best practices. The easy answer, therefore, is to say they can't. That makes things simpler. So, let's make it a rule: admins cannot alter the content of quizzes after the fact.

But what if we're wrong about that? This one simplification might lead to a lot of discontent among Enable Quiz's users. They may want to make minor changes to quizzes, and they lose the ability to easily compare results among students if the system makes them create a new quiz at that point. One way around this might be to issue a warning (and link to best practices in which Enable Quiz writes about comparative quizzing) when customer admins want to modify an existing quiz. Ultimately, though, I don't think it's a good idea to block the admins from modifying the quizzes.

Another question: At what point in preparing a quiz for students does the system formulate the list of questions? Should the entire list of questions be compiled as soon as the students are registered for the quiz, when they begin the test, or do you pull up questions step by step as the students take the test? The best option seems to be to compile the whole list when the students begin the quiz. It doesn't make sense to do it when the admin registers the students, since it could be awhile from this point until the students take the quiz. You want to have the students answer the newest set of questions to reduce the possibility of their obtaining the answers from another student. Also, we would need a place to store the list of questions if we formulate them for all the registrants in advance. If, on the other hand, we create the list at the moment the student begins the quiz, we don't need to store that set of quiz questions.

When I'm making notes on Controllers, I like to organize them around the questions the Controllers answer. Let's call this current Controller the "How do you select the list of questions when registrants take a quiz?" Controller. It could work as follows:

1. The student is registered for a quiz by the customer admin.
2. The student initiates the quiz.
3. The Enable Quiz Controller does the following:
   - Gets the total number of questions for the quiz.
   - Sums up the number of questions from each question source attached to the quiz (these are references to one or more question banks).
   - Ensures that the total number of questions in the quiz and the total number of questions that we're pulling from each bank are identical.
     - If so, proceed.
     - If not, present an error to the student: "There's an error with this quiz. Please contact [insert name of customer admin for the quiz]."
       - Send an error notice to the account owner via e-mail.
       - Note: Even though the number of questions from each bank should always be consistent with the total configured for the quiz since we force that to be the case, we should perform this check

in advance to make sure everything's all right, especially in the early days while we're working out the kinks.

- For each designated source of questions for the quiz (these are question banks), do the following:
  - Check the date on the account's subscription for the bank
  - Pull [n] questions where [n] is the number of questions that this question source should contribute to the quiz.
  - Do not pull any questions newer than the subscription's expiry date on the account.
  - If a static list is absent, select the questions in random order.
  - If a static list is present, use all the questions from the static list first.
  - Randomize the response set for each question (the order of the available answers).
- Put the set of questions in a random order through the various slots for the quiz.

We'll step through a specific example story to see if it all makes sense. Let's say we have a quiz on the Unix operating system that's supposed to have 23 questions. The customer admin created the quiz to pull questions from two sources: the Enable Quiz Unix 1 bank, which is available to the customer by way of subscription, and an Acme Internal Unix Quiz bank that Acme's IT Director created to ask some custom questions they've deemed to be important. The quiz is supposed to pull 19 questions from the Unix 1 bank and four questions from the Acme bank. First, we check that the 19 questions from the Enable Quiz bank and the four questions from their customer bank add up to 23; we're doing fine so far. The Controller selects 19 questions at random from the Unix 1 bank, excluding questions that have a date/version more recent than the subscription expiry on the account. It then selects four questions from the Acme bank, and randomizes the order of the questions as well as each question's available responses. Now we have our questions ready to present to the quiz taker.

Iterative Learning and Design

We've spent a lot of time on how to use short cycles and quick tests to verify we're on the right track. The design material here implies deep thought and detailed preparation. How do we balance the two? There's no pat answer. Two symptoms of underdesigning are that you're having to do a lot of rework and that lots of new work is incompatible with things you've done before. A symptom of overdesigning is that you spend too much time thinking and not enough time doing and seeing if things work. If you're waiting to acquire a team for implementation, sit down and do as much design as you possibly can. Just don't present it to your implementation team as an absolute prescription but rather as a set of ideas. And make sure you remain open to revising it.

Pulling It All Together

The right amount of design depends on your situation, but ideally you have a Product Design that paints a picture of your audience and solution and spells out some core ideas and operating principles behind the solution. Next, you will want to ensure you have a prioritized backlog of stories for your team to implement.

Chapter 3 Summary

1. Study Your Audience

   The first step in formulating a good product design is painting a picture of your audience. Be as vivid as possible and keep in mind that you're not the core audience. You're working like an anthropologist to describe the audience to your implementation team.

2. Use Stories

   Once you've identified and described your audience, create stories that describe how your product helps the audience members do what they want to do. Epic stories encapsulate an activity with multiple sub-activities (stories), like a play with individual acts. Use test cases to add further detail to your stories. Remember the INVEST guideline.

3. Understand the Basics of the MVC Framework

   Though you don't need to become a computer programmer to do this, understanding the MVC framework will provide you a core toolset to flesh out your design and constructively engage your developers. It's best to approach the View first, then the Model, and finally the Controller.

4. Let User Stories Drive Your Views

   Just as you're probably not a database designer, you're probably not a user interface designer either. Nevertheless, you can give yourself a huge head start on the user interface process by organizing your application's content into a site map and identifying a few sites you think do what you want to do well. Relate the focus of what you like back to your audience description and stories.

We look at the product implementation process more in Chapter 6. There's an example product design and example user stories on Alexandercowan.com/pdesign.

Checklist

I can't tell you how many bad products I've seen that were the result of the implementers misunderstanding the designer's intent. A graduate student in psychology at Stanford did her dissertation on a game where one person tapped out a song on a desk and the other person tried to guess the song. The listeners got the song right around 3.5 percent of the time. Here's the wild part: the tappers thought or assumed that the listeners had understood the song 50 percent of the time.[5] The point is that we're almost all better talkers than we are listeners, and we think what we have to say is clear, obvious, and interesting. However, our audience rarely agrees. Take extra care to articulate your design goals clearly to your implementation team.

Let's cover the items you'll want to produce a fully articulated product design:

1. Audience Definition

    Finish fleshing out a description of your audiences. Focus on customer audiences but remember internal ones, like the questions designers that will be updating Enable Quiz's "banks".

2. User Stories

    Organize user stories around your audiences. Think of every last little thing the various audiences will want to do with your product. Put them in your product design, Google Docs, or your issue tracking system, whatever works best for your team.

3. Model

    Have you thought through the model? Do you understand the concepts behind it? Work with your team to draft some general ideas about the Model if you think it's applicable. If you don't have a team, go ahead and rough out some ideas of your own. Though it may not be the final thing you implement, it will probably provide your team some useful insight.

4. View

    If you have time, draft a site map and write notes comparing best practices across popular websites and how that applies to what you want to do.

5. Controllers

    Think about important checks and processes your application needs to execute and write them up in the simple step-by-step format we used. In particular, be thinking about controllers when you formulate your views and vice-versa.

[5] *Made to Stick*, by Chip and Dan Heath.

Specialty Reading by Topic

If you want to know more about …	… then read
Product Design	*The Design of Everyday Things*, by Donald Norman
	This seminal book on product design introduces many fundamentals of the discipline, most importantly the relationship between people and objects. The author has several other similar works if you can't get enough or one of the others catches your eye. They are all useful.
Thinking Like a Designer	*The Ten Faces of Innovation*, by Thomas Kelley and Jonathan Littman
	This provides the layman a vivid and actionable introduction to design thinking.
Visual Communication	*Visual Explanations*, by Edward Tufte
	Edward Tufte's groundbreaking work catalyzed a superior union of data and graphic design. Even though a thorough reading of this book probably won't make you a graphic designer, it will work wonders on your ability to take a disciplined approach to visual communication. Edward Tufte has several good books in this area.
Programming	*The Art and Science of Java*, by Eric Roberts
	A lot of excellent (free) resources are online that deal with programming. If you're new to programming, or even more so, engineering, this book will give you a strong grounding in the foundation ideas of how to approach it.
	To reiterate, you do not need to learn programming to be successful in a technology-enabled business. I've provided this reference in case the material here has stoked your interest in sitting down and writing code.
Creating Views	*Designing Interfaces*, by Jennifer Tidwell
	This is a thorough and highly readable introduction to best practices design patterns.
	See also Alexandercowan.com/views for a collection of resources
Modelling Data	See Alexandercowan.com/models for a collection of resources
Designing Controllers	See Alexandercowan.com/controllers for a collection of resources

The Architecture

Unravel the Python of Monolithic Architecture

4

Chapter

In today's environment, your ability to leverage available components is as critical as building software. The Python of Monolithic Architecture is a solitary creature with its own particular twists and coils. You want to assemble your tech business using as few custom components as possible. This chapter will take you through some of the most important trends in systems development, applying them to the example of Enable Quiz.

Industrial Revolution 2.0

The goal of this chapter is to provide you with the fundamentals needed to establish your product's high-level architecture by defining the major building blocks of your system. You may want to draft a high-level architecture before contracting developers, since knowing what piece parts and technologies you'll use will inform the kind of talent you need to recruit. Making smart choices about architecture is an increasingly important part of getting a product out the door.

The Industrial Revolution in Europe and the United States took place around the turn of the 18th century and one of the big catalysts for this event was the introduction of interchangeable parts. Before this time, a rifle maker would have to chop down trees, mill rifle stocks, pour steel to make barrels, and assemble the

Figure 4.1

Industrial
Revolution
2.0

		Pre	Post
Industrial Revolution 1.0		custom goods built one by one	standard goods built from interchangeable parts
Industrial Revolution 2.0		monolithic software custom built from the ground up	purpose-built software created from best practice/ off the shelf components

rifle. Post-Industrial Revolution, rifle makers specialized in making whatever piece at which they were the most efficient, such as stocks, barrels, or triggers, but they weren't building the whole thing anymore. Once you could get piece parts from anyone you wanted, price decreased and quality increased to the point where broad generalists were no longer competitive. The same thing is happening in software. Call it Industrial Revolution 2.0. Rather than building applications from scratch, software companies are increasingly creating specialty items on top of existing components, which means we have to be smart about using existing piece parts where we can.

Designing an Architecture

The first step is to lay out the required functional blocks and the second step is to define how these pieces connect to one another. The last step is to evaluate available, off-the-shelf software packages to see what you can buy and use versus paying someone to build them from scratch. How do you determine this? The following is a sequential list of questions:

1. Are there off-the-shelf components that meet key functional needs?
    If the answer is no, then your evaluation is over.
2. How much do they cost to buy and to maintain?
    Licensing and support contracts are easy to measure. You should also consider the ease of operational maintenance. For example, if you're using a large, complex, off-the-shelf component to fulfil a simple function, it may be costing you more to keep that component running than it would to build your own software internally to perform the same function.
3. How much would it cost and how long would it take to build internally?
    Be careful here. Internal engineering projects are rarely overestimated. Ensure you've factored in all the less tangible, less obvious benefits of an off-the-shelf product. For example, an off-the-shelf product

probably has documentation, it's probably been field tested by other customers, operational infrastructure (like logging, upgrades) is likely to be more advanced, and the vendor is probably making continual updates. As a bonus, there's probably a population of engineers who know how to use it. None of these is a foregone conclusion, but they're important to consider to ensure you're looking at the whole picture.

4. What is the integration cost for the off-the-shelf option versus the internal build?

You'll have to integrate the component with the rest of your systems, and this may be more or less difficult with a third-party, off-the-shelf component.

If the consideration is at all close, my advice is use the off-the-shelf option. In most cases, you'll have something that's more cost-effective and has a better upside in terms of evolving with best practices and standards.

Identifying Functional Blocks at Enable Quiz

Table 4.1 shows the functional blocks for the Enable Quiz system, complete with a little metaphor to keep it from getting boring.

Organizing their website views with a CMS will make maintenance and internal consistency easier for Enable Quiz. The Quiz Engine chunk is basically the innards behind the website views. Then Enable Quiz has

Table 4.1

Functional Requirements at Enable Quiz

Piece Part	Description	If Enable Quiz were a restaurant, this would be the . . .
Content Management System (CMS)	The CMS deals with keeping the front end of the site organized and easy to update.	Seating Area
Quiz Engine	This is the core application that deals with creating and managing quizzes.	Kitchen
Customer Relationship Management (CRM)	This CRM deals with overall management of customers, i.e., where they were acquired, what services they use, sending specials they might be interested in via e-mail, and tracking any issues they've had or need resolved.	Sales Office
Billing	This section deals with invoicing, tracking payments, and clearing payments (e.g., credit cards).	Accounting Office

the back office, or the systems that it uses to manage its customers from a business standpoint. Specifically, they'll have a customer relationship management (CRM) for tracking and a billing system to issue invoices and collect payments.

Understanding Integration

Two foundation concepts before we start: clients and servers. You've probably at least heard those terms. It's another one of these things that sounds complicated, but it isn't. A client makes a request and a server responds.

Figure 4.2

Clients and Servers

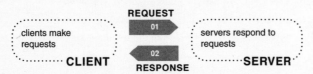

The most ubiquitous example is your web browser (Internet Explorer, Firefox, and so on) bringing up a web page. When you type "cnn.com" into your web browser, your browser acts as a client and sends a request to the cnn.com server. The server responds with a series of content files that your browser renders on your screen, allowing you to read the news. We're covering this concept because when we review the high-level architecture, we're describing the way in which a set of components connect to each other. As part of that description, you should know which component is acting as a client versus a server.

Functional blocks in an architecture will generally connect to each other in one of three ways:

1. Code integration
2. Add-in (plug-in) integration
3. Arm's length integration through an application program interface (API)[1]

Code-level integration means you're taking a software module from someone else and including it directly in your application. This usually means the code you're using is written in the same programming language as your own. For example, I was recently working with my team on some stories that required an online calendar. Rather than building one (it's a component that's deceptively complex), we licensed one from a small company in Sweden and included it in our application.

Add-in integration means you're creating your application within a predefined framework where it will be hosted by another application. The host application (Application A in Figure 4.3) has an add-in manager that deals with hosting the various add-ins. For example, I have a Norton add-in that provides enhanced

---

[1]Technically, add-ins will use some kind of API as well. The idea with #3 is that this is a stand-alone application that you're connecting to another stand-alone application, rather than something you're building specifically to operate on a host application as an add-in.

spam protection. The host application is Microsoft Outlook. While they don't all fit the generally accepted technical definition for add-ins,[2] there's recently been a proliferation of applications written on top of platforms that are like add-ins in that they're designed to operate in a highly prescribed environment, both technical and commercial. I'd put the games and other apps on Facebook in this category. Online CRM company, Salesforce.com, has a successful online store with similar kinds of purpose-built applications. Though iPhone applications are not add-ins, since they're generally written to the iPhone operating system (iOS), they

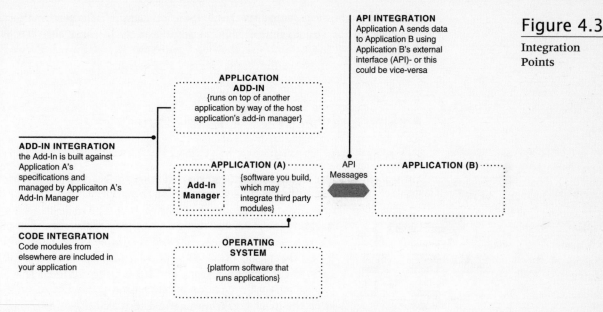

Figure 4.3

Integration Points

live in environments similar to the ones I mentioned in that Apple simplifies the creation of applications (as well as making them easy to sell and distribute by way of Apple's app store).

The last type of integration, by API, means that one application ''talks'' to another through a specific set of commands the server-side application makes available. APIs are external interfaces that applications make available so other applications can send and receive data to and from them. Figure 4.3 summarizes these three different types of integration:

Integration at Enable Quiz

The architecture for Enable Quiz has several examples of API integration. When customers request a sales contact from the website, they'll be created as a sales ''lead'' in Salesforce.com, where Enable Quiz tracks

---

[2]Generally, an add-in requires a host application to function and talks to some kind of an add-in manager.

information about its customers. How does that happen? Customers fill out a web form with their information and click on the submit option. At that point, a piece of client software embedded in the Enable Quiz website processes those inputs and puts that lead into Salesforce.com using its API. The Salesforce.com API specifies a way to format a message that says, "Here's a new lead."

Architecture Piece Parts at Enable Quiz

Content Management System (CMS)

Figure 4.4

Content
Management
System

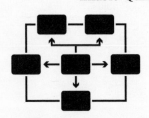

CMS

organizes the application's
front-end/view content
and allows for easy
editing

Let's get into more detail concerning the components of the Enable Quiz architecture, starting with the CMS. Enable Quiz has a substantial user interaction component, and though it's not going to have as many pages of content as, say, a news website, it will have quite a few. So, they should probably use a CMS. Building the front end using a CMS may require more overhead up front for the developers, but it's worth it in the long (or even medium) term. The CMS implements an organizing hierarchy for all the application's content, maintains a consistent set of visual templates, and provides an easy-to-use graphical front end for editing content. The bottom line is that you won't have to pay or wait for a developer every time you want to modify something on the site. And it will keep the front-end content consistent and organized.

Many CMS's exist. Joomla! is one popular choice with lots of circulation and support, which is particularly important since it's open source. Open source means the product's source code is publicly available, and in Joomla!'s case, many of the software's updates and enhancements come from a community of volunteers. Unless the people building the Enable Quiz site have a strong feeling otherwise, Joomla! is probably a fine choice in this area.

Though Enable Quiz will use Joomla! for creating the View portion of its application, Joomla! is its own application with a complete set of MVC components. Joomla!, therefore, has its own views (for administering the site), its own controllers (that present parts of the site to users and internal admins), and its own model (a database that houses all the site's content). That will be the case with most of the remaining components we look at here. Enable Quiz's proposed architecture consists of four applications (CMS, Quiz Engine, CRM, Billing) where they'll be doing API-level integration to tie them together.

Let's begin by sketching out how the Joomla! application talks to the rest of the system (Figure 4.5).

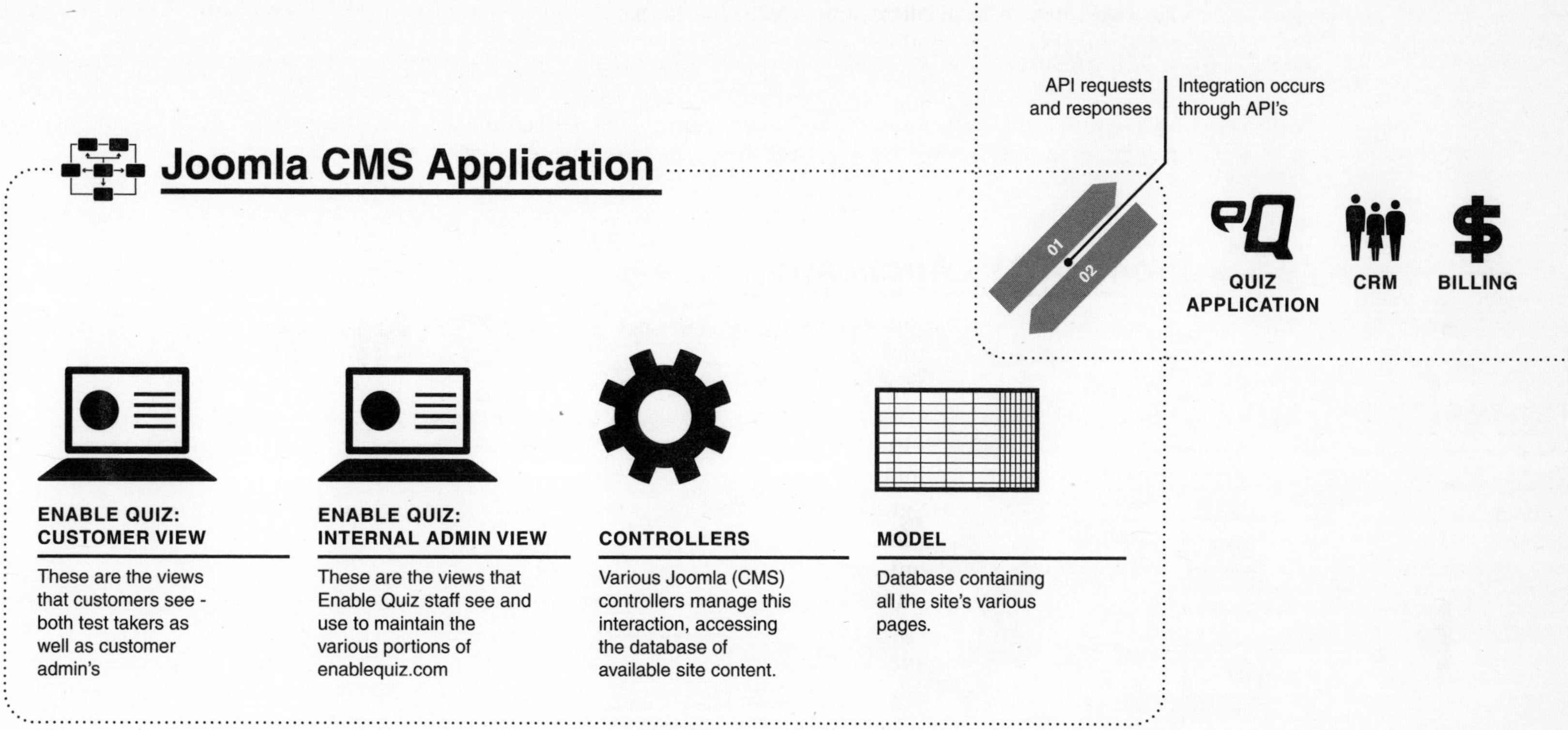

API requests
and responses

Integration occurs
through API's

QUIZ
APPLICATION   CRM   BILLING

Joomla CMS Application

**ENABLE QUIZ:
CUSTOMER VIEW**

These are the views
that customers see -
both test takers as
well as customer
admin's

**ENABLE QUIZ:
INTERNAL ADMIN VIEW**

These are the views that
Enable Quiz staff see and
use to maintain the
various portions of
enablequiz.com

CONTROLLERS

Various Joomla (CMS)
controllers manage this
interaction, accessing
the database of
available site content.

MODEL

Database containing
all the site's various
pages.

Figure 4.5   Joomla! Integration

Joomla! has its own native Views that Enable Quiz staff will use to edit content on Enablequiz.com so this content is, in turn, available as Views to Enable Quiz's end users. Joomla! has its own data model, a database that tracks all the site's pages and how they fit together, as well as its own Controllers that implement the logic Joomla! uses to process pages, making them look right and fit together. Joomla! is its own application, with a discrete set of MVC components. It will interact with the quiz engine, CRM, and billing through API integration.

Let's go through a specific example with five steps:

Step 0: First, someone from Enable Quiz has gone in and created the front-end pages that a student will see. Remember, Joomla! has two views: It presents the site to users, and it has its own internal view for admins to add and modify site content. Someone from Enable Quiz built the quiz-taking page. Let's say an end user is logging in to take the "Unix 1" quiz for steps two through five.

Figure 4.6

Joomla!
Transaction

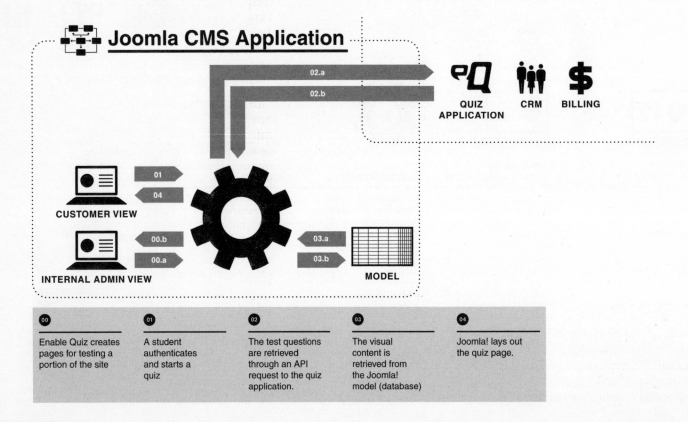

00	01	02	03	04
Enable Quiz creates pages for testing a portion of the site	A student authenticates and starts a quiz	The test questions are retrieved through an API request to the quiz application.	The visual content is retrieved from the Joomla! model (database)	Joomla! lays out the quiz page.

Step 1: Joe, the student, authenticates to the Quiz Application with his username and password, and we present him a page (by way of Joomla!) that says "click here to take the Unix 1 quiz" and (step 2) he does just that.

Step 2: The quiz application does not reside in Joomla!. Instead, Joomla! is the application that deals with presenting and managing front-end content. The quiz application is its own application. In step 2, the controller associated with the Joomla!-based page that displays the quiz will have a command that makes an API request to the quiz application and says "this is Joe Simmons from Pillsman's and he wants to take the "Unix 1" quiz, at which point the quiz application responds with the corresponding quiz questions for Unix 1. At this point, we have a bunch of questions to show, and we need to know how to show them.

Step 3: That same Joomla!-based page will lay out the quiz questions and go and grab the rest of the content it needs to display the quiz page from the Joomla! database of content.

Step 4: Joomla! will organize the visual content and the quiz question content into the quiz-taking page we present to the user.

Let's revisit the restaurant metaphor we introduced in Table 4.1 since the way these applications fit together is an important foundation concept. In this situation, the CMS is the seating area and the waiters. The quiz application would be the kitchen. Have you noticed that restaurants have a little window into the kitchen where the waiters drop off and pick up orders? Think of that as the API interface where the CMS application talks to the quiz application. Waiters in the seating area request a particular menu item from the kitchen, and the kitchen returns the requested dinner to the waiter in the seating area through the window, which is their interface to each other.

Quiz Application

Let's move on to the quiz application itself. We spent the previous chapter getting clear on what this part needs to do. It doesn't look like there's anything off the shelf that resembles what they need at Enable Quiz, so this is something they'll have to build.

How does the quiz application fit in with everything else? Since Joomla! is written in the programming language PHP, does that mean the quiz application has to be in PHP as well? The technical answer is no. All the APIs that Enable Quiz will be using are web service APIs, meaning they exchange standard message types independent of programming language. The practical answer, however, is that it depends on the number and breadth of Enable Quiz's development teams. If they use an agency that has capabilities in multiple technologies and a track record of managing them together coherently, they can use more than one implementation technology. Alternatively, they might split

Figure 4.7

Quiz
Application

QUIZ APPLICATION

the core application that
deals with creating and
managing quizzes

up the teams between the applications, which would create flexibility around technologies. With everything else being equal, it's simpler to stick with one programming technology wherever you need to write your own software code.

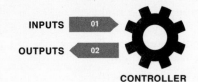

Figure 4.8

Inputs and
Outputs

I mentioned the integration is by way of API, specifically a language-independent web service API. Let's look in more detail at how the CMS (seating area) interfaces with the quiz engine (kitchen). An API is a way to expose application Controllers, which always have a distinct set of inputs and outputs. You pass inputs to the Controller, and it returns you outputs. Even if the controller isn't returning information, as a search function would, it will always at least return a response that indicates success or failure. However, the mere fact an application has an API doesn't tell you much because there are many types of APIs. Some are transparent, robust, and modern, and others are opaque, touchy, and antiquated. Having an API used to mean that you published information about some of your application's controllers which meant that the person who wanted to integrate with your application had to be using the same implementation technology (Java, PHP, etc.) and would have to rely on whatever documentation you made available to make the integration work. The generic statement for a controller within a program is the following:

output f(args);

The "f" means "function," which is just another name for controller. Args (arguments) means inputs. Let's look at an example for our Get Quiz controller:

questions{} getQuizContents(quizID);

This function takes a quizID as input and will return a set of questions as output. (It knows the user since they are logged in and have a session.) Though this is a simple function, the description doesn't tell you a lot about the inputs and outputs. Most APIs today are implemented as web service APIs, an implementation standard that is language-independent. Basically, this means you can publish web services in the same way across development languages. For example, if we have a PHP-based front end and a Java back end, using a web service interface to the back end would work fine.

The most important thing about a web service is the contents of the inputs and outputs, which are encapsulated in Extensible Markup Language (XML). XML is basically a system to create information that describes itself. For example, if we had an item called a greeting, we'd enclose it in a set of tags like this:

<Greeting>Hello, world.</Greeting>

The tags are enclosed by the < and > characters. <Greeting> means "here comes an item of type greeting" and </Greeting> means "that's the end of the greeting." Everything in XML is enclosed in these tags. This is what the function getQuizContents might look like if it was rendered in XML (details omitted for clarity and brevity):

```
<getQuizContents>
        <annotation>this take a quizID and returns a set of quiz questions</annotation>
        <quizID>abc123</quizID>
</getQuizContents>
```

The first element declares the name of the XML-based request, getQuizContents. After that, there's a note (annotation) describing the request, followed by an element called quizID. The quizID is the one input that this particular request needs to include since that's what we need to find the right quiz and return its contents. Notice the difference between this and the simple one-line function above. Though this XML-based version may not look like a big deal, the additional structure helps when you are receiving larger and more complex requests. The important thing to understand about code-level APIs versus web service APIs is that the latter will almost always be better organized, more standard, more modern, and you can communicate with them from a program written in any language. It's a bit of a red flag these days if a system has an external interface other than web services.

The architecture for Enable Quiz is to have a CMS-based front-end application (seating area) talking to the quiz application through a web services API. The CMS-based front end will send web service requests to the quiz application (Figure 4.9).

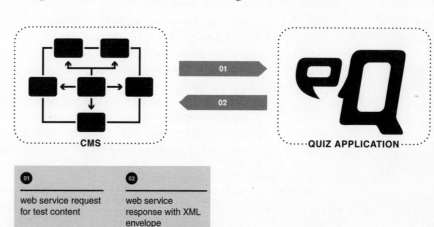

Figure 4.9
CMS to Quiz Engine

CMS

QUIZ APPLICATION

01 web service request for test content

02 web service response with XML envelope containing test content

Customer Relationship Management (CRM)

The CRM (Figure 4.10) provides a way to organize information about current and prospective customers. Though Enable Quiz could keep track of our customers on a simple spreadsheet for the first few months, this tactic tends to use up a lot of time. Companies are generally better off initiating some kind of CRM system from the beginning. The CRM does more than organize information about customers. It allows you to do things like track where your new customers are coming from (via online ads, promotions, Google, and more) and manage e-mail campaigns to sets of customers with common characteristics. Anytime a customer contacts support with an issue, it's logged in CRM and tracked through to resolution.

So, how would the CRM integrate with the rest of the application spheres? How would a new customer flow through the systems? Generally, a new customer will flow from CRM to billing to the quiz application. At a high level, it's a three-step process:

Figure 4.10

CRM

CRM

deals with the overall management of customers

1. Let's say a prospective customer arrives at the site and is ready to buy. All of the site's content is generated by the CMS, so this prospective customer would be going through a set of account sign-up pages that Enable Quiz maintains by way of the CMS. The CMS, in turn, talks to the API on Enable Quiz's CRM when creating new customers. So, let's say the prospective customer visits the purchase page. They need to create an account before they can sign up, which happens in CRM with inputs from the CMS-generated web pages. Then the customer goes through to buy a subscription. They pick what they want, supply a credit card, and submit.
2. CRM makes a request to the billing system to clear the payment and, assuming it clears, sets up the customer for monthly billing.
3. At this point, the billing system returns success to CRM, and CRM creates the customer's account or updates it if they were subscribing to an additional question bank.

Figure 4.11 summarizes these steps.

There are a few good options on CRMs, but Salesforce.com has emerged as the most dominant for this kind of general purpose application. Though it's one of the most expensive options, the company charges based on the number of internal users (people that work at Enable Quiz as opposed to customers) and Enable Quiz doesn't expect it will have that many users.

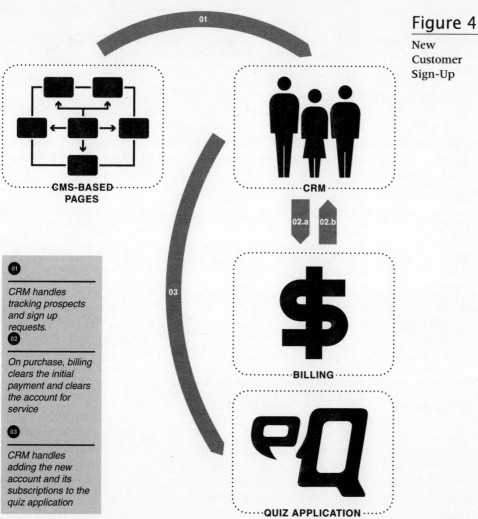

Figure 4.11
New
Customer
Sign-Up

01

CRM handles tracking prospects and sign up requests.

02

On purchase, billing clears the initial payment and clears the account for service

03

CRM handles adding the new account and its subscriptions to the quiz application

Billing

Since we all get bills, we intuitively understand the process of billing. To make this a standard operation in the Enable Quiz system, we'll formalize a few things and run through some details. Billing has three main elements:

1. **Orders:** This is an agreement to buy something on a non-recurring (one-time) or recurring basis. When I buy a television set from Walmart, that's a non-recurring order. When I subscribe to a cable service, that's a recurring order for which I pay every month.
2. **Invoices:** You receive invoices based on the terms of your order. They are an obligation and notice to submit a payment. Basically, an invoice is a bill. Invoices might be due right away, in 30 days (net 30), in 60 days (net 60), etc.
3. **Payments:** This occurs when the seller gets your money.

If we summarize the relationships between the key items in billing, it would look something like Figure 4.13.

All of this is simple in the case of nonrecurring purchases. If I walk into a gas station, put a stick of gum on the counter, that's an order. When the clerks asks me for $1.50, that's an invoice, and when I hand the $1.50 to him, that's a payment. If I dashed out of the gas station without paying, that would start the dunning (nonpayment) process. Buying something online that has a one-time charge isn't much more complex. You say what you want, usually by putting it in some kind of a purchase list or shopping cart and that constitutes your order. Once you input in your credit card details to finish the purchase, that's the invoice and payment.

Recurring payments that get billed after the fact make this process more complicated. Customers who sign up for Enable Quiz will have a few initial charges, and will pay a fixed amount per month based on what they want.

Figure 4.12

Billing

BILLING

handles order, invoice, and payment management as well as dunning

Figure 4.13

The Billing Process

the customer agrees to buy something: an order
········**ORDER**········

the customer receives the invoice: a notice to pay
········**INVOICE**········

the customer pays
········**PAYMENTS**········

DUNNING PROCESS

in the case of non-payment, the seller works through their business rules on non-payment

Let's say a customer pays $200 to sign up and $50 a month after that based on the contents of their order. That means they place two orders: one for a nonrecurring $200 sign-up fee and another for a recurring $50 monthly subscription fee. Assume that all invoices are due on receipt. (When customers pay by credit card, that's typical.) Most services like this are prepaid, meaning that if customers sign up on the 17th of March, the $50 monthly subscription is a prepayment for the next month's service (March 17 to April 17). On April 17th, Enable Quiz will issue another invoice against that recurring order and collect payment. The payment is usually automatic since companies require a credit card on file. That April 17th payment covers their service through to May 17th, and so on.

Now, what if it turns out that the card on file has expired? This is when the dunning process starts. Dunning is a generic term that refers to your business process for dealing with overdue customers. Most companies send increasingly severe notices at fixed intervals, then stop service, and then some send customers to collections agencies.

Billing is a fairly complex thing to implement. I don't generally recommend developing this system yourself, especially since many good off-the-shelf options are available. One open-source package is called Freeside, and a SaaS service called Zuora is tightly partnered with Salesforce.com. A hosted storefront service called Shopify is even more inclusive.

Let's sketch out the Enable Quiz architecture as an example of how all this might fit together (see Figure 4.14).

The data Models are linked by account ID. Notice the linkage between the customers' question banks and their orders within billing: Those recurring orders in billing are driving the customers' subscriptions. If a customer doesn't have an order open for a question bank, they shouldn't have access to any new questions in that bank beyond the expiry date of their subscription. The question bank would be linked to the orders with part numbers from the product catalog. Let's say the Unix question bank is part number EQ1001. That would go into the user's shopping cart, be cleared by billing, and added to the quiz application once billing is validated, using that same part number.

What about the data model for the CMS? Since it's not part of the inter-system data architecture, we won't deal with it in any more detail. The data structure in Joomla! is mostly invisible and is a way to keep the views organized. It doesn't connect to anything else from a data Model perspective.

We didn't previously cover data Models for the CRM and billing system in the product design and didn't write them up, which is fine as well. We don't need to know about those Models in any detail since they're abstracted away in a somewhat similar fashion to Joomla!. The CRM and Billing systems have their own front ends that abstract the data Model. The Enable Quiz system will talk to them using an API that is another

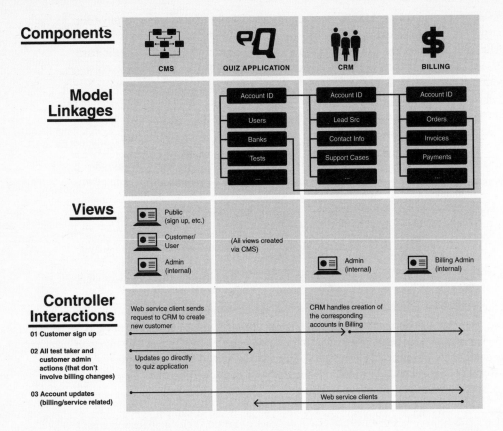

Figure 4.14

Draft
Architecture
for Enable
Quiz

type of View even though it's geared toward a computer program versus a human being. The API presents the important parts of the Model so you don't have to worry about all the details.

Enable Quiz will create and maintain three views in the CMS. First, there's the public website which includes static items like the company's address and marketing materials, as well as more dynamic content like the sign-up and purchase pages. Second, the CMS manages all the Views for the quiz application. Finally, the CMS has its own native interface that Enable Quiz personnel will use to manage these second two Views.

The CRM and billing applications will have their own native views for internal staff at Enable Quiz to use. Most people inside Enable Quiz will have access to the CRM, which includes sales, support, and management. Only a few people will have access directly to billing (accounting, finance) since that provides a lot of leeway financially, such as the ability to do refunds.

Now we come to the interfaces these systems will use to communicate with each other. Everything will operate around web service APIs. When a customer signs up (01), a web service client on the Enable Quiz server will talk to the CRM's API to create the new account. The CRM will in turn have its own web service implemented against the billing API that creates the account there as well as creating the order and the invoice and clearing the payment. Next, comes all nonbilling-related customer interactions with the quiz application (02). In this case, a web service client will make requests to the quiz application using its API. This is what happens when students take a quiz. Lastly, we have account updates (03). These work in a similar fashion to the initial sign up.

Evaluating Piece Parts

The key to evaluating piece parts for your architecture is to piggyback. You never want to answer a question someone else (indeed, probably many people) has answered. Aside from the specific questions about whether it's the right fit for what you need, you must ask six questions about an application you're thinking of using as part of your system:

1. Does this application have staying power?
2. Are we using the application in a manner consistent with the rest of the base? If not, does our use require special support or compatibility that's at risk?
3. Will the application's authors keep it current and respond to community-driven and market-driven requests for enhancements?
4. How abundant are add-ins the application supports? Do they align well with our intended use? An active third-party development community is a positive sign.
5. How large is the population of experienced engineers we can hire to work on this application?
6. How does its price compare with substitutes?

Let's take two of Enable Quiz's proposed piece parts: Joomla! (CMS) and Freeside (billing) and run them through this list of questions.

Example 1: Joomla! as Enable Quiz CMS

Joomla! looks pretty strong in terms of staying power. It's an open-source project supported by a nonprofit, which means that their storyline differs from the typical software company that creates a product, sells it to as many people as possible, and competes in the marketplace. We'll cover open source in more detail shortly, but the key thing is that Joomla! has the hallmarks of any successful software application. For starters, when you search for Joomla on Google, pages and pages of results turn up. Searching on Amazon shows dozen of Joomla! books from reputable publishers. Those are good signs. Though we should ask around and get a few data points from actual users, it's reasonable to assume that there are more than enough serious users to keep the project breathing.

The next question to ask is whether Enable Quiz is using the application in a typical fashion and whether Joomla!'s authors will keep it current. What they're looking to do with Joomla! is the most basic kind of content management. Given the number and spectrum of contributors, I think they're safe. If Joomla! stopped adding new functionality today, I don't think Enable Quiz would run into anything major that they would need. One of the most reassuring things about Joomla! is the marketplace for add-ins, many of which are commercial (meaning that you pay for them). Joomla!'s site shows a total of almost 7,000 add-ins for things like an interface to Facebook, making payments, and more. That's a great sign in terms of staying power as well as finding anything additional they might need off the shelf. Getting a critical mass of third-party developers on your application has been the key battleground for high-tech's biggest players. Since Enable Quiz's intended use is so basic, there isn't anything in particular I can see checking for in the add-in store. However, it shows that Joomla! has longevity and that Enable Quiz is likely to be able to find something off the shelf if they do need extended functionality.

When sizing up the population of qualified engineers Enable Quiz could hire, we want to determine how long it's going to take them to find people, how quickly those people can get up to speed, and how much they'll cost (since rarer, more specialized skill sets will cost more). As I mentioned, there doesn't currently seem to be any need for custom development on top of Joomla! itself. The virtue of Joomla! is that once a systems administrator installs it, it makes the content easy for users to access, with little or no technical training. I don't think Enable Quiz will need engineers to modify Joomla! or even build an add-in; however, since they're not that far into implementation, it's worth checking. If we go to Monster.com, and search for an engineer with Joomla! experience, we get over 100 results. Joomla! is written in a widely used programming language called PHP. Since this is probably what Enable Quiz will end up using for the front end, those engineers are likely to be familiar with Joomla! or at least comfortable with the underlying technology. Therefore, a Joomla! developer should be easy to find if they need one.

Example 2: Freeside for Enable Quiz Billing

Now let's look at Freeside. Though this application is free, the company does sell consulting and support, making it a for-profit, open-source operation. The key element in terms of their staying power is how they're doing financially. The number of people out there who need a billing engine is a tiny fraction of the number who want a CMS to manage their website, so we wouldn't expect to see nearly the volume of information out there on Freeside that we saw on Joomla!. Quite a few results for ''Freeside'' appear on Google, but they're articles and listings, not the kind of dedicated third-party websites we saw for Joomla!, like www.joomlatutorials.com.

One thing you want to look for on these niche applications is a couple of large customers. I don't see any customer testimonials on Freeside's website. That doesn't mean it doesn't have any impressive customers, but Enable Quiz will have to discover that by talking to them. Enable Quiz will need to do some more digging on their continuity and staying power.

Enable Quiz is planning to do basic subscription billing with the application. Based on a review of Freeside's documentation, Enable Quiz's requirements seem to fit well inside Freeside's existing functionality. Enable Quiz will probably be paying Freeside for support and maybe some consulting as well, so they'll probably be willing to have someone do a follow-up from a sales inquiry, particularly if Enable Quiz sends them the use cases and design notes they've assembled to show Freeside that it's a serious prospect. I think we can assume that Enable Quiz's requirements are well within the application's current capabilities. The next step is to verify that in consultation with Freeside. One of the positive aspects of these commercial open-source operations is they generally have technical salespeople that will answer your questions.

It's a little hard to tell what the story is with Freeside's responsiveness to new requests and add-ins, based on what's publicly available. Enable Quiz will need to ask the company for a brief history of how it has been evolving the product and compare that to the direction Enable Quiz is headed with billing. Though Freeside has some partners on the consulting side, a few quick searches didn't turn up any third-party developers of add-ins, which is something Enable Quiz will have to ask it about.

Freeside is written in a language called Perl, and many developers are familiar with Perl. However, Freeside itself is a complex application, so Enable Quiz would need to hire an engineer with Freeside experience or use consultants from Freeside. A search on Monster.com shows seven hits for engineers with references to Freeside, which isn't great, but, again not overly surprising since it's a niche application. Enable Quiz should ask Freeside what it charges for consulting. After evaluating how big a job they have to make it work for the Enable Quiz system, they'll have a solid answer on the economics of using that application. Even if the application is free, the biggest cost it presents is its set-up, integration, and maintenance. Therefore, it's critical to include estimates of all those costs in your evaluation, even if the licensing costs are zero.

Joomla! and Freeside, half of our four-system components, are open source, something we'll review in the next section.

Understanding Open Source

Open source software is generally free or inexpensive. Why would someone write free software? Well, the first thing to know about open source is that it doesn't mean free overall since the biggest cost attached to using an application is its set-up, integration, and ongoing support. Various reasons exist as to why people write open source software.

First, it's important to recognize that open source does not equal nonprofit. Open source is a business model that many companies have used successfully, usually by offering support, training, and consulting for the application they've released. Red Hat, for example, offers training and support on the open source operating system, Linux. MySQL is an open-source database company that was purchased by database giant Oracle.

Consider Freeside's situation: To date, billing software is usually sold by large companies to other large companies, mostly in telecommunications and media. Freeside could have gone head to head with those corporations using a closed-source model with some kind of angle, such as cheaper or better for specific situations. However, that would have required a lot of money and risk. Instead, Freeside went open source and has emerged as one of the leaders in open source billing, probably without spending a lot of money on marketing and sales. Anyone who wants a low up-front cost, code transparency, or likes open source will give this company a serious look. Additionally, it's probably profitable and didn't have to put forth that much cash to get going.

You should evaluate a for-profit, open source supplier as you would any supplier. You cannot assume the whole thing is free, as there are costs for support, training, and consulting. If you need a specific feature implemented outside of a company's plan, it'll likely ask you to pay. This might occur with documentation, too: Since these companies are not charging you for software, some of them, particularly the smaller ones, don't feel an obligation to keep their documentation current. All this is not to say that open source is a bad way to go: It's simply a caveat that you need to look at the total cost of the option, which may include things you'd take for granted with a commercial or closed source product.

Next, how do you evaluate a nonprofit's staying power and direction? We've talked about a number of ways to check the circulation of an application (hits on your search engine, books on Amazon, people who mention it on their résumés). Another important data point for these operations is how long they've been in business. Prestige open source projects form much of the current core of industrial computing, like the Apache web server and the Linux operating system. These have been around for over a decade, are in massive circulation, and are not going anywhere anytime soon. However, consider again the case of Joomla!. Though it has a lot of traction, what if one of the key players storms out on the project? Or it could be as simple as something more interesting coming along. Though it's not going to evaporate in the near future, the currents do shift on these things and it's important to be wary of them. The basic solution here is to look at how long the project has been around, how stable the core is, and the general strength of its circulation and user community.

It doesn't look like Enable Quiz will need to extend any of the open source applications it is evaluating. However, it's worth understanding the basics of the General Public License (GPL) that applies to this kind of software. The basic idea is that if you take that application and change it somehow, you can't go and sell that extended work to someone else. You are, however, allowed to use it internally. One critical item here is the question of whether someone using modified GPL software offering a SaaS service is obliged to provide that modified code to the public. This is an ongoing debate, so you should check with an expert on your particular item of interest. The principle is that the application is a public item, and you should make what you've done available to the public if you modify it. However, this doesn't mean the source code/content for a website is public domain if they use an open-source tool like Joomla! to manage it. Those rules would only apply if Enable Quiz were modifying Joomla *itself*.

Understanding Development Tools

This chapter provides a brief primer on system development tools. Unless you have a background in software development, I don't recommend making a decision for your team on what technology tools they use based on this section. The idea here is to give you a succinct synopsis of the most popular development tools as well as a few foundation concepts so you can ask the right questions when collaborating with your team.

What's in a Language?

Four of the most popular languages in the world of web application development are Java, PHP, Ruby, and .NET. In the abstract, most programming languages are similar. If you asked your average web developer to give you a quick layman's characterization of the four, they'd probably say something like this:

Java is good for heavy-duty development (like the Enable Quiz engine).

PHP is good for lightweight development (controllers to support front ends, like the interface to Enable Quiz).

Ruby is a more modern take on what PHP sought to do and has more structure.

.NET is for developers that prefer things prepackaged and don't mind paying some licensing to Microsoft for platforms.

Though the reality is more nuanced, those glib statements have some validity. Looking at it from an economic perspective, you'll want to ask the following three questions regarding technology selection.

1. How well does our selected technology dovetail with our customers' operating environments?
2. What is the quality and availability of compatible development environments and libraries?
3. What is the cost and availability of developers with applicable experience?

These technologies have their own complex sublayers and subcomponents. Since these vary quite a bit, we organize them here into five conceptual layers. (See Figure 4.15.)

Like any simplifying framework, this obscures detail that can be important for certain purposes. But we're not worried about the details here. Instead, we're concerned with getting a basic organizing framework to make sense of our options and trade-offs.

The five layers are:

1. Your Software
2. Helper Packages
3. Foundation Packages
4. Operating System
5. Hardware

Figure 4.15

Technology Stack

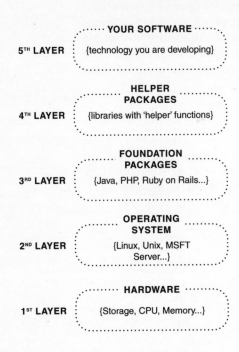

5TH LAYER — YOUR SOFTWARE
{technology you are developing}

4TH LAYER — HELPER PACKAGES
{libraries with 'helper' functions}

3RD LAYER — FOUNDATION PACKAGES
{Java, PHP, Ruby on Rails...}

2ND LAYER — OPERATING SYSTEM
{Linux, Unix, MSFT Server...}

1ST LAYER — HARDWARE
{Storage, CPU, Memory...}

If you're creating an add-in or operating on a development platform like Facebook, the iPhone, or Salesforce.com, everything but the software and maybe helper packages is taken care of by the platform and its developer community. In the next few paragraphs, we'll run through an example of how these layers look if you're building and hosting your own web application, which is the plan for Enable Quiz.

Hardware is the physical servers you use. That's consistent these days no matter which technology you chose in the upper layers—most of it's comparable in price and does the same things. In web applications, there are two popular choices for operating systems: Unix/Linux and Microsoft Server. The things you install on top of a server operating system are called packages, which is the third layer and that's where you actually run your programming language, such as the PHP packages, Java packages, etc. Let's call these foundation packages. Next, you have all the libraries other people have written for your selected technology, which we will call helper packages. These are a big deal because every helper package you can leverage is that much less software code you have to write and maintain yourself. Your Software is the quiz application, for example.

The first question you have to ask yourself is this: How well does our selected technology fit our customers' operating environments? This encompasses the operating system, the foundation packages, and the helper packages you'll require the customers to install and maintain. Your application's compatibility with customers' existing infrastructure will drive your costs and how readily customers adopt your application. For example, if all your customers run Windows Server, then you will want to build your software on .NET, which is Microsoft's development environment. Even though you could run a Java or PHP application on Microsoft Server, it will be more difficult to install and maintain the required packages on Windows Server because in this context Java and PHP are primarily run on Unix and Linux operating systems. Fortunately, Enable Quiz doesn't have to worry about customer environments for software installation and maintenance since it is offering the software as a hosted service. This means that the customers never have to install or upgrade a server to run the software, which is one of the big advantages of pursuing an SaaS model.

The second driver is the availability of development environments and supporting helper packages (libraries), the items in the fourth layer. A development environment is an application that developers use to organize, author, and debug the software they're building. Supporting libraries are existing software you can include in your code instead of writing the applicable code from scratch. A developer's ability to identify and use supporting libraries instead of building them from scratch has a major impact on how much software you have to create and maintain. The development environment and libraries are often organized into what is called a framework. For example, PHP has something called the Zend Framework, which includes a development environment as well as helper packages.

Evaluating all of this is difficult until you've worked in the environment in question. The quality of the helper packages has to do with subtle things like ease of development and the applicability of the helper packages for what you're doing. If you don't have a development background, you'll need to rely on your team's experience for this part of the process.

The third and last driver is possibly the most significant: What's the supply of experienced people you can hire to build your software using the selected technology? We've talked a bit about how to determine this. The short answer is that you'll be in good shape using established technologies. When you use newer or more exotic technologies, you're generally going to have fewer choices which will drive your development costs and timelines. This is one of the problems with Ruby at this moment: The developer population is relatively small and highly sought after for popular social media and other Web 2.0 projects. Figure 4.16 summarizes these drivers.

Figure 4.16

Technology
Stack with
Drivers

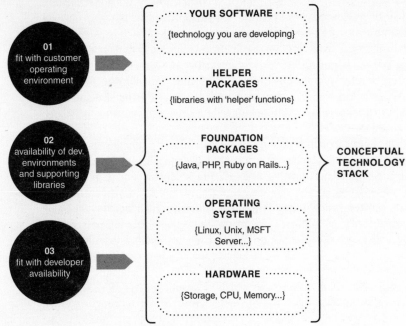

**DEVELOPMENT TECHNOLOGY
SELECTION:
THREE KEY DRIVERS**

01
fit with customer
operating
environment

02
availability of dev.
environments
and supporting
libraries

03
fit with developer
availability

YOUR SOFTWARE
{technology you are developing}

**HELPER
PACKAGES**
{libraries with 'helper' functions}

**FOUNDATION
PACKAGES**
{Java, PHP, Ruby on Rails...}

**OPERATING
SYSTEM**
{Linux, Unix, MSFT
Server...}

HARDWARE
{Storage, CPU, Memory...}

**CONCEPTUAL
TECHNOLOGY
STACK**

Java: Pros and Cons

Java started as a modernization of more traditional languages like C and C++, and it remains similar. One element of Java that was considered to be a big deal is that it was written to run on a virtual machine. The idea behind that was you'd have a virtual machine for every available operating system. This would allow developers to write Java code once and run it on any type of host machine: servers with different operating systems, PCs, phones, and so on. That aspect of Java has succeeded. With a lot of languages, you have to redevelop your software for every operating system.

Java is considered to be heavy duty in the sense that it forces you to do things in a relatively structured and organized way, which is what you want if you're building a large-scale application like the Enable Quiz quiz engine. However, it's not as good if you need to build some Controllers for your front end to do a few simple things, since it probably creates more overhead than you want. For example, to print the text "Hello, world!" in Java would take 191 characters; it would take 25 with PHP.[3]

After weighing its options, Enable Quiz has settled on Java for the quiz engine. The application has to be heavy duty since it's going to have to manage its own databases of account and quiz information, implement a lot of involved logic, and present a web services-based API for the front ends to use. The development environments and helper libraries are diverse, mature, and well supported. For example, you could write a set of books on all the different Java tools available to connect your software to a database. Lots of Java tools are available for publishing web service APIs and because of Java's relative age and popularity, Enable Quiz will be able to find plenty of developers for hire.

PHP and Ruby: Pros and Cons

Java is not always the best choice for the front end since it requires a lot of overhead. Even though plenty of Java tools for implementing front ends exist, they're not as abundant as those available for PHP and Ruby. Java implementations are more complex. In regards to our third driver (What's the supply of experienced people you can hire to build your software using the selected technology?), a very large portion of developers who specialize in web front-end development focus on PHP or Ruby.

PHP is at the other end of the spectrum from Java in terms of structure. It was originally developed as a scripting language to allow web pages to present content dynamically, using Controllers to present pages instead of being limited to static content. Developers will tell you that it allows for sloppy and potentially insecure code because PHP code is interleaved with the HTML[4] View content. There is truth to this claim because though writing sloppy insecure code in any language is easy, it's even easier to do it with PHP. That said, PHP is lightweight and a good fit for building the kind of dynamic front ends users expect.

Ruby is an increasingly popular alternative to PHP. They have material differences from a technical standpoint: Ruby is more robust and structured, but like PHP, it often plays a similar role as a language

---

[3]Based on writing a Java applet for the purpose.
[4]HTML, hypertext markup language, is the syntax that web browsers use to render web pages.

for building dynamic front ends. Enable Quiz didn't choose Ruby mostly because Mike has never used it. Additionally, because it's the "hot new thing" with so much excitement around it, developers' rates are through the roof.

.NET: Pros and Cons

Though Enable Quiz is not using .NET for anything, we should touch on it since it's extensively deployed. .NET is a framework, so it encompasses development environments as well as helper packages. It's made up of three programming languages: C# (pronounced "C sharp"), J# (pronounced "J sharp"), and Visual Basic. C# is .NET's core heavy-duty language, J# is a transitional language that allows you to run Java code on the .NET framework, and Visual Basic is a lightweight language for front ends (with a similar intent to PHP and Ruby). The benefits of .NET are that it's put together well and works effectively with the whole ecosystems of Microsoft products for businesses. For instance, Microsoft offers CRM applications, finance applications, and so on. The environments do a good job of masking complexity, all of which is the technical underpinning to their People Friendly ad campaign targeted to businesses. The disadvantages are that there are licensing costs for their operating systems as well as many of their helper packages, like the Microsoft database suite. In terms of web applications, Microsoft, for all intents and purposes, is not much a part of the robust ecosystem of open source piece parts from which you can choose in environments like Java, PHP, and Ruby.

In terms of staffing, a lot of .NET developers are out there, but I would say they're mostly focused on building enterprise applications around the Microsoft ecosystem. If you choose to go .NET, you can find developers.

Examples

Let's look at an example that many of us use to help see this all in action: What language is Facebook written in? It's best to think of Facebook as a system, rather than a discrete application. Enable Quiz has four piece parts to its system: front end, quiz application, CRM, and billing. Facebook probably has a dozen or more pieces like that, each one pretty substantial. Like other Web 2.0 infrastructure, a general term for the current generation of rich media web applications, Facebook engineers started out writing a lot of the system in PHP, most likely since they wanted something quick and flexible. I imagine they leverage a lot of helper libraries, as all PHP developers do. Libraries are sets of prewritten code you can leverage in your own applications. Later on, Facebook developed a way to translate PHP code into C++ code.[5] C++ is more efficient than PHP, and with the gigantic scale of traffic at Facebook, being more efficient makes a difference in the amount of resources they have to consume. Enable Quiz doesn't need to worry as much about it for its scale. I'm sure Facebook has components written in a number of other languages as well.

Back to Enable Quiz: what's the overall development strategy with the CRM and billing pieces? The engineers are using those as finished applications with some configuration on top of them, so they don't have to go under the hood and deal with the underlying software code. I'm not sure what language Salesforce.com is written in. Third-party developers write applications on top of it using Salesforce.com's own proprietary language, called Apex.

Will Enable Quiz have to use Apex to do their integration? That great question touches on a subtle but important point, and the answer is no, they won't because they're interfacing to Salesforce.com's API to read and write information, rather than building an application on top of Salesforce.com. For example, when new customers sign up on the Enable Quiz website, Enable Quiz will add them to Salesforce.com using the Salesforce.com web services API. That API is a programming language–independent way of reading and writing data to your instance of Salesforce.com. The Enable Quiz website is the client; Salesforce.com is the server. For example, if Enable Quiz didn't want to do the API integration, it could have all new leads come in to an inbox as e-mails. Someone from Enable Quiz would go to Salesforce.com and enter the information the prospective customers submitted by hand. Instead, when a customer signs up, the Enable Quiz website sends the information directly to Salesforce.com using their API, which automates the step of transferring the prospects' information from a web form on the Enable Quiz website to Salesforce.com.

As a counterexample, what would be a case in which you would use Salesforce.com's Apex programming language to build an application? Let's say you wanted to port your trouble-ticketing system to operate as a Salesforce.com application. You write a Salesforce.com application using Apex when you want to extend the functionality of Salesforce.com itself. For example, you might have an enhanced trouble-ticketing application which would run as part of your Salesforce.com account. When you logged in to Salesforce.com, you'd open a new tab labeled XYZ Ticketing System with additional functionality. That's different than wanting to read and write information from your plain Jane Salesforce.com account.

---

[5] http://developers.facebook.com/blog/post/358.

Chapter 4 Summary

1. Get on the Right Side of the Revolution

    Industrial Revolution 2.0 means you should be in the business of building specialty items for your particular market, using as many commercial, off-the-shelf components as possible. Avoid building complex software and platforms unless you see a compelling need to do so.

2. Applications versus Systems

    Many web applications are systems, rather than a single piece of software. For example, there is no single application that is Facebook. It's a system of many interconnected applications. When you're designing your architecture, you may need to divide your system up into functional blocks. This decomposition will help you more clearly evaluate alternative approaches for the various blocks, including use of off-the-shelf components.

3. Types of Integration

    Three primary modes of integration are code, add-in, and API. Code-level integration means that you're pulling in modules of someone else's code into your application. Add-in means that you're building your application in an add-in framework on top of another application that will host it. Arm's length API-level integration means that your application is talking to another stand-alone application by way of a defined external interface.

4. CRM

    If you're going to have contact with individual customers, consider the use of an off-the-shelf CRM like Salesforce.com or SugarCRM. These are offered on an SaaS basis where no software has to be managed. The CRM system provides you an economic means to manage your customers. These systems have mature integration interfaces (APIs) if you want to tie them in to another system.

5. Billing

    If you're going to be billing customers, be sure you understand the fundamentals: orders, invoices, payments, and the dunning process. Commercial billing systems for the small to medium-sized businesses are an emerging area. That said, several good options exist that offer built-in integration with leading CRM systems. Avoid building your own billing system unless you're billing on a small scale, as the nuances are deceptively complex.

6. Selecting Piece Parts, Selecting Partners

Use the checklist provided here (at least) to evaluate your system subcomponents and piece part partners. Make sure you make sense as a customer for them as well as the other way around as a way of ensuring a long-term fit.

7. What's in a Language?

No programming language is inherently better or more efficient than another. You must evaluate a language based on your customers' operating environment, the availability of supporting toolsets, and relative abundance of qualified developers.

8. Java

Java is one of the most popular core programming languages and is a likely candidate for substantial application development.

9. PHP and Ruby

PHP and Ruby are popular choices for front-end development and are highly popular for web applications in general.

10. .NET

.NET offers developers a complete development toolkit built around Microsoft technologies.

11. Open Source: There's No Such Thing as a Free Lunch

Most open-source software has no license, which is deceptively attractive. Ensure you evaluate everything you'll need to do with the open source software and how much that will cost. Things you might take for granted with a commercial system, like documentation, support, and the availability of certain features, may be unavailable in an open-source application and acquiring those things could be more expensive than a commercial alternative.

Checklist

1. Functional Blocks

   Have you worked with your team, and are other resources available to you to identify the functional blocks you need? These should include the following:
   - Function description
   - Requirements
   - Current candidates and notes on our evaluation

   Have you reviewed ideas concerning off-the-shelf options?

2. Integration Strategy

   If you are using piece parts, has your team arrived at a general integration strategy?

3. Open Source

   If you're using open source, have you evaluated the full cost of what it will take the get the components where you need them? What about keeping them current for your product?

4. Development Environment

   Have you validated that the talent and infrastructure is available to support your selected technology?

Specialty Reading by Topic

If you want to know more about …	… then read
CMS	See Alexandercowan.com/cms
CRM	See Alexandercowan.com/crm
Open Source Software	See Alexandercowan.com/opensource
Software Architecture	See Alexandercowan.com/arch
Joomla!	See Alexandercowan.com/Joomla
Web Applications	See Alexandercowan.com/webapps
Java	See Alexandercowan.com/java
PHP	See Alexandercowan.com/PHP
Ruby	See Alexandercowan.com/ruby
.NET	See Alexandercowan.com/MSNET

The Team

Dodge the Magpie of Discord

Managing a technical team is part art and part science. Those that do it well can write their own ticket. The Magpie of Discord rankles developers with its dissonance and inconsistency. This chapter walks through some of the most common disconnects between engineers and businesspeople, the type of talent you'll need, how to identify them, and how to acquire them. We also review the pros and cons of using resources offshore.

Who Are These Software People?

If this is your first time working with engineers, you have a substantial challenge ahead of you. If it's not your first time, you still have a challenge (at least, I know I do). Keep in mind that challenges are one of the best parts of building a business. They help us grow intellectually and professionally, and understanding a few key things about developers will dramatically increase your chances of having a fruitful, enjoyable relationship with this part of your team.

Though individual engineers' personalities, aptitudes, work ethic, and preferences differ as much as any other profession, you can say three things about most engineers:

1. They're expensive.

    A global shortage of engineering talent and an acute shortage of high-quality talent exists. By the law of supply and demand, you'll be paying these people a lot, especially if they're good and if they're specialists.

2. They have a different perspective.

    Even if some of your engineers happen to have a business background (most won't), they're in the role of engineer. Things that are obvious to you about what's important to the health of the business won't necessarily be obvious to them.

3. They're part of a profession.

    George Bernard Shaw famously said, "All professions are conspiracies against the laity." This is as true of engineers as it is of any other profession. Though you can expect some challenges understanding what's going on in engineering, few technology systems are impossible to explain to the laity. If your technical staff doesn't seem to be making an effort to help you understand what's going on with the system, they're probably hiding behind their profession for one reason or another. It could be something as innocuous as they don't want to talk about it, perhaps they're struggling with the work, or they are antisocial and hard to work with. (All are bad signs, of course.)

What can you do? First, prepare; second, execute. The single best thing you can do in terms of preparation is to formulate an outstanding product design. Engineers resent having to redo their work and change their approach because you didn't do your homework to figure out what you want. Completing a thorough product design and setting aside time to review it with your technical team is a great way to introduce yourself. If your team has more than two people, it's particularly important to spend the time and money (within reason) to find a strong technical lead. This should be someone with a lot of experience, as well as the ability to communicate with you, the businessperson, about key aspects of the project.

Once you start, you'll want to take the role of an anthropologist. Ask probing questions and abandon any preconceived ideas you have about how things work in this area. This won't be hard if you're new to the area; be free but earnest in your ignorance.

Let's talk a little about the sociology of the engineer and the businessperson. We'll start off with the stereotypes since they're simple and they lurk in the back of everyone's mind. We'll then move on to the truth, which is more complex.

I'm going to guess your stereotype of developers: They sport a World of Warcraft–inspired wardrobe,[1] they're late to bed, late to rise, they drink a lot of Mountain Dew, they like to be left alone, and they love to make things complex because it keeps you out of their hair. In reality, a wide spectrum of personality types gravitate to engineering jobs, but the stereotypes exist for a reason. While I'm not claiming this is scientific, I always have everyone on my staff take the Myers-Briggs Type Indicator (MBTI) personality

---

[1]This is an online multi-player game, traditionally popular with the IT crowd.

quiz.[2] I've found that it helps give a basic sense of how people operate. Here's something that may surprise you: I typically see only about half the technical staff fall into the quiz's introverted classification. Believe it or not, the rest were extroverts.[3]

However, this doesn't mean most engineers spend their off hours at cocktail parties. Most have gone through an engineering or sciences track at college, and they typically enjoy problem solving and building things. They tend to be patient, quiet, and cautious with strangers. In contrast, people in a discipline such as sales, customer service, project management, general management, finance, or law are more accustomed to talking through problems instead of sitting down and penciling them out. The engineer is used to other people asking them for things instead of asking others. Because they deal more often in absolutes (right vs. wrong) than most professions, I've found they tend to be more judgmental than your average person. Using the MBTI, I typically found over 90 percent of the technical staff rated as being in the "judging" category versus the less judgmental "perceiving" category.

I've swapped between roles that were more business-y and those that were more technical. I went into my first software internship having run my own company. However, I had light technical experience, with just one programming class under my belt.[4] The company had a great team that devoted a huge amount of time to helping the interns. One of my assignments was to build a demo front end for a new product idea the company was evaluating. It was a relatively good fit since it involved understanding the prospective user as well as the (lightly) technical aspect of building the front end. It was a little bit of a stretch given my level of experience but doable with reasonable exertion.

That said, I had growing pains because of my background as a small business owner, which involved a lot of communication. I would ask the engineers more questions than was necessary or appropriate. I would frequently get stuck on relatively trivial things, and because of my training, I was more inclined to talk to someone about these issues rather than work through them on my own. The other engineers were helpful and patient, but after a week or so, they rightly judged that I wasn't sitting down and grinding through the problem as I should (as an engineer would). I started hearing things like "Well, step through it and I'm sure you'll find the problem" or "Check the documentation and see if you find an answer." This was the right advice. What I found when I started thinking through my questions was I often arrived at the answer in the process. I needed to make a major cognitive transition to thinking in a more detail-oriented, structured fashion and to getting comfortable opening up the hood on new technical topics.

---

[2] A personality questionnaire (http://en.wikipedia.org/wiki/Myers-Briggs_Type_Indicator).

[3] I do not, of course, maintain that this is anything but an anecdotal result. I'm unaware of a large-scale survey of engineers using the MBTI, though I would be very interested to see the results.

[4] CS106A at Stanford University, where we used the predecessor of the Eric Roberts book listed at the end of Chapter 3.

Even though the best engineers are usually great collaborators, it's generally a loner's game on a daily basis. Imagine salespeople who can't close a deal and keeps asking their fellow salespeople for advice. Even in the kindest and most supportive sales offices, those people's peers will regard them poorly. Anyway, I worked like a dog that summer and the prototype turned out fine. Was that enough to make me a great programmer? No, I wish. Being a great programmer takes most people years of experience, ideally preceded by a thorough education in engineering as an undergraduate (which I don't have). All this can be intimidating, but remember, many great innovators, Steve Jobs and Eli Whitney for instance, had no formal engineering training.

Another important point to touch on is the stereotypes engineers have about businesspeople. If you've read comic strip *Dilbert*, you're off to a good start. Scott Adams's parodies about engineers oppressed by incompetent bosses and businesspeople are pinned on many an engineer's cubicle. Though the description of bosses and businesspeople is a caricature, the cartoon has its origins in reality. These stereotypical businesspeople don't do their research, don't appreciate the difficulty of what engineers have to do, and they dump extra work on engineers when their sloppy preparation gets the company in trouble.

A prevalent stereotype exists that businesspeople are privileged and got where they are not by hard work but by being part of some type of old boys' (or old girls') club. Though that might be unfair or inaccurate in most cases, it likely stems from the demographics of engineers versus business people. Many engineers are first, second, or third generation immigrants, at least in the United States and Canada. Their parents pushed them toward concrete things like medicine and engineering, partly because of the inherent job security and partly so they could rely on their skills to make them successful instead of having to compete for influence with colleagues who were more embedded in the system. This might sound overly conspiratorial but even if you've grown up with parents that have been in country for several generations, you probably have more intuition about how your countrymen operate, a perspective that frequently makes the business side of things easier. Of course, these patterns are path dependent. Many engineers with this profile had a parent or grandparent who came to the United States and worked as an engineer for a lot of the reasons I described. Their kids grew up watching them work as an engineer, which makes them more likely to do the same kind of work.

How do you spot the engineer who's able to make the transition from engineer to engineer/manager and/or businessperson, becoming that rare gem which helps you bridge the divide? This is a critically important question for startups as well as mature companies. These managers are like the nuclear armament of high-tech: difficult to get and powerful (not as dangerous).

One sign is that such candidates will consistently ask questions in team meetings about your customers and strategy. When they're developing things, they come back to the product people with suggestions and ideas, sometimes good, sometimes a little misguided. But that is okay, better than okay because they're operating with limited perspective. It's more important that they have the interest and aptitude to make these suggestions. So be sure to go out of your way to be encouraging. When it comes to expanding professionally, I've found that most people are limited more by whether they have a genuine interest in learning than by their ability. If you have such individuals, you can test the potential transition by giving them small assignments in the business area, like researching a competitor. One of their biggest challenges is likely to be learning to work with people from different backgrounds, perspectives, and abilities. These people are probably bright and work hard. They may expect everyone else to be the same, otherwise, they'll become dismissive of them. They are apt to be ruthless when it comes to getting to the right answer. Sometimes, especially when dealing with customers, the right answer is subjective and a matter of perspective. Statistically, few people make these kinds of transitions, so keep a close eye out and foster interdisciplinary talent whenever you can.

Roles and Skill Sets at Enable Quiz

Figure 5.1 shows an example organization chart for Enable Quiz.

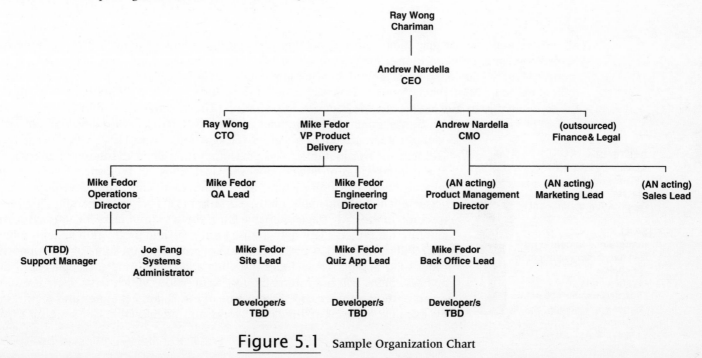

Figure 5.1 Sample Organization Chart

Let's say Andrew has augmented his cast of characters by three people:

1. Ray Wong: Angel investor and mentor.
2. Mike Fedor: A friend of Ray's who is acting as development lead.
3. Joe Fang: A friend of Mike's they've brought in part-time to do systems administration (more on that further on).

You'll notice lots of people repeated in different slots. This is important. Just because you're a small company and people play several different roles doesn't mean you should institutionalize around them. In fact, the opposite is true. You must identify the discrete roles all the team members are playing so others know where they're coming from on certain issues, and whom to go to on specific questions so the structure of the organization is built to scale. We'll review these roles in more detail in the following sections.

Systems Administration

Mike is responsible for operations and engineering. On the operations side, he has a part-time contractor, named Joe Fang, he plans to use. Joe is available at $68/hour if the company commits to at least 30 hours a month. Mike would do the work himself, but he's going to have his hands full getting the development project rolling, not to mention that he's on the expensive side for that kind of work. Why not use one of the developers the company has to hire anyway to do systems administration? They're engineers, after all.

They shouldn't for a number of reasons. First, software development and systems administration are different career tracks. Though they share a number of overlapping skill sets, the two jobs differ. Systems administration is an interdisciplinary job function at the intersection of engineering and operations, and, as such, experienced systems administrators (sysadmins) have a different set of skills from developers. A developer gets better at building applications; a sysadmin gets better at operating high-tech infrastructure. In the early stage of Enable Quiz, the sysadmin tasks include setting up servers and Internet Protocol (IP) networking for the lab and production systems where Enable Quiz will run, as well as installation and maintenance on some of the supporting applications like Joomla!. It includes installing and configuring the applications developers and sysadmins will use internally, like Subversion, which developers use to store and organize their software code base. Some of this is fairly complex and requires planning, for example ensuring redundancy works and Enable Quiz can scale up capacity as it

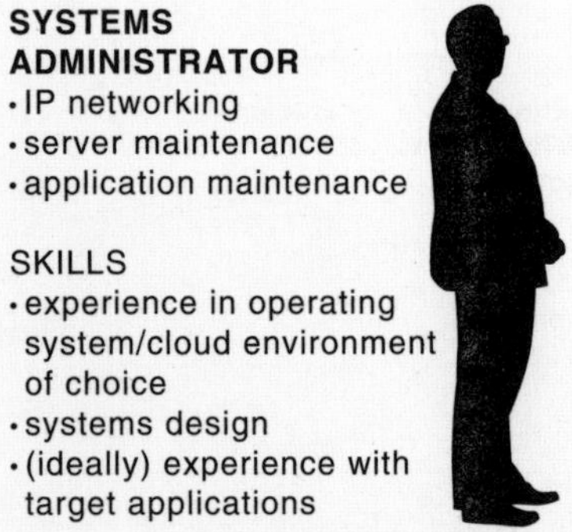

Figure 5.2

The Systems Administrator

SYSTEMS ADMINISTRATOR
· IP networking
· server maintenance
· application maintenance

SKILLS
· experience in operating system/cloud environment of choice
· systems design
· (ideally) experience with target applications

needs without tearing up the whole infrastructure. Another benefit of an experienced sysadmin is that you'll have an engineer outside of development with a more operational perspective looking at the maintainability of your application.

Sysadmins are a fascinating bunch. Though most developers have a formal engineering education, many sysadmins have self-taught. Since their responsibility lies at the variable intersection of engineering and operations, they're often attuned to the company's operational realities in a different way than developers. You can learn a lot by talking to sysadmins about how your system is deployed and operated. Since the job is in large part operational, there's a lot of judgment involved. As in any situation where the right or wrong answer isn't black or white, sysadmins often display a lot pride and ownership in their decisions. The fact is experience does make a huge difference in the role. You can test software and see if it breaks. A sysadmin's operational design has to take into account a much wider spectrum of factors, and they're usually preventing things that could happen under a certain set of circumstances versus things you can deterministically reproduce. Some recipes for doing things work well, and others do not, and it takes experience to determine the right way to go. It helps a lot if the individual is focused on the discipline and solely doing systems administration. In the case of Enable Quiz, this is why Mike brought in Joe Fang, because Mike knows Joe's an experienced syadmin and he can count on him.

Many startups have ceased hosting their own infrastructure, outside of labs. A number of outfits will host it for you. Rackspace is one leader in what I would call the full service segment. It maintains the server hardware and operating system for you, as well as the networking and connectivity to the Internet. Rackspace is more expensive than the alternatives; however, it provides good service and it rarely goes down. They do a lot of the things you would normally pay a sysadmin to do, like upgrade your operating system. Amazon offers an entirely cloud-based service, meaning that your servers are completely virtual. You get a bare bones Linux image which exists on this infrastructure grid it has. Though it costs substantially less than a managed server at Rackspace, I have heard of and experienced horror stories about it going down. And there isn't much account service if you need help.

Another option, which can be handy in the early days, is to have one of your techies run a few servers at home. The speeds may be just fine if they have one of the new higher speed data services (like FiOS from Verizon and U-Verse from AT&T).

Development Lead

Like all managers, development leads have to be able to operate at a level of abstraction. If they used to be engineers, they have become accustomed to the idea that they don't get to understand all the details anymore,

Figure 5.3

The
Development
Lead

DEVELOPMENT LEAD
- software delivery per process/specifications
- developer recruitment, training, management, retention
- (bonus) product improvement ideas

SKILLS
- interdisciplinary perspective
- experience with modern development techniques (adaptive/agile)
- experience in development environment of choice
- general management

meaning not being experts in every domain of their project is all right. Mike's comfort level on the Enable Quiz project is an overall 8 out of 10. It's a 9 out of 10 on the quiz application and a little lower on the back office part—a 9 or higher on the CRM part and a 6 on the billing part. Though Mike used to do Salesforce.com development, billing is new for him. He gets the basic idea because it's just software, but he'll be looking for a bit more senior-level resource in that area to lean on for experience.

At the most basic level, development managers receive a set of inputs and objectives describing the software they need to build, and their job is to deliver that software on time and on budget. Doing that requires they be highly capable in several key areas. First, they must have an interdisciplinary perspective. Their job is to interact with the rest of the company, product management in particular, so they must understand their perspective. More than anything, achieving that understanding requires that they care about the other people's perspective: As long as they want to understand, they will.

The next thing development managers need to be is good project managers. This means being on top of anything that could block development progress, ranging from a gap in the design to an infrastructure issue to a workplace disagreement. This requirement needs extreme discipline about the dull business of creating a project plan and keeping it current. The third thing development managers need is being able to manage the developers. A lot of that is core general management things, such as understanding what the team members want out of the job, helping them get it, and putting the right players on the right tasks.

Development managers should be familiar with formal software development methodologies. Though there are a ton of buzzwords, these methodologies mostly break down along the lines of predictive versus adaptive methodologies. A predictive methodology is one where you have a specific, prescribed set of requirements and plan out all the deliverables over a relatively long period. It's difficult and messy to change plans in this case because you have this elaborate long-term plan. This kind of methodology is popular where budgeting, fixed-price contracting, or predictability are high priorities. It works best when you're doing something similar to what you've done before; otherwise, it's hard to predict with that kind of foresight. It's well-suited to developers who need a lot of specific direction and/or who are working in large teams.

Adaptive, or agile, methodologies are more popular with small companies who operate in dynamic environments. The idea is to break development milestones into smaller intervals, usually into one to four weeks each. At the end of each of these segments (usually called "iterations") you integrate everything together, test it, show it to the parties concerned (such as product management), and ensure you're on track for the next iteration. This works well in smaller teams who are operating against product requirements that are likely to evolve. Enable Quiz is a brand new product so even though Andrew produced a good product design, the team is likely to find things they want to change as they go along and have their initial contacts with customers.

It probably makes sense for Enable Quiz to organize more toward the adaptive end of the spectrum. One downside to this is that adaptive methods work best when everyone's in the same office, including the business people, which won't be the case at Enable Quiz. That's probably okay because they are starting with a good design and will be investing time in producing even better documentation for the developers to use.

While adaptive methods emphasize working software over documentation, it's still important not to underinvest in this area, particularly if you're selling enterprise solutions to businesses. Companies that release great products with weak documentation end up in a situation where users don't know how to engage with the product and internal teams don't know how to maintain it.

Let's look at what Enable Quiz needs to do on the documentation front. The first step is to produce the user help files. Andrew's product management role suggests he is a good candidate to produce those, though it's a lot of work and he may need to bring in someone on contract to help. Having experience with at least basic multimedia (such as screen recording) for producing multimedia tutorials will be a huge asset. Camtasia Studio is a popular tool in the personal computer (PC) environment, and there are a number of offerings for Macintoshes.

Mike will be responsible in his various team lead capacities for producing lower-level technical documentation. Two documents that are particularly important are the installation and maintenance guide and the integration guide. The first of these will provide the sysadmin and support personnel everything they need to install and troubleshoot the application. The integration guide will detail the integration points between the site, the quiz application, CRM, and billing. It will also keep the various teams' work internally consistent. A good first step to getting your documentation tasks organized is to publish an outline. Google Docs is a useful tool for making such an outline generally available and editable at the same time.

What will Mike be doing as Development Lead? The first area to tackle is the web front end. Aside from finding a qualified developer, the main task will be to facilitate timely interaction between the designer and Andrew on the user experience. Beyond that, the main success factor is to ensure they set up everything properly in Joomla! so the website is easy to maintain on a go-forward basis. The next step in that area is for Mike to screen some candidates and have Joe Fang set up a web server with Joomla! so the designer can go to town.

Mike is doubling as a developer and the quiz application is where he will spend most of his time. If he finds good personnel on the front end and back office, he may be able to do a substantial part of the initial software development himself. This kind of green field application development is something guys like Mike usually enjoy. Mike must acquire an intuitive understanding of the specification so he can fill in all the gaps that arise while he's writing the software with all the little decisions he has to make. This was the primary purpose of Andrew's product design document as a starting point. Beyond that, Mike must organize the implementation into sensible pieces and consult with Andrew on the product part as they go along.

The crucial items on the back office part are design and planning. Customizing a CRM system is like finger painting: easy to do, but hard to do well. The product design is a good place to start, but Mike will need to work together with Andrew to take it to the next level of detail, in particular integrating the billing system. Ideally, he should find someone who's integrated Salesforce.com and whatever billing system they select. Though Mike's not an expert on billing, he knows the five steps he needs to take to select, customize, and deploy enterprise software:

1. Document the applicable business processes.
2. See how those processes fit in to the standard operating model for the software.
3. Customize where necessary.
4. Ensure the output works for the users.
5. Document.

The next step in that area is for Mike to finish researching billing systems, make his recommendation, and source a contract team to work on it.

Let's review the type of people Mike's looking for on the three development teams.

Developers

Your ideal developer has genuine professional enthusiasm. You can often get a sense of this when perusing their résumés by looking at their personal website or searching for their name online in conjunction with a couple of areas they've worked on, such as their name and a technology they have used (example: "Bob Smith PHP"). Have they posted on forums? Are they involved with any technology-related organizations? If you ask them about a project or technology during their interviews, do they have something interesting to say about, for example, the pros and cons of their approach? It's also perfectly okay to ask them brain teasers in an interview to see how well-organized they are when solving a problem. It's understood that the ability to reason through complex problems is part of the job. A developer who's an unclear and undisciplined thinker is likely to produce sloppy work.

Price should not be the number one consideration. Even though you don't want to pay through the nose, the difference in the quantity and quality of output you'll get from a great developer versus a middling or bad one is enormous. A bad developer is worse than no developer at all because, if you want to move forward, someone will have to go back and clean up the previous work.

If you're going to use an adaptive methodology, you need a developer with good communications skills and a team orientation. Weigh these heavily along with technical expertise if you're planning to use an adaptive methodology since, without them, the engagement's success is at risk. Do not mistake a language barrier for a communication issue. If your developer is offsite and has English as a second language, try using Instant Messaging (IM) chat as a communications medium. You may find the developer is more comfortable with written communication.

You want to ensure you know what you want and align your hires' work with their interests and experience. Enable Quiz has a few different areas. Their front-end developer needs website and application design fundamentals, in addition to a track record with Javascript and Ajax, two of the main technologies for making the kind of highly interactive front ends users expect. Although anyone can learn those technologies, the learning and experience curve is steep, and a lot of intangible knowledge is required to implement them effectively. Enable Quiz doesn't have nearly enough time to teach someone these, so it'll be looking for people with a track record.

Then Enable Quiz has the quiz application. This has a few facets: front-end design, web service API implementation, database design, and controller/workflow design. To complete something like this from the ground up, you must find a strong generalist who's built a substantial application from scratch. Mike has that experience building applications on Salesforce.com and that's part of the reason Ray (the Enable Quiz chairman) identified him as such a great fit for the project.

Aside from his experience in all these different areas, Mike is willing to go ask experts for guidance when he needs it. That's a key quality to have in your senior developers: If they're biting off something big, they need to be the kind of people who will seek and receive advice. This is a good interview question for people in that role: "What would you do if you needed to find out more about [insert topic that's new to them but relevant to the project] on short notice?" Their answer should include seeking advice from a peer.

DEVELOPER
- responsible for discrete portions of product implementation

SKILLS
- genuine professional interest and enthusiasm in their field
- track record/portfolio in area of interest
- good communications skills
- team orientation
- experience with modern development techniques (adaptive/agile)
- experience in implementation technology of choice a plus

Figure 5.4

The Developer

As the development lead and senior developer, Mike's job with the quiz application is to rough out the basics, put it on a good footing, and carve out specific tasks for someone else if he runs short on time. Marek, who Mike is bringing in to help on the quiz engine, developed an online application for managing custodial staff. It's similar to Enable Quiz from a software development perspective in that it's a web-based application with substantial front-end requirements and a substantial database back-end component. That's why Mike thinks he'll be good as a supporting developer in that area. He has not done much with web service APIs, so Mike will do most of the initial work on that.

Finally, there is the back office task with the CRM and billing system. This work needs a different type of developer. The CRM and billing systems are applications that have their own configuration and customization layers that any nontechnical layperson can use. However, integrating all the systems together is complex and requires experience with the CRM and billing applications. Enable Quiz will need someone with a developer background to integrate the two back office systems with the Enable Quiz website and will be specifically looking for someone who likes to do integration-oriented development on top of existing applications. This is a little trickier than it sounds because, as I mentioned, most developers like to build things from scratch. Having done development on the Salesforce.com CRM, Mike knows some people in that area as well as what to look for in candidates. He has the general idea on the billing piece as well, since it's what people would call enterprise software or software for businesses to run their operations. Mike doesn't think Enable Quiz will need a lot done in that area so he'll be looking to outsource the need for that expertise. He'll have to pay more for that, but it will be worth it.

Quality Assurance

Mike believes Enable Quiz should hire someone relatively senior in this area. They should have enough perspective to work directly with Andrew. The traditional view of Quality Assurance (QA) is that they take the software, see if they can break it, and then give it back to the developers to fix. Even though this is true, it's also the minimum you could ask of QA. Mike would like to find someone who can read the product design and be responsible for designing the test plans and asking questions where necessary of Andrew (as the product guy) if something doesn't makes sense. It's not that Mike's not ready to manage this person, but you don't want the fox guarding the chicken coop. The QA lead should be a somewhat independent check on the development teams, making sure their output complies with the letter and intent of the product design.

Mike is a big believer in automating QA, meaning that a software application automatically runs the same tests a human would otherwise execute by hand. A lot of great tools are available for doing so, many of them open source and free. Selenium is one example. Think of it this way: Every test case you automate is one you don't have to pay someone to execute and can run as often as you like. This doesn't mean you'll never have to test anything manually, since some items like layout are easiest to test with human inspection, but it makes an enormous difference in the cost, quantity, and reliability of your testing.

To regress means to move backward. The idea with a regression test is to make sure you didn't break anything that was working with the new features or changes you've added in the new release. It's something you do in addition to testing all the new stuff. It's easy to enter a wasteful cycle where you are pressed for time and preoccupied with getting the latest release tested and out the door. Someone must take the time to automate the testing up front and maintain that automated regression test suite as you progress. It took us a week to do a regression manually at Leonid Systems; however, once we automated it we could run it as often as we wanted. We were also able to run it for compatibility with different browsers, like Internet Explorer, Firefox, and Chrome. This is especially important since, after a long period of relative stability, the number of browsers in the market is increasing. Once we automated regression, the QA team members were able to take more time to look at new features, which is what they should be doing rather than turning into zombies from running the same test plan repeatedly.

Product Management

We'll briefly cover the product management job since it's so closely tied to what happens in engineering and development. You have several ways to organize this area. I learned a lot about this type of role when I worked at Nestlé, one of the largest, oldest, and most enduring companies in the world. At a lot of tech companies, product managers are kind of toothless—they do their thing but they're treated like a cog in the wheel. At consumer packaged goods companies like Nestlé, products are managed by brand managers who are like mini CEOs for their particular products. They often get their bonuses on profits for the product, not just sales. Managing this way in high-tech means that your development managers will have to account for the time they worked across the various products to allocate engineering costs accordingly. It's a pain but it does show you where you're investing your development dollars.

Since Andrew is the company CEO and one of the owners, he has the accountability aspect of the job going for him. However, as Enable Quiz grows, and adds more people to

QUALITY ASSURANCE (QA)
- review output from developers and evalutate its conformance with the product's specification and intent
- design and maintain test plans
- create and maintain automated regression tests

SKILLS
- general interest and understanding of customer experience with the product
- attention to detail and organization
- experience with modern development techniques
- experience with test automation tools

Figure 5.5

The Quality Assurance Engineer

PRODUCT MANAGEMENT
- responsible for particular product- to extent possible a "mini CEO" for their product
- assess market needs and formulate product design and delivery to fufill them

SKILLS
- customer-facing experience in relevant market
- understanding of product development process and drivers of efficiency
- competency in design thinking to pull together approach on product

Figure 5.6

The Product Manager

product management, it should consider organizing the job with a high degree of accountability, ideally against the profit on its products. It's a great way to attract outstanding people to the job.

Product managers will succeed or fail based on their ability to figure out what the market wants and to deliver it to them. That being the case, product managers need to have experience with customers, whether those customers are businesses or consumers. If product managers are out of touch with the customers, they're going to miss the market. Additionally, they need to know how to give engineers the right inputs so they can deliver efficiently. That means asking the right questions about cost/benefit and delivering good, clean, clear product design inputs. The product managers need to understand the operational side of the product, specifically what drives support costs. Part of this is allocating support costs by product so that product managers understand how things like documentation and design for maintainability drive operational costs.

How do you design for maintainability to keep down operational costs? The first step is to do a good job on documentation, particularly around the process of turning up new customers. The most pressing problems often originate from the sysadmins' and support personnel's lack of training on how to manage and troubleshoot the application. If you don't do a good job on documentation, you'll end up with one or two people who know how to fix things because they've been at it from the beginning, but that doesn't scale.

Once you're clear on documentation and training, then you need to continuously examine what's driving time on operational issues. Is it customer education? Bugs in the product? Improper configuration? Ideally, you want at least a basic post-mortem on every single trouble ticket that comes in from customers. You want to organize these areas so you can answer the question "How could they have been avoided?" for every complaint or issue.

Evaluating New Hires

Tell Me about Yourself

After you've written job descriptions, identifying the key skill sets you need, the hard part is evaluating candidates with the limited information you'll get from a résumé and a job interview. Beyond the technical credentials of the developer, you have different mindsets and things that drive them. On an anecdotal/non-scientific basis, I've put together a set of buckets that I use to help me think about what kind of person a developer is and what they want. These are particularly important if you plan to use one of the adaptive or "Agile" methodologies popular with tech startups. Those methodologies require close collaboration and teamwork, meaning that communication skills and team orientation are as critical as technical skills.

The percentages look silly, but I like to put together specific data points and adjust them based on experience. The first category—Climbers—are rare but valuable. They work hard and happily take on new challenges as long as they see an upside. They can sometimes get in other developers' hair, so you need to ensure you give them a big enough project to keep them focused and prevent them from disrupting others. You can help Climbers do what they want to do by giving them as big an opportunity as you think they can handle and giving them a long leash.

The second category—Scientists—will acquire fantastic expertise in topics that interest them. These developers are perfect if you have a complex new technology where you need expertise or otherwise need people to go do a lot of technical learning. These individuals' natural priority and interest is to learn and understand, so you need to keep them focused with specific goals that have timelines attached. If not, they'll go off on tangents. Scientists are the opposite of Climbers. Climbers see technology as a means to an end, and Scientists take great interest in the technology. You can help Scientists do what they want to do by giving them a technically difficult problem in an area that interests them.

Climbers (15%)
Scientists (20%)
Artists (15%)
Day Laborers (20%)
Mixed (30%)

Artists are the hardest to manage but can be enormously productive. If things go right, these individuals fall in love with the product and its relationship with the audience. You and Artists can reap wonderful results from this kind of partnership. They will regard the technology with interest, but they care a great deal about how it performs in the real world. The downside of Artists' dispositions is they are easily turned off if they don't see the product as worthy and they can develop a strange, stilted view of the world. Their belief about what's great and wonderful can go far afield from the market realities. And they get mad and hurt more easily than most developers. Offending these individuals is easy, and they tend to hold a grudge though they will change their attitude quickly if you approach them sincerely with an apology or resolution. The term Artists doesn't necessarily mean that they work in particular on visual things: You could have a database artist. The best way to help Artists is to give them an abstract goal, a minimum set of parameters, and let them complete the project the way they want. Your interpersonal relationship with Artists is more important than with any another category, and you have to sit down and want to understand their approach.

As far as Day Laborers are concerned, this job is a means to an end: Their dominant interests lie elsewhere. This isn't to say that the other types don't strike an acceptable work/life balance, or that Day Laborers don't get a solid amount of work done. It means you shouldn't expect a lot more than the minimum from them. In fairness to other types that are producing more deliverables, you should find a way to supplement compensation based on achievement or overachievement of objectives. Success-based bonuses are a good way to approach this kind of variation among employees. It sets the expectation that you have a minimum expectation for them, and they will receive a larger bonus for going beyond that. The way you help Day Laborers do what they want to do is to set a minimum set of expectations and give them a clear, consistent view of what they need to do so they can manage their time.

The Mixed category is the largest by far and contains people with elements of more than one of the personality types above, such as a Climber-Scientist.

The most constructive way to think about these classifications is as attributes that coexist in larger or smaller degrees in everyone. Many people become Day Laborers as they get older and have families. Of course, all people will perform better on a project they enjoy, working for a company they like. That's universal. But within those parameters, different things motivate them.

There are a few things I make sure I do before an interview. If we're doing an interview, I've already read their résumés. If they look promising, I'll see what I can find out about them online. I don't want to know about their personal life because that's their business. What I look for are notes on their personal website that reference a relevant professional interest, postings to a technical forum of some kind. The goal is to do a basic screening on whether they have the interests and experience for the job in question. Following that, I want to assess what drives them, starting with the personality typing I described above, and dig through their experience and analytical capabilities. Table 5.1 lists key interview questions I use to categorize the candidate.

These are the questions I generally lead with to get a sense of who a qualified candidate is and what he or she wants out of the job. There is an extended list of questions on Alexandercowan.com/recruiting. Some firms use brainteasers to see how a candidate works through a complex problem. If I haven't been able to find much about their previous work, I'll ask them some questions about that, to give me some specific details on a project, for instance. I'm looking to see how they describe what they did and why.

Question	Climber	Scientist	Artist	Day Laborer
What do you want to be doing in five years?	I'd like to be in a management job or running my own company.	I'd like to be a world-class expert in [field of interest].	I want to be working on a project I love for a great company with great people.	I'd like to be retired if I could.
How do you feel about your workload?	It's fine.	I'd like to have more time to dig deeper into things.	I'd like to have more time to get things right.	I'm so busy.
What is the one thing you've done professionally that makes you the most proud? Why?	Something they did where they saw the upside for the business. Here's an example: I was involved in the launch of [a product], and it was a huge success for the company because it [delivered tangible results].	Some difficult problem they solved. Here's an example: When [some technology] was in its early stages, we [did something difficult or cutting edge with it].	Some deliverable (opus) where they assessed it to be great and wonderful. Here's an example: I was the lead on [a deliverable], and it was just a beautiful piece of work, really great.	Could be a number of things but probably not especially heartfelt: Well, let me think. I guess [answer].
What are the pros and cons of the job you do now?	The pros are that I'm learning a lot about the business. The cons are that I'm down in the weeds, the details a lot.	The pros are that I get to work on some interesting problems. The cons are that there is a lot of daily stuff that has to get done.	The pros are that I do get to do good work a lot of the time. The cons are that sometimes you have to do things that are arbitrary because of management's or a customer's insistence.	Every job has its pros and cons. I guess [answer].

Table 5.1

Nontechnical Interview Questions

(continued)

Table 5.1

(*continued*)

Question	Climber	Scientist	Artist	Day Laborer
Tell me about the most and the least exciting projects you've done, and why you'd rate them as such.	The most exciting project was [x] because I learned a lot and it was a big success. The least exciting was [y] because it didn't add up to much in the end.	The most exciting was [x] because we accomplished something that was cutting edge. The least exciting was [y] because we were doing housekeeping on a mature or aging technology.	The most exciting was [x] because I was able to do the right thing and it turned out great. The least exciting was [y] because I was a cog in a machine that was fulfilling the same old prescription.	I guess [x] because we finished early. [y] was probably the least since it ran over in time, and there was a lot of pressure on the deadline.
Do you prefer sending an email or using the phone?	Usually phone unless there's a lot of detail that needs to be laid out.	E-mail, but I love a good talk with the right people.	Phone as long as I'm talking to people who know what they're doing.	Either way I guess.
Tell me about a difficult situation or circumstance with a colleague or customer, and how you handled it.	I got involved with a customer situation where the account team and the engineering team were not putting their heads together to get things done. I helped sort it out and the customer was happy.	We had a new guy who was having a lot of trouble understanding [x technology]. I sat him down and we went through it and he got it after that.	We had a customer that did not get what we were doing and kept trying to turn the product from a race horse into a donkey. I got the account team involved to sort it out.	This could be a number of things, and it's likely to have to do with the amount he [or she] had to work instead of the quality or relevance of the work.

Question	Climber	Scientist	Artist	Day Laborer
Tell me about a time you went above and beyond what was called for and did what you knew needed to be done. How did you know what needed to be done and why did you do it?	We had a situation where I had seen repeatedly that the lack of [x feature] in the product was causing a whole cascade of problems. I went to the right people, convinced them we needed to fix it, and I put in the extra time to do it since no one else was available.	We were working through a difficult problem with [x technology]. I had expertise in the area and dug in, talking to a few colleagues. I figured out the nature of the thing. I could tell we needed a better understanding based on my experience with [x technology].	We had a deliverable that was just going to be garbage. You could see it coming, like a big freight train of junk. I stepped in front of the train and just fixed the problem.	Hmm. Let me think. Several years ago [answer].
If someone senior to you criticized you or your work unfairly, what would you do?	It depends on the situation, but I think I would present the facts, assumptions, and results around whatever was the source of the criticism. If the manager was bad, I'd find a way to avoid working under him [her].	I would explain to them as best I could the facts. But sometimes they just don't understand and that kind of thing happens.	It happens all the time. I take it, like a knife in the heart.	Whatever, it happens. If it happens a lot, I find another job.

Table 5.1

(*continued*)

At this point, I've decided if they're on the short list or not. If they are, I call the references. This process allows me to look for any red flags and confirm my assumptions. As you might be aware, there's a lot of legal touchiness regarding references. Many big companies will tell you an employee's dates of employment and confirm salary. Whenever you're able to get a reference, you need to learn to read between the lines.

Evaluation at Enable Quiz

In an ideal world, Enable Quiz would luck out with the following three people.

1. Artists on the front end who know the complex front-end technologies but still want to know the user
2. Climbers who want to summit the challenge of building the quiz application from scratch
3. Scientists on billing whose expertise they can leverage.

The CRM part needs a reasonably priced doer. They have Mike screen candidates and get additional opinions from Andrew and the rest of the technical team.

Evaluating Third-Party Firms

Evaluating third-party firms requires a somewhat different approach, since you're looking to form a relationship with a whole company instead of an individual. That said, if the firm is comprised of a couple of people, I'd interview them as I would an employee, with less emphasis on the interpersonal stuff.

The number one thing to remember with a third-party firm—for example, an offshore contracting house or a web development firm—is to look for success on projects similar to yours. I find out as much as I can about the relevant projects and then I ask to talk to references at those companies. An inability to supply a reference is a red flag, and you need to check that. One other thing I check when examining the references is whether they've completed the project with the firm in question. If they're still actively engaged with the client I'm talking to as a reference, that client reference may hesitate to say anything bad about the firm even if they're not delivering because they won't want to risk making a bad situation worse to help out a stranger.

Table 5.2 shows a hit list of questions for references. These assume that you have an understanding of what the project was and how long it took.

Question	What You're Hoping to Find Out
Would you use them again?	Relationships with third-party firms for custom development are difficult to manage and often fail. That's just a fact, and you can double that failure rate for offshore firms. So a few negative responses here aren't necessarily a deal breaker. But if I receive a negative response, then I need to satisfy myself that the failure was a bad fit or the firm's poor management over this client. Otherwise, that's a deal breaker.
How was the engagement planned and scoped out?	The answer tells me a lot about the firm's ability to do the initial design and scoping. You may not expect the firm to do your design, but you should expect it to be able to provide accurate estimates on hours and timeframes for a well-defined project. If the third-party firm did the design on the project in question or helped the client clean up its design, then terrific.
How did you communicate with the firm on status? How predictable were deliverables, timelines, and costs?	I'd like to hear that the firm's team members had a place, a ticketing system or extranet for example, where they posted questions and got answers from the client. I'd like to know the firm scheduled regular demos to make sure they were on the right path before they went too far. I'm looking to hear that timelines, deliverables, and costs were on target.
	If they weren't, I would want to relate the answer to the above items about scoping and planning. There are two high-level possibilities, and they're not mutually exclusive. The first is that the client did a reasonable job with their design, and the firm did a bad job of reading it and estimating the job. That's bad.
	The second is that the client decided to change things as it went along, which is a common occurrence. Some clients will freely admit to throwing in changes, and it's a feature of those adaptive development methodologies and sometimes perfectly OK. Others see it as a bad thing or are bullying the firm into doing free work. If I get that sense, then I know I have to take everything I'm hearing from the reference with a grain of salt.

Table 5.2

Questions for References

(continued)

Table 5.2

(*continued*)

Question	What You're Hoping to Find Out
	Both of those things commonly happen simultaneously, so it's important to see if the firm is willing to talk about specific examples so you can get a sense of which case you're looking at and how much of each case.
Did you have them do documentation? If so, how was it? If not, why not?	If I hear the client say it didn't want to pay for documentation and it complains about the handoff, I know it's likely bad management of the firm by the client instead of bad work by the firm.
	If they did do documentation, I want to understand what kind of quality to expect and how prescriptive or specific I need to be about the contents of the documentation.
How did you do the handoff to your own people for maintenance (if applicable)? How well did that work?	I've answered the documentation question, so this question's goal is to get a sense of how maintainable the firm made the code. I'm also looking to understand how maintainable the firm made their application: Was every configuration parameter hard coded somewhere deep within it or did they make it easy to configure aspects of its behavior?
Who worked on your project? Who did well and who didn't? Any particular strengths or weaknesses regarding those individuals? How was their English (if applicable)?	This question tries to unearth the level of talent at the firm. This is getting into the firm's kitchen a little bit, but, hey, I'm going to find out whatever I can. When you're a new customer and you're small, you'll often get a company's newbie if you're careless, and that's not what you want. If I do end up with newer employees, I want to negotiate rates so I'm not paying senior development prices for someone junior. You have to accept some junior developers: After all, a company doesn't have its superstars sitting on the bench. However, the junior developer has to be balanced by a senior developer who is not the team lead a lot of the time. A lot of the time, the team lead is checking schedules and managing at a high level. The lead is not going to be controlling enough to coach a junior developer to do things right.
What would you do differently?	This is the general catchall to see what else they have to tell me.

What about questions for the third-party firm itself? I primarily ask it about its internal processes, and of course, I request anonymous staff résumés to ensure the team we're getting has the skills we need. I compare the résumés to anything I've been able to learn about particular team members from talking to the references. I make sure I know what development methodologies the firm uses and how it organizes its source code that tells you a lot about their level of organization. For example, I've learned that two types of firms do development on top of CRM systems: consultants and developers. Consultants are customizing a single CRM instance for a particular company. They tweak things until they get something the client likes and don't design for extensibility and maintainability. That may be all right if it's your own internal system, but Enable Quiz is developing a product. The consultants don't usually use source control and though this is common for firms that do customizations on top of CRM platforms, it does tell you the prospective firm is of the consultant ilk versus developer.

If the firm is abroad, I ask for a phone call with a couple of the team members in an attempt to get a sense of how strong their English skills are. In many cases, their written English will be adequate even though they can't speak well. The only somewhat reliable method I've found is to ask developers to explain back, often by way of a translator, something I've sent them, like a product design. You can tell from the kinds of questions they ask: They probably have a language issue if they consistently ask questions answered in your product specifications. If they have no questions, that's probably a language issue, too. These are serious problems since they cause soft failures where the developers have understood your specifications somewhat but not completely. If they understand 70 percent, that's a lot of stuff that will be messed up.

Motivation

How do you motivate these teams and get them to feel the same way about the project that you do? That's hard. The idea was not theirs, at least the initial concept, and they don't have nearly the upside that you do. You can give them ownership, and that is the most consistent recipe for increasing performance. First, developers care more about their deliverables when they have a discrete, identifiable patch of grass, so to speak, that's their own. Giving the employees ownership means investing them with confidence and trust, giving them basic direction, minimal supervision, and giving them the latitude to accomplish their objectives. Second, you want to avoid overreliance on equity. Overreliance on equity is a no-win situation: Employees will wonder if their equity will be worth something, or they will walk once they can cash in the equity. A bonus structure with a portion going to a retention bonus is the best way to align reward and retention.

Going Offshore

Here or There?

There's layer upon layer of misperception surrounding the concept of offshoring. One misperception I call the Alice in Wonderland view, where people see outsourcing as a magic pill you swallow that defies the laws of time and space. I hear this refrain a lot: "We tried outsourcing, and it didn't work." That's like saying, "I tried hiring a programmer from Texas, and that didn't work." You don't try something like that once and write it off if things don't work out as you'd hoped. The best way to view offshoring is to see it for what it is: recruiting and managing developers in another country.

Do you still need to make sure you get good people? Yes.

Do you still need to train them? Yes.

Do you need to give them incentives? Yes.

Do you need to spend lots of time making sure they understand the company's objective? Yes.

You need to spend lots of time training them in best practices and familiarizing them with your target users, especially since those kinds of customers may not exist in their environment. You have to make sure the offshore employees understand written English (if not spoken). You'll want to be aware of any cultural differences. Better yet, understand them in detail. Wow, you might be thinking, that sounds like a lot of work. Why go to the trouble?

The answer is money. You can change your economics if you have a team of offshore developers who are well qualified, well trained, and well integrated into your company. A lot of raw talent lives abroad, but you'll probably need to have the time and scale to make a major investment in training them on best practices. A U.S. software developer of the caliber Enable Quiz needs will run in the neighborhood of $80,000–$110,000, adding 20 percent for benefits. A senior developer in Eastern Europe will run around $30/hour or around $62,000 a year. If you average the 80K to 110K level to 95K and add 20 percent for benefits, that's around a 40 percent savings, which is a big deal if you have a larger team. That's the theory, at least.

Those savings are hard to get in practice. Most offshore teams are not that well managed, so they're not going to be at parity with a domestic development team. The developers are not inherently any better or worse than U.S. developers, but outside of a few development hotspots, they're not as trained in best practices, and that makes a big difference. You're probably lucky if you save 25 percent in the end. The savings may be worthwhile if you're running a sizable operation, and you include your QA resources. Many people are looking for the lowest hourly rate when they first go at it, which is a huge mistake. As I mentioned before, a mediocre developer is almost worse than no developer at all. If you pay bargain basement prices, you're likely going to get a less productive developer who's thousands of miles away and who probably isn't well trained or managed. The results are predictable and not very good. If you want to use adaptive and agile methods, scoring lower on communications and teamwork skills will be a huge handicap to the potential effectiveness of those methods.

Tips for Success

Given the wide range of what offshoring can mean in practice, it's not easy to prescribe a single formula for success. However, I've summarized a few things that I've found helpful in the past:

- Minimize Jargon

  High-tech is notorious for its jargon. This is justified, in part, since there's a steady stream of new concepts. I've found it's best to avoid jargon, and use simple, direct, descriptive terminology instead.
- Manage to the Right Level of Specificity

  The agile methodology emphasizes lightweight documentation that's augmented by conversations, an approach that may not work as well if your team is in a different location, has a different first language, or is new to a lot of the concepts you're introducing. This isn't to say you can't use adaptive and agile methodologies, but if you have less currency with the person-to-person conversations, you will have to supplement it with more detailed documentation. That may come in the form of more detailed design notes and/or write-ups in whatever you're using (Rally, Bugzilla, etc.) to track the progress of development items.
- Maintain a Healthy Backlog

  Time zone and communications differences may cause your team members to get hung up on items, and it could be awhile before the right person is able to get them unstuck. Therefore, you want to ensure you have a long list of prioritized items for the offshore employees to work on. These are often referred to as evergreen requirements. This way, they can move on to something else if they get stuck on a particular item.

- Organize Your Time Zones

  Most cross-shore teams adjust their time schedules a bit to have more working hours together. Additionally, if your team is in Europe, you'll want to get those extra few notes to them before you leave the office. Remember, they'll be having lunch by the time you wake up.

- Use Careful, Close Diagnostics

  Set up systems to track progress as well as Q&A. You want to encourage informal discussions, but put as much as you can into your tracking system so everyone has access to the written notes. Make sure you can see what team members have accomplished on a daily basis. The standard way to do this in agile is a daily stand up meeting in which team peers update each other. This may not work as well if there are language, geography, or time zone barriers, and you may want to substitute a written update and ad hoc conversational updates.

- Employ Backup Systems

  The following scenario occurs: Your (choose one: test system, source control, wiki, ticketing system) goes down in the United States, and your offshore team is delayed for hours until daylight U.S. time when someone gets the message and fixes it. You never want to let this happen. Whether the procedures are manual (a process) or technical (a backup instance), you need to make sure your team knows how to keep rolling if everything in the United States goes offline.

- Use Frequent Commits

  One of the key tasks is to engage in regular, explicit communication where all the team members are on their deliverables. Frequent code commits allow you to get your QA and the rest of teams involved earlier, uncovering any misunderstandings sooner so they can be resolved.

- Design Your Processes

  We review this more in Chapter 7, but process increases in importance with the complexity of your team composition. You can fudge a lot of things when everyone is in the same office, but that won't work if you have distributed teams. Ultimately, these more structured processes will help you scale (as long as they're designed well). Above all, communicate with your offshore teammates regularly, and it will probably be pretty obvious to you both the best ways to collaborate.

Offshoring and Enable Quiz

Does offshoring make sense in the case of Enable Quiz? It does not make sense unless the number of team members increases and they find a great team abroad. Marek happens to be in Slovakia, so that will save them a few bucks, but that's a coincidence. What's important is that he's someone Mike knows has the right skill set.

And that's the other reason to go offshore when you're looking at a specialty area because, of course, not everyone's in the United States. You may find clusters of experts abroad whose expertise may make the distance and cultural and language barriers worth overcoming.

Contracting

Getting the right contracting agreement in place is critical. A typical form will basically state that the employer owns everything developers do for them on an exclusive basis. If a developer has any pre-existing intellectual property they want to exclude, they need to identify it explicitly. Though it might sound draconian, there's no other way to do it, and most developers understand this. If your company does not own the intellectual property outright, you will have a huge liability for you and your customers even if you're using an open source model. Hence, employment and contract agreements with those terms are typical in the industry.

Then you must consider compensation. Do you do things with a fixed price based on a statement of work, or do you use an hourly rate? Recall our discussion of adaptive versus predictive development methodologies. It's like taking a cab. If you know where you're going, say from the airport to your hotel, you might ask the cab driver how much the trip will be. But if you think you might want to stop at the ATM, pick up a friend, see the sights, and so forth, then you'll need to pay the driver by the mile.

Enable Quiz has a good idea of what they want to do, but not nearly good enough for a fixed price statement of work. Also, they'll probably use an adaptive methodology, all of which suggests that they contract to pay hourly, but make sure they're getting their money's worth as they go along.

Internal Tools

If your team's not all on site, good tools and processes (which we'll cover in Chapter 7) are important. Make sure you have consistent communications systems in place across the board: a phone system with a company-wide block of numbers (even if they forward to mobiles), email (Google Apps is free and solid), and IM (there are a number of options and many systems include presence to tell if someone's on the phone, which is handy). Table 5.3 shows a few notes on IT systems.

Table 5.3

Notes on
Internal
Systems

Item	Requirements	Example Options
Customer Relationship Management (CRM)	At a minimum, this is a contact database for all your customers and a place to keep track of potential sales. Depending on the sophistication, you may want to manage email campaigns here. Ideally, you're doing issue management (next item) in the CRM as well, so the data are integrated with the rest of your customer's profile.	Salesforce.com has an all SaaS (hosted) offer. SugarCRM has a strong solution, particularly if you prefer open source and would like to run the system locally, and it offers both deployment options.
Issue/Trouble-Ticket Management	You want something that can manage issues by queue (type) and severity and make it easy for you to update customers on status. Ideally, it provides a ready-to-use portal for customers as well.	The above CRM systems are suitable for this purpose (usually with some minimal customization). Some operations prefer to manage these in their bug tracking system (below).
Feature and Bug Tracking	You want something that will facilitate an agile methodology where you have a prioritized backlog. Beyond that, it's important the system provide tools to track status and progress by developers, particularly if they are off site.	Bugzilla is a popular open-source option. Most of these systems are highly customized. Your development team will probably have experience and preferences for a particular system.
Source Control	This system deals with organizing your source code for releases.	Subversion and Git are popular open-source options. Like the previous item, your team members will likely have experience with a particular system. If they are more than one person and they are not using source control, you may want to ask why.
Test and QA Management	This system deals with organizing test cases and tracking their execution across iterations and releases. Such a system helps keep your test plans organized and doing post-mortems on bugs that reach the field.	Test Link is a popular open-source option. Various commercial options are available, and some are integrated with other example items below.

Item	Requirements	Example Options
Functional Test Automation	This system deals with creating automated test suites. These will save you lots of money and heartache as you scale. Once you automate a test, you can run it free as many times as you want or until it finds a bug, which is its reason for being.	Selenium is a popular and easy to use open-source option. SilkTest and IBM Rational are proprietary options. Your team members are likely to be familiar with a specific platform. If they're not, Selenium is a cheap and easy way to get started.
Project Management	This system deals with internal and possibly external project management. If your team is collocated, index cards and bulletin boards are the classic tool for agile project management.	If you have a requirement for external project management with customers, Basecamp is a popular tool. Google Docs provides a sharing framework. Your team may use specific tools for Agile project management, such as Rally and Atlassian JIRA, many of which handle test management as well.
Document Management	Document management deals with organizing and versioning documents: customer documentation, internal documentation, etc.	Basecamp provides such a facility, as does Google Docs.

Table 5.3

(continued)

Chapter 5 Summary

1. The Engineer

   Being the businessperson, you must understand that the engineer is accustomed to deep, measured problem solving while you may be more used to talking back and forth. Engineers will, therefore, appreciate your preparation and articulation of what the product needs to do. More than anything, they want to see that what they produce is relevant and useful to the end user. Engineers will resent last-minute changes to product definition, especially if those changes stem from a lack of preparation on your part. Using an adaptive or agile methodology provides for more flexibility on changes but doesn't remove the requirement for research and preparation.

2. The Team

   Even if you're working in a small team with members assuming multiple roles, make sure you lay out the functional responsibilities of product management, development management, development, QA, and systems administration. Do your best to confirm that the applicable team members have the right skills set as each of these areas requires a distinct set of skills and experience.

3. Characters

   Your people will be stretched to their limits in a small team, particularly if you're a startup. Take some time to understand what motivates them. Though most people are a mix of things, currents of Climbers, Scientists, Artists, and Day Laborers run through most engineers and understanding these characteristics is worthwhile.

4. Evaluating Third-Party Firms

   The easiest way to evaluate third-party firms is through relevant references. This chapter provides a list of key questions to use during these discussions.

5. Offshoring

   Offshoring is often regarded as a silver bullet, but it isn't. The best way to think about offshoring is as what it is: a team of developers in another country who probably speak another language and have another cultural frame of reference. Running a high-performance team under those circumstances has all the challenges and requirements it would in your home country, plus the need to bridge the language and cultural barriers. If you look for the lowest prices, you'll probably get what you pay for, and a bad engineer is worse than none at all. Offshoring is most likely to work with a larger team and as an alternative if you need specialists that are unavailable in your home country.

Checklist

1. Job Descriptions/Roles

   Have you and your team defined all the necessary job roles even if multiple roles per person exist? Do you understand the skill sets required for each one?

2. Team Organization
    Have you arrived at an organization for these roles that you like?
3. Interviews and Staffing
    Do you have new hire sources identified and a strategy for systematically evaluating candidates?

Specialty Reading by Topic

If you want to know more about …	… then read
Creating Job Descriptions for Tech Positions	See Alexandercowan.com/jobdesc for sample job descriptions
Development Management	*The Mythical Man Month*, by Frederick P. Brooks This is an early and enduring classic in the area of development management.
Offshoring	See Alexandercowan.com/offshore for notes on offshoring.

Getting to Beta

Discipline the Chihuahua of Unruly Development

6 | Chapter

A few recipes for software development have proven particularly successful, most under the agile rubric. We'll look at how to apply these frameworks in a practical fashion. The Chihuahua of Unruly Development runs hither and thither dissipating its energy. A good development program retains structure and productivity while being adaptive and responsive. We'll review these methodologies and their application to Enable Quiz's progress to beta.

From Here to There

Predictive versus Adaptive Development

Enable Quiz has a plan, a team, and an objective. How does the team get its system to launch? We briefly discussed the predictive versus adaptive approaches to systems development in Chapter 5 and noted that Enable Quiz will organize around an adaptive or agile methodology. Why would anyone not want to be adaptive or agile? Uncertainty makes managing a business more difficult. It would be hard to justify an adaptive approach if you could predict which features customers would find most important and the pace of your development. It would be much better to know what's coming when.

The cost of uncertainty generally grows as you move down the technology stack we reviewed in the introduction. For instance, an adaptive methodology is harder to apply to an operating system as opposed to an add-on to an existing application because the interfaces and protocols are optimized for more prescriptive operations as you go down the stack (from applications to operating systems to hardware). For example, if your job is to build a router with a new 100-gigabit interface that complies to a certain standard, you will have less flexibility in what you do and how you do it than if your mission is to build a Facebook app for families. If you publish a database program, your developer community will want a fair amount of visibility on what facilities and interfaces you'll be providing since its development depends on your specifications.

Let's look at the adaptive versus predictive question from a customer's perspective. Not every company is obliged to publish its release plan to customers: Think about, for example, how much buzz Apple generates by keeping its particulars secret. However, many firms that sell to businesses do provide plans since their customers have to do their own operational planning around the features of their vendors' products.

Let's consider a typical customers' reaction to an adaptive versus predictive explanation of your product's roadmap. If you present a predictive approach they'll love that they can see what they'll be getting 18 months out because they can plan around that. However, if they realize they need some critical capability three months from now, they won't enjoy hearing that you can't deliver their feature for 24 months since all your resources are committed for the next 18 months and it will take six months to plan and execute what they want. Worse, if you're a small organization and they're a big customer, you may be forced to break up and redo your roadmap to accommodate them.

If you present an adaptive roadmap, your customers will like that you're able to react quickly. They won't like that they can't see your whole plan for the next 12 to 18 months. This approach has another aspect to be careful of: If you have larger customers, they may seek undue influence over your plan if they know it's flexible. Customer management strategies exist for all of this and we'll review those in Chapter 8.

One of our products at Leonid Systems (the company where I work) is a portal application for users to manage their hosted phone service. Let's say you have an office phone at your desk and you want to add a key that dials your assistant. Our portal allows you to do that by interfacing with a call processing system called BroadWorks through its API, functioning as a kind of customizable overlay. BroadWorks is the software that handles the phone calls. The relationship is similar to Enable Quiz's quiz engine (like BroadWorks) and the CMS (like our product, Loki). BroadWorks supports standardized protocols for voice over IP (VoIP) communication, and as such, is at the center of an whole ecosystem of interoperable telephony devices. Its customers and partners need a lot of visibility on what they have planned, so BroadSoft is primarily predictive in its development in that they can tell you what to expect 18 to 24 months out.

Our customers at Leonid Systems have two divergent needs. One is that they need us to keep pace with new BroadWorks features. After all, they can't offer a new BroadWorks feature to their customers if we don't support it, and this slows down their innovation. On the other hand, customers use Leonid's portal application because it gives them a highly flexible platform for presenting services to their customers. We're constantly coming up with new ideas for the portal with our customers. Even though we need to be highly predictive in keeping up with new BroadWorks features, we need to be adaptive and innovative with new things. The result is that we operate along the lines of what is shown in Figure 6.1.

We still use four-week iterations to do our development, which is an adaptive practice. However, we split our resources between a set of predictive resources, which we allocate in advance to keep pace with new BroadWorks features, and a set of more adaptive resources, working on ideas we come up with every few months. As a manager, it's always easy to say "yes" or "both." However, it can be impractical. In Leonid Systems' case, the practice of having a predictive stream flowing through our adaptive process works well but not perfectly. I drew the dotted line (minimum resources to keep pace with BroadWorks) as a flat line. It's bumpier in practice, and we have to adapt to that, but the

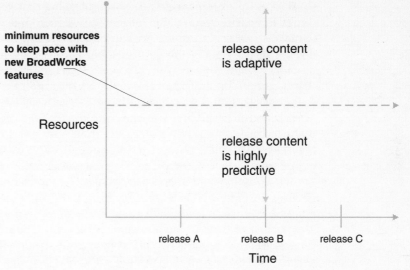

Figure 6.1

Resource Planning at Leonid Systems

alternatives are not as good. One alternative is that we could go fully predictive and say everything's planned for the next 18 to 24 months. The problems with that are we don't conceive all our ideas that far in advance and our customers require us to be able to implement new ideas quickly, otherwise they don't have much reason to use our nifty portal overlay. We could go fully adaptive, but as I mentioned, we have to keep up with the BroadWorks feature set in a predictable fashion. Just because everything doesn't neatly fit into your planning principles doesn't mean they're wrong. The key is to make sure they're better than the next best alternative.

Applying a Development Methodology

Which approach is best for your system development? How do you know if it's working? The short answer is whatever system generates the least overhead is the best system. What do I mean by overhead? In business process terms, every working moment of an employee's day can be placed in one of the following three buckets: Real Value-Added (RVA), Business Value-Added (BVA), and Non Value-Added (NVA) (Figure 6.2).

RVA: "Real Value-Added", time spent delivering to customers (**good**)
BVA: "Business Value- Added", time spent managing the business (**necessary evil**)
NVA: "Non Value-Added", time wasted (**bad**)

Figure 6.2

Process Evaluation Tools

RVA is time employees spend on something that goes directly to the customer. In our world, that includes things like writing software, setting up systems, and writing customer-facing documentation. Your job as a manager is to maximize the proportion of RVA time in your employee's day. BVA is time spent on work that doesn't directly go to the customer but is necessary for operating the business, like creating schedules and providing status reports. Your role here is to minimize the time your employee's time on BVA tasks, knowing that a certain amount is unavoidable. NVA time is a nice term for wasted time, spent on things like waiting, fixing mistakes, and working around organizational issues. Your job is a manager is to eliminate NVA.

If adaptive development means introducing BVA in little chunks around planning, and predictive development means doing it one big chunk, then why not go for the big chunk you get when you use a predictive approach? It would reduce the amount of context shifting your technical personnel have to do between planning and development since it's once every 18 to 24 months. Your release schedule would be more of a known quantity, simplifying management of the business overall. This sounds good. If you knew what would be most important 18 to 24 months from now, and you could describe it to your developers in a document and you knew the pace of your development organization—well, you probably would be better off with a predictive approach. The issue is you almost never have this much forward visibility in practice. Most technology-driven ecosystems change quickly. Your customers, partners, and competitors don't operate in perfectly synchronized, visible, 18- to 24-month planning intervals. If your system is complex, even an experienced development organization will usually see material deltas between their estimates and their actuals. You can always pad the estimates, but that becomes inflationary and leads to wasteful hedging. If you're using a predictive approach and your priorities or your timing on individual items changes, you will be redoing the whole big schedule, which consumes a lot of hours and roughly doubles your BVA time.

Table 6.1 describes a few key factors that weigh for and against an adaptive versus predictive approach. None are completely deterministic in and of themselves, but you may want to weigh them and see where you fit.

It's easy to see why most tech startups use a form of adaptive/agile methodology. If you're running lean and have a lot of learning to do, it's about your only choice. If you're using an offshore or remote team, you may need to put a little more product planning infrastructure in place, but the method is still likely to work for you. If you're doing a deliverables-oriented, fixed price statement of work for a large buyer, agile may be the wrong option. For most, agile doesn't have a particular orthodoxy and has several flavors. The main thing is to balance the use of organizing frameworks with the need to do what's practical.

Table 6.1

Adaptive
versus
Predictive

Item	More Adaptive	More Predictive
Release schedule and content	is flexible and mostly at the company's discretion.	is something that must be provided to customers and/or partners many months ahead of time.
Billing model for resources on contract	is hourly or salaried (plus bonus).	is based on contractually agreed to deliverables.
Team	is experienced, has good communication skills and team orientation, experience in agile, and located at the same place (ideally).	is junior and/or has challenges with communication and/or lack of team orientation and/or no experience in agile and/or remote.
Product/market fit	is unknown and lots of learning remains.	is well understood.
Product design	is an idea at this point.	is well articulated.

Personally, I learned the more formal tenets of the methodology from Leonid System's development manager, Lii Ling Khoo. We'd been doing a lot of the things agile prescribes naturally, and the more of the method we put in place, the better things went. More demos and collaboration? Worked great. Shorter delivery cycles to increase visibility and agility? Fantastic. More integrated testing? I was sold. We haven't applied agile across the board. Some of the specifics weren't a good fit for our situation, in part because many of our developers are in Europe. Even if some of the practices aren't a fit for you, the methodology may still work. The many different variants of agile are proof that the right implementation varies by operator (See Figure 6.3). Few communities of practice are more prolific online. If you're wondering how agile's working for you, I've organized a few resources under Alexandercowan.com/agilestuff.

Figure 6.3

Balancing
Methodologies

Development Methodologies at Enable Quiz

Enable Quiz will use an adaptive methodology. Figure 6.4, excerpted from the Wikipedia page on agile software development and originally created by VersionOne, describes the agile process.

Figure 6.4

Wikipedia
Diagram on
Agile

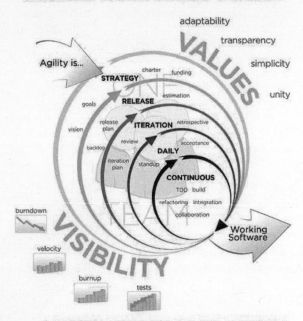

Source: VersionOne, Inc.

If you reference the layers in Figure 6.4, you'll see they move from high-level items to more specific tactics, starting with strategy. On strategy, specifically goals and funding, Enable Quiz needs to be at beta in 16 weeks and general availability (GA) in 20 weeks, which dictates a Release plan. This is compatible with agile. However, if Enable Quiz is going to fix their date for beta, they will need to be flexible on what content to include. They've completed a starter product design, which describes the contours of what they'd like to have for the release. Andrew now needs to go through and prioritize the various stories to ensure Enable Quiz delivers a minimum viable product for beta in 16 weeks. The last thing they want to do is be late and in the midst of implementing essential functionality. The next few sections describe how Andrew, Mike (his development lead), and the rest of the Enable Quiz team apply an adaptive methodology to arrive at the Enable Quiz beta. The first section, Planning, describes how they planned their iterations. The second section, The Reality, tells the story of how thing went, including the bumps they encountered on their way to beta.

Planning at Enable Quiz

Organizing Around Iterations

Figure 6.5 summarizes the planning process Andrew and Mark completed for beta.

First, we have the story backlog. Here, Andrew prioritizes the list of stories based on his assessment of what he feels is critical for a minimum viable product and some input from Mark on dependencies between iterations. The classic method of doing this is to use index cards to create the stories and post them on bulletin boards to monitor their progress. Because the team is distributed, Andrew and Mark did this with a few custom fields and reports in the open-source feature and bug tracker, Bugzilla. The planning and prioritization exercise is iterative: Andrew prioritizes, Mark estimates the size of the stories, and Andrew may reprioritize based on the size of the stories. Sizing in agile is typically done with story points or some other arbitrary measurement calibrated over iterations to determine the amount of units per iteration the team can complete. The team plans to use four-week iterations. In each iteration, the team estimates and agrees on a target list of stories, executes them, tests them, and delivers them. They plan four iterations to beta, the fourth being the beta release. With agile, a fixed date means flexible content, so it will be important for Andrew to keep an eye on things as his team moves along in case he needs to change customer expectations on content. The diagram above shows a release that includes several iterations. An iteration differs from a release, in that you may keep it internal. However, in the case of Enable Quiz, after beta,

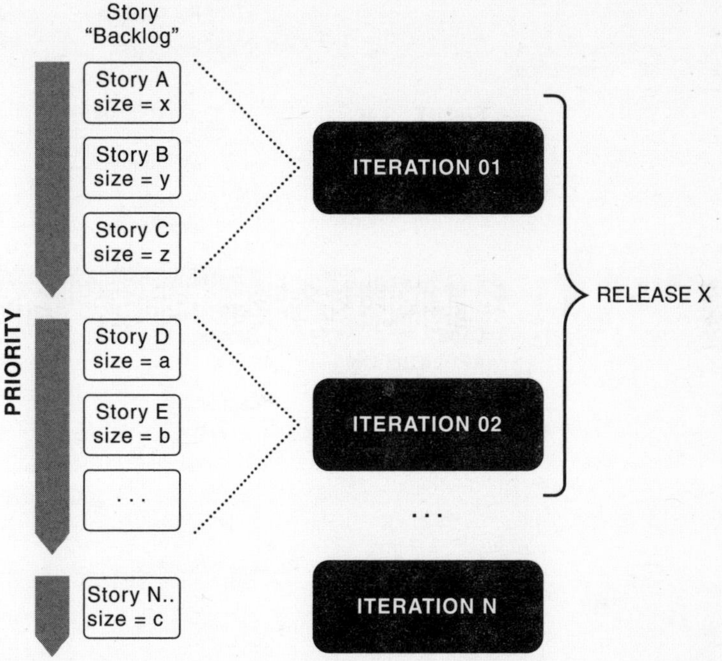

Figure 6.5

Organizing
Iterations

the team members will continuously deploy each iteration to an alternate instance of Enable Quiz where they have permanent beta users. The beta users will always be one iteration ahead of the general market and receive free service for user testing new product.

Andrew, in agile terms, is the product owner, meaning he is the primary representative of the customer and responsible for making calls on product function. As product manager, he's responsible for going to the market and getting feedback. While Andrew will be out doing some customer demos, the first four iterations to beta will be mostly an internal item. Following that, Andrew, as product owner, will be consistently soliciting customer feedback for the most recently released iteration, reviewing implementation of the current iteration, and doing planning and design work on the forthcoming iteration.

Figure 6.6 shows a high-level release plan to beta.

The exact content of each of these items will be left up to the planning process in the individual iterations. Highly predictive planning is not a feature of agile.

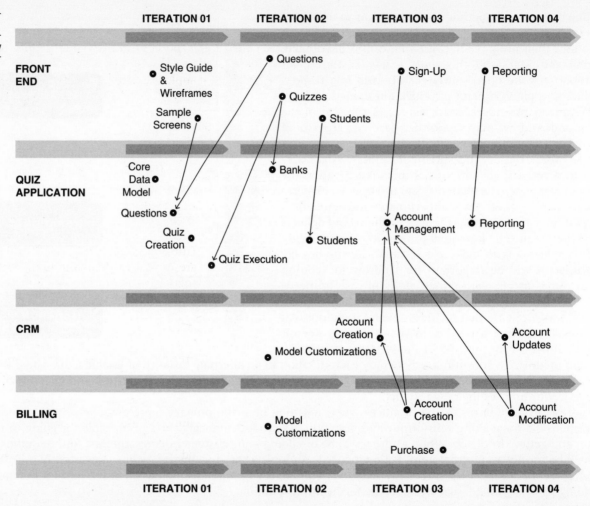

Figure 6.6   Enable Quiz Release Plan

Enable Quiz has filled out its team as follows:

Front-End Work: The team is using an outside firm called Snoetrope that specializes in web application front ends.

Quiz Engine: Mike's cousin, Marek, will help Snoetrope with the more complex Controller aspects of the front end and contribute to the Quiz Engine.

Customer Relationship Management (CRM): The team is using an outside firm in Chile that specializes in Salesforce.com development.

Billing: They're using an outside firm that specializes in billing.

Quality Assurance (QA): They have Raul, the QA lead, on board.

Mike will be performing the initial work on the Quiz Engine, which he will taper as the rest of the team ramps up and his responsibilities as development management increase.

Though the team members foresee the need for flexibility and recognize the limits of their ability to estimate some of the more novel items, their strategy implies certain specific requirements for each iteration to beta. They agree on an adaptive approach within a set of predictive contours. To define the predictability they need, Andrew and Mike went through and defined which development deliverables are critical to their minimum viable product at each phase of their development. They also defined a simple language of intent for each four-week iteration:

Iteration 1/Early Demo: Have something we can show customers so they can visualize what we'll be delivering.

Iteration 2/Demo: Have a working prototype of the quiz application for reality testing with prospects and to accelerate sales to key early adopter customers.

Iteration 3/Alpha: Have a basic working version of the quiz application with the commerce back end to conduct early field testing with friendly customers.

Iteration 4/Beta: Have a working version of the quiz application for a limited launch. If possible, have the commerce functions working to test the end-to-end sign-up process.

Iteration 5/GA: Have a complete system, including web-based sign-up and billing.

Iteration 6/1.1: Take on the most urgent items they weren't able to do for GA.

Mike's gone through and done some skeleton planning for the next six iterations on this basis. Within those, Mike and Andrew will use adaptive techniques to fill out the specifics of what they'll deliver. Planning that far in advance is not necessarily pure adaptive or agile development, and that's okay. The key is to balance a purposeful, organized framework for your development with your own judgment on what makes sense for your particular circumstances.

The following subsections describe Mike's planning for the first six iterations to GA.

Iteration 1/Early Demo

The team members plan to deliver something Andrew can demo to prospective customers at the end of the first iteration. It won't have anything near all the functionality in the product design, but Andrew's identified the key stories he wants to tell prospects and has worked with Mike to organize the Iteration 1 priorities around those. In terms of development, they'll be focusing on the web front end and supporting back-end functions in the quiz application.

They have a two-person team at web design firm Snoetrope on the front-end design. Virginia is the designer and Andre is the developer. For this iteration, Snoetrope is planning to complete the style guide, base wireframes, and quiz screens. The style guide defines the basic rules of the road for how the site looks: colors, design patters, logo usage, and the core paradigm for site navigation. The wireframes apply the style guide to example pages. The style guide will enable developers to complete basic screens by themselves using templates from the style guide. The last thing they plan for Iteration 1 is to have completed the front-end screens for students taking a quiz. These are important for Andrew's first round of demos.

It's not a lot of output, but Snoetrope is going to have to deal with the initial learning curve of communicating with the quiz application's API. They may have to wait on Mike's work on the quiz engine to some degree. Though he has roughly determined the basics of the API, it will require another week or so of work to document it and make it useable for someone else. Andre will probably be working on other things, but it's possible that Mike will delay him some.

That brings us to the quiz application. Mike's gotten a bit of a head start on this during the concept phase, before the team members start formal iterations. That said, it's a substantial application with a fair amount left to do. Now that Mike is managing six other team members, he'll be doing this in his "free time" with Marek's help. Marek's getting ramped up but Mike needs to finish the foundation of the application before he can use Marek effectively. Marek is a little less experienced than Mike had originally thought. He'll still be a valuable contributor, but Mike won't be able to let him loose on the core design as he has tentatively hoped.

Mike thinks he'll spend around two-thirds of his time managing. This is less than normal, but they have a relatively senior team working off a well-articulated design. During this dash to get to market, Mike's working around 11 hours per day during the week and five or six hours per day on the weekend, which is not a sustainable pace. He thinks he'll be able to spend about three hours daily during the week and most of the time on the weekend working the quiz application. He needs around one more week of work to complete the foundation and break the subsequent tasks into pieces that will be soluble for Marek. Then he can delegate most of the balance of the work, which is what he should be doing as manager.

The quiz application functions that Mike plans to finish in this iteration relate to creating questions, creating quizzes, and taking quizzes. The front-end team only needs the functions for taking quizzes, so this puts the functions available on the quiz engine a few steps ahead of what the front-end team needs. This is good but the lag between the back-end API and the front raises a practical question concerning the demos: How will Andrew create questions on the system to use during demos? It turns out Mike has a back door for creating questions and quizzes, a set of database queries he runs with a script. It's nothing close to as easy as it will be to manage once they have the front end, but once Andrew sends along a spreadsheet with questions, Mike can load them no problem.

They're not doing anything with CRM or billing in this first iteration. That's partly because the team won't be available and partly because Mike thinks the team at large should be very focused on the application itself. They'll begin the back office stuff on the next iteration.

Mike is kicking off with the QA lead engaged, something Enable Quiz should do if they're going to make QA an integral part of their development cycle. Raul is ready to start and he has set up Test Link to keep their test plans organized. Raul's job during this iteration is to take the user stories and convert them into engineering test cases. He thinks he can finish automating all the test cases for this iteration using their automation suite, Selenium.

Iteration 2/Demo II

If everything goes well, they'll be moving into the second iteration with an organized development program and a team that knows how to work together. Andrew's business goal with this iteration is to have a product they can demo to an expanded audience of prospects for the beta.

On the front end, they'll add the screens for managing questions, quizzes, and students and will create the screens for managing the quiz banks. Mark and Marek should be tracking a week or so ahead of the front-end team on the API side of the quiz application, so the work on the quiz engine won't delay the front end.

On the back office, they'll kick off the CRM and billing contractors. The main focus will be to finalize a working version of the Integration Guide that describes key parameters that link the back office to the rest of the system, and then customize the CRM and billing data models as needed. It sounds simple, but this is one part of the program where Mike feels that some risk exists, mostly because he's not an expert on billing. One thing they need from Andrew before this iteration starts is the final product catalog: an Excel spreadsheet with each product name, part number, and price.

On the QA side, Mike expects Raul to be caught up on automating the test cases, so they can regress the product nightly. They need to have three critical documents completed at the end of this iteration. First, their sysadmin Joe will work with Marek to complete the installation guide. This is the definitive guide to getting a new server online for the quiz application. This critical step will allow them to ensure that the production servers their customers will be using are set up properly and they can turn up new servers quickly if needed. The second document is the Integration Guide which covers every aspect of how the quiz application integrates with CRM and billing. Finally, there's the User Help, which is Andrew's department. Snoetrope will set up an environment in Joomla! that Andrew can use, and then he will take it from there.

At the end of all this, they plan to have an application that looks like what they plan to take to market. It won't have account management functions but will be supportable by the operations team. Andrew would like all the initial quiz application development to be completed after this iteration, leaving time free to respond to bugs and requests that come during alpha. Unfortunately, substantial work remains to finish the account management functions and back office, things like creating accounts and making payments. Andrew will likely need to temper the amount of new stories they schedule until the 1.1 iteration, four iterations out from here. This gets into a question of how to accommodate some predictive elements in the adaptive environment. Andrew may need to provide key customers specific dates on new features they feel are important.

This raises another practical question: How does Enable Quiz organize written descriptions of new features, and how do those updates make it into the relevant product documentation? Figure 6.7 describes this process. The Product Design described the original 1.0 version of the product. The implementation team will describe subsequent product updates, where necessary, in functional descriptions (FDs), and these will supersede the product design document. The FDs are not formal documents, they're just repositories for working descriptions of the features after implementation, and their primary purpose is to serve as inputs to the admin guides and user documentation. Enable Quiz will keep the following current as working documents:

- The user help (how they explain the product's current operation to users)
- The installation and Administration guide, which describes how to install the product
- The integration guide, which describes how the whole system fits together

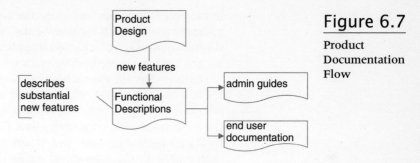

Figure 6.7

Product
Documentation
Flow

Iteration 3/Alpha

For Alpha, Enable Quiz will need to get the basic back-office infrastructure working since the idea is to put the full working system through alpha testing. The key focus in this iteration is getting the sign-up process functional.

Mark will be focusing Snoetrope on the front-end tasks like the sign-up and account management screens. Andrew will be submitting examples of what he considers to be comparable best practices. There isn't much explicitly scheduled for the quiz application, which they plan to have complete for three reasons: (1) for the back office to be done, the quiz application's API needs to be in a final working form, (2) Mike needs to focus on making sure the back-office items close on time, and (3) Marek will be busy fixing bugs.

They'll be dealing with account creation in the CRM, as well as billing. This will include details around recurring orders, invoicing, and payments. Since they're only accepting credit card payments, they only have to worry about clearing credit cards, no paper bills or checks to worry about. They plan to use Authorize.net as the credit card payment gateway, which is a system that allows you to transmit credit card information and initiate payments securely. Modern payment systems offer a service that allows you to post the credit card and receive a code for the customer's profile. Vendors use this to initiate payments, which is helpful for vendors because it keeps them from having to store credit cards numbers on their system. No matter how well you secure the system, having sensitive data like credit card numbers is a material risk. This implementation allows Enable Quiz to store the code they receive from Authorize.net, so they can initiate payments for their service. A security breach would compromise sensitive information like addresses and names but would not expose actual credit card numbers since those are stored on the Authorize.net system.

Some partners, vendors, and insurers will ask you about payment card industry (PCI) compliance, which is a big, scary topic for companies that are starting out. PCI is a set of technical and operational standards around keeping your customers' credit card data safe. I'm no expert on it. Auditors are available who specialize in helping companies understand and manage compliance. However, one thing I've consistently heard from payment processors is that the best way to achieve PCI compliance is to reduce your PCI footprint. This means storing credit card information in as few places as possible. In the case of Enable Quiz, this would be nowhere since it's all up on Authorize.net.

Let's review the interaction between CRM and billing. Basically, when Enable Quiz creates a new account, it's first added to CRM, which then initiates the creation of the account in billing. Billing is updated based on what the customers buy. The customers have accounts on the CRM and billing applications though the Enable Quiz site masks that complexity by showing them a consolidated account screen in the portal. CRM knows the billing ID for the account and that ties the accounts together. But CRM doesn't hold much more than an ID with regard to what's going on with a customer's billing data. A core design guideline is not to repeat the same information in multiple places, especially complicated items like orders. So, CRM knows about the customer but doesn't need to know about the details of billing. Billing knows who the customers are but doesn't need much detail about them; it only needs the status of their orders, invoices and payments.

What happens when someone from support gets a call from the customer? How will they know about the customer's billing status? As a customer, it drives me crazy when I have to stay on hold while someone accesses another system to check my account. I always wonder why organizations can't have that information in front of them once they pull up my account. Enable Quiz's design will do better than that for its customers because the CRM will pull in data directly from the billing system for display purposes. CRM has a window on the customer's account in billing, which gives Enable Quiz employees a single view of the customer's account without having to worry about having multiple copies of the customer's billing profile that could get mixed up.

On the QA front, Enable Quiz will continue to update its automated test suite with the new features, and it will keep the documentation current in the same fashion. Its goal in terms of systems administration is to have the internal applications (the quiz application and the front end) completely, to use the term, Puppetized. Puppet is a popular systems administration platform that automates the installation and upgrade of new web application servers. By way of background, software companies and their customers have historically spent a lot of time and money to install operating systems on servers and install and configure their applications. In the early days, and with new stuff, there's always some tinkering and integration. After that, a lot of the daily sysadmins' work involves staring at a screen, waiting, and clicking through to the next step. Lots of technologies exist to help automate this process, and they all work to varying degrees. However, the ultimate goal is to have a standard operating system and application configuration you can load on a piece of hardware with a click of button to turn up a new instance of your product. Puppet is pretty close to that. The tool's name comes from the idea that you're controlling the hardware and software as if they were a marionette, automating the whole install process. Basically, it's a way to turn up new hosts quickly and inexpensively. The Enable Quiz team members will need this if they're going to keep their headcount down and respond quickly to spikes in demand. Joe will be setting up a monitoring system using an application called Zenoss that will alert him to any issues with the system.

On release of Alpha, Andrew will be out pleading for feedback from early alpha users to see if Enable Quiz can learn anything about usability he can use to inform the work during the beta iteration.

Iteration 4/Beta

As far as the front end and quiz application go, Mike has left the beta iteration mostly empty to make room for bug fixing and critical features that he can't launch without. He has some work set aside for updates to the company website and reporting on the system, but he can defer all that if he needs the cycles to work on more critical items. The front-end team at Snoetrope will work on the screens for the quiz application reporting and Marek will help with the back-end queries. The CRM and billing systems have their own built-in reporting, which is one more example of the virtues of using an off-the-shelf application versus building your own.

They will have a few big items to finish up on the back office. Account updates are the main item here. Let's say customers want to add or remove services. That's one of the more complex parts of the back office since it requires tasks like prorating their bill for the new level of service. This iteration doesn't handle the closure and deletion of accounts, which is slated for version 1.1. If customers want to delete their account, they'll have to call Enable Quiz. Some companies prefer to have customers speak to a retention agent before they disconnect anyhow.

Iteration 5/General Availability

This is what Enable Quiz will use for launch. Any substantial issues it faces at the beginning of this iteration will require it to delay the launch. Mike left this iteration open for medium and small bug fixes. If by some miracle none occur, the team members will surely have a number of stories queued up and the implementation team can jump on those.

Subsequent Iterations

The next iterations are basically open. They'll probably be crammed with prioritized feature requests (in the form of stories) by the time Enable Quiz gets halfway through beta. The process for those will be for Andrew to write user stories for new features and prioritize them. Mike will estimate them and, on the basis of priorities, schedule them into an iteration.

See Alexandercowan.com/iterations for more documentation on the Enable Quiz implementation cycle.

The Reality

This section describes the outcome the Enable Quiz's iterations.

Iteration 1/Early Demo

Enable Quiz gets through this first iteration with minimal cuts and bruises. The only person who hasn't finished is Mike, something that he finds satisfying as a manager but frustrating as an individual contributor. Fortunately, his day job is manager. Keeping the teams rolling has taken more time than he thought, and Marek is still coming up to speed, though he's doing well now.

Mike thinks they can make up the time on Iteration 2. Since everyone else has finished on time, Mike has given them a day off and he's going to use the breathing room to complete the lion's share of his remaining work and hand it over to Marek for final testing, cleaning, and documentation.

They are on time, on budget. On QA, Raul organized the test plan framework well and he's working well with the development teams. They'll have automated regression running early in the next iteration, and Raul has the developers set up with a simple process for them to fix their bugs.

The thing that worries Mike most is the back office, particularly CRM and billing since these are new to him. In the worst of worlds, he can stay up all night and fix anything that needs to get done on Salesforce.com. However, he's unsure about billing. As far as the rest of the program is concerned, this is where everything stands:

- The front-end team at Snoetrope is solid.
- Marek will do fine on the quiz application.
- QA is better than expected.
- Sysadmins are fine, and they'll see how Joe does as they get into the more complex stuff for production.

Iteration 2/Demo

This iteration did have a couple of cuts—they weren't terrible but, in Andrew's opinion, not trivial either. Material issues occurred with student management. Often it would take over 30 minutes for the e-mails inviting students to take new quizzes to arrive. The issue embarrassed Andrew more than once during demos when he had offered to e-mail prospective customers an invite. Andrew realized that even though the issue would be an irritant to customers, it was not a showstopper. What worried him more was that sometimes a quiz would show up as taken when it shouldn't have, keeping students from taking the quiz. It didn't happen often but it had shown up recently, and Andrew was worried that Mike hadn't found the root cause.

The last and most pressing issue was that the stories in the initial product design hadn't included a way for customers to bulk upload students or questions. This was Andrew's fault since he wrote and prioritized the stories. The bottom line was that alpha prospects had told Andrew they regarded the system as nonfunctional until the issue was resolved and weren't interested in participating until bulk upload was available. Andrew was grinding his teeth at night because Enable Quiz wasn't where it needed to be on the current iteration, and they needed new, unplanned features to bring customers online.

Mike thinks all of his team members are doing pretty well overall: but he recognizes the issues that the quiz application has in managing invitations to students. The application is taking a long time to post the invitations, and cases occur where students initiate a new quiz and the application has marked it as having been taken. He's isolated the issue about the slow sending of the quizzes and has a straightforward fix for it. But he's still determining why some quizzes are showing up as completed when they haven't been.

Everything else looks good on the quiz application and front end. Mike has the back-office team rolling and the data models customized. The Integration Guide has explained and documented those customizations. The billing consultant is not much on documentation, which worries Mike some, but he's understanding the system better and edited the guide for the billing component himself.

QA and sysadmin are going well. Raul has the automated test suite running nightly with the full suite of tests on the product. Raul is working with Andrew on formulating cases and working with the developers on rapid bug resolution. On the sysadmin front, the production system is up and running and looking good. Joe, the sysadmin, plans to run a set of redundancy tests to make sure the system stays up if one of the servers fails, but it looks good overall.

The key question at this point is how the team members are looking for alpha. Mike feels they're at risk. He hates to admit it, but the issues with the quiz application put them at least a few days out. He can't say he's

100 percent comfortable with what he's been seeing on the billing side, and between the two of those they're delayed around a week. Andrew doesn't love the news, but he appreciates the candor. They agree to change the duration of the alpha iteration and shift initiation of alpha out by a week.

Iteration 3/Alpha

Andrew has kept a low profile during the current iteration. Mike was frustrated with the back-office contractors, particularly the billing team members. His frustration was no doubt exacerbated by their being a week off on the current schedule, having extended the iteration an extra week. During their meetings together, Andrew reviewed the items Mike wanted to discuss and got the schedule updates. However, he avoided probing too deeply, knowing that Mike would update him if he saw something wrong.

Surprisingly, Mike announces they can declare alpha, subject to Andrew's approval on the current state of the system. The sign-up process for new customers works if users follow the "yellow brick road." If they stray in any way, for example, by signing up but paying later, this could potentially break billing.

Mike asks to explain a few things before Andrew assesses whether that's a blocker that would delay alpha. First of all, though the error conditions around sign-up aren't fixed in the code, Mike's worked out checks that will allow them to post a message that instructs customers to get in touch with support. That's not a good user experience. It will drive traffic to support, which will costs them money, but it might allow them to launch. Rather than waiting until the next iteration, Mike's planning to have the fix patched back to the alpha release during the beta iteration.

Patching is a process where you take a particular piece of software from a current release and layer it on top of an earlier release. The term is quite apropos. For example, in the case of Enable Quiz, a rip in the software is preventing the purchase process from working in some cases. They don't want to put on a whole new pair of pants (the beta release) since it won't be done, so they take the section they want and put it on the old pants (the alpha release).

Mike estimates they can issue the patch for the alpha version in about one week. He doesn't want to be the stereotypical engineering manager who's always talking about how hard everything is, but some cautions exist concerning the patching process. Patching is often a contentious issue within companies, and even more so with their customers. The audiences, who are usually the customer-facing teams inside the company and the customers themselves, want something quickly and without the trouble of a full upgrade, often pressing for more things to be patched into older releases. Two big problems exist with this. First, the farther back in the release stream you patch something, the more complex the patching process becomes because newer releases are continually diverging in structure from old releases. Second, the time your development and QA teams spend creating and testing patches is time taken away from getting new releases out the door. The basic moral of the story is that growth in patching creates a drag on resources and that slows new releases. The issue becomes more complex in an environment where you're deploying software to customer sites and various customers have different releases, and patching has to be managed individually at each account. Since Enable Quiz is operating the software, they have only one internal environment to decide on, which simplifies the issue.

Unfortunately, Mike thinks they're off by at least a week on beta for two reasons. First, they have the sign-up issues from the alpha iteration bleeding into the beta iteration that they need to patch back. That's in billing, which Mike has regarded as the highest risk part of this execution. The billing consultant is not bad but he's not great either. The bottom line is that even if they didn't have these issues now, Mike would be concerned about whether they can finish the account update functions in time.

Andrew's first reflex is to push Mike to pull in the schedule. After further consideration, he decides to give beta an extra two weeks. More things are likely to go wrong during beta on the engineering development side of things. This is always the toughest part of development because lots of things the product team thought were getting done by someone else or were unnecessary come out of the woodwork when they're putting the product through its final paces.

The second problem is that the billing modifications feature is progressing poorly, and they have too few staff with that expertise to make up the difference. Of course, customers don't like delays, but they like uncertainty and the appearance their vendor isn't in control of their development program even less. If the Enable Quiz team members delay beta by one week and have to return to the customers and delay it another week, Enable Quiz will do more damage than breaking it to customers there's going to be a two-week delay. If they go to beta early, which is unlikely, customers will be pleasantly surprised.

Could they take the quiz application to beta on time, removing some features, and update the back office later? The first related question is this: Do they think they could go to beta without the account update functions? Those wouldn't be ready without the back-office infrastructure in place. Second, per Mike, though doable, considerable overhead exists to reorganize iterations, this one in particular. They could do it, but it would take additional time to reorganize, and Mike's not sure the net gain would be all that great.

Andrew concludes they can't declare beta without the ability to update the account's purchases. One silver lining exists though: Since most of the work is on the back-office team, Mike thinks the front-end and quiz application teams will now comfortably be able to fit the bulk upload of questions and students via Excel in the revised beta iteration.

Iteration 4/Beta

They were right that they barely finished even with the two weeks added to the beta iteration. Even though Andrew wondered whether the work had expanded into the available time to some extent, he realized Mike had been working hard and fast with the back-office team to pull things together. Mike thinks he's ready to call beta.

Documentation

We Need to Write this Down?

Before I became accountable for an engineering team's performance, I considered documentation to be one of those dull managerial things you do when you can. However, once I became accountable for a team, I realized how documentation drove performance. When I looked at cases where the team developing a new feature had gone off in separate, noncomplementary directions, usually they had done it because they didn't understand the others' intent. As a manager, I had to ask myself how that had happened and how I could have prevented it. Documentation was usually a big part of the answer, partly because much of our team is distributed and we aren't able to have the frequent in-person interactions agile prescribes, though we have many chats going on Instant Messaging (IM). Engineers aren't the most talkative lot by nature, but most read documentation if they know where it is and what it's for. Plus, if your system is complex, it's impossible for everyone to talk to everyone else about every part of the system. Once we designed documentation into the development process earlier and with more structure, performance improved and not just in development. Operations and support had a much easier time delivering and supporting the product with customers.

One corollary to this is easier said than done. Most people hate doing documentation. After you get something working, you have a natural tendency to want to pop the cork and consider it done. Some engineers like the esteem and job security they get by making what they do as a kind of black magic. A lot of development managers bring in a documentation person to deal with this supposedly dull business of documentation. The dedicated documentation person approach never worked for me. First, this means documentation will always get done after the fact rather than making it an integral part of the process. Second, the documentation people rarely have the technical skills to write the documentation properly, so they end up needing help from the developers. When you add the developer time consumed by interviews with the documentation people, the time you have to spend reviewing the work for accuracy and completeness, and the money spent on the documentation people, it has rarely made sense, in my personal experience.

What about paying extra for a more technical documentation lead? This approach has two problems. First, it's hard to find people with that profile because few developers want to do this job. If they're good enough to figure out and write up everyone else's functionality, they'd be more valuable as a technical lead or architect. Second, if you did find such a person, they'd have to spend so much time backtracking over the implementation that the cost-effectiveness would probably remain lousy. One approach is to hire a company-wide documentation editor who is responsible for maintaining the documentation program at large and checking submissions for consistency and quality, while individual contributors do their own documentation. This does not apply to end user documentation, like help guides. These are often economically executed by specialists.

Documentation at Enable Quiz

What documentation does Enable Quiz need, how will the development team write it, and who's going to act as documentation editor? Mike will act as documentation editor for now. As far as getting the developers to write the documentation, Mike's given all the departments a distinct area of ownership and explained how documentation fits into their turf. That's the "pull side" as Mike explains it. The push side is that he's created documentation outlines, assigned responsibility for each piece, and made completion of documents a part of every iteration. They need an installation guide, an integration guide, and an operations guide. They have working versions of all three up on Google Docs. Let's describe each of the three guides and the intent, audience, and content for each of these documents.

Installation Guide

If your software is installed on a server or PC, as opposed to a more structured environment like an app store, you'll need an installation guide. This guide describes how to take a server out of the box and make it a member of the cluster of quiz application servers. The goal of a good installation guide is to make the software installation and upgrade process boring. Enable Quiz wants the operation of the system to be humdrum with no surprises. Without such a guide, every installation becomes its own unique puzzle, and it becomes like a murder mystery troubleshooting these servers once they break because they're installed in a nonstandard fashion. Customers don't want that kind of excitement, nor does your operations team if you are delivering your application on a hosted basis. Instead, they want a hive of humming clones, created in the same fashion that your QA team used in software test.

The following six items outline the Installation Guide:

1. Hardware Requirements

    This lays out the minimum hardware requirements for a new server: CPU, RAM, storage space, things like that.

2. Operating System Requirements

    Enable Quiz uses Red Hat Linux as their servers' operating system and pays a certain amount per server even through it's open source. Red Hat maintains standardized documentation and operating system (OS) packages, which saves them time and money.

    a. Version

        Enable Quiz has a specific version of Red Hat they support to make sure everything's consistent and has been through QA as a complete package.

    b. Disk Layout

        All computers have a hard disk, which is the permanent storage of all the information on the server, including the operating system. You usually partition this storage into distinct and separate chunks on a server for a few reasons. The most important is you don't want a process running on the server to fill up the whole hard disk because this can crash the server. If you isolate processes that create a lot of data to a particular partition, they can only fill up the specified space instead of bringing down the whole server. The most common example is logs. The Enable Quiz application records all of its actions. A scheduled process runs every day to remove logs older than 15 days to keep the amount of logs under control. But even if someone forgets to set that up properly, having the logs in their own distinct space keeps that mistake from crashing the server.

    c. Network Interfaces

        You plug servers into the network, connecting them with the rest of the system. Since you never want servers to become unreachable, they almost always have two or more network interfaces. Utilities inside the OS provide facilities for the admin to specify how and when these interface work together. For example, do they both stay on all the time or does one take over if the other fails? Sysadmins will have different ways they want this to work depending on their approach. The key thing is consistency. The interface should always be set up the same way so when you have a problem you know what the servers will do and can troubleshoot accordingly.

   d. Other Configuration

     Disks and network are a couple of the biggest items here, but you must set up lots of other hooks and dials for things to work right. Again, the key is consistency, and this section specifies configuration of the remaining hooks and dials to that end.

3. OS Package Requirements

    Helper programs and utilities sit on top of the operating system and allow our application to operate. The developers continually update the required packages so it's critical to keep this list and the releases current.

   a. Package Configuration

     Some of these packages, like the helper libraries their programs use, don't require much in the way of installation other than making sure you apply the right version. Others require some vetting to get them right. For example, the Apache web server needs specific configuration. It responds to requests from users' browsers and requires a number of settings for when and how to respond. Enable Quiz uses MySQL for their database, and they have a number of options they set in a particular way based on their use of it.

4. OS Checklist

    Trust but verify. Once these steps are complete, Mike will create a quick checklist the sysadmin will run to make sure the installation was completed properly.

5. Software Installation

    This section deals with the installation and configuration of the quiz application. Since the application is new, we'll see a lot of updates here over the next few months.

   a. Configuration Guide

     This section describes where to put the software and how to set its various configuration options.

    b.   Checklist

        Likewise with the operating system and its packages, Enable Quiz's sysadmins have a series of checks they'll run to make sure everything has come up and works.

6.   Software Upgrade

       This section covers and references the above steps with some differences for the case where you're doing an upgrade from one software version to another versus a fresh installation.

    a.   Configuration Guide

    b.   Checklist

How does this fit in with the automation, the stuff based on Puppet? All this will form the basis for the Puppet recipes that Joe will create after they have the process working reliably. It's an inefficient use of time to invest in Puppet until development and systems administration have these processes working reliably and have them documented, and they don't have either yet.

What about installing the billing and CRM systems? Since Salesforce.com and Zuora (the billing system they've selected) work on a hosted basis, Enable Quiz doesn't have to worry about installation or upgrades, just as their customers don't have to worry about installing or upgrading Enable Quiz.

In summary, the installation guide provides a way for the development team to specify for the sysadmin team how to bring up a new server.

Integration Guide

The integration guide describes how Enable Quiz's three subsystems (quiz application, CRM, and billing) fit together. The primary audience is the development team members, and the guide informs them of how changes to one part of the system affect its overall integrity. Better still, it describes the underlying principles they used to design the end-to-end system, particularly, the back office. This way, no one is reinventing a new and inconsistent approach to the whole thing when they need to extend its functionality or change or replace a piece of it, at least not inadvertently. When the system breaks, the integration guide is the document people in support or engineering will use to guide their troubleshooting. If Enable Quiz is publishing this material externally, they'd probably create a separate troubleshooting guide. Since the audience is strictly internal, keeping all this in one place is economical. The following is an outline for the integration guide:

1. Scope and Design Goals

    This first section summarizes answer to the questions: "What is this system, what is it supposed to do, and how does it do it?" The Product Design isn't something they'll maintain; Mike quickly created this section based on the material Andrew produced.

2. Subsystems

    Here they go through each subsystem in more detail. Each subsystem has its own Help guide, so they reference those on particulars. Things they describe for each are the scope of its functions and, in the case of the off-the-shelf applications (CRM and billing), any additional fields or modules they've added in any customized instance of each:

    - Quiz Application
    - CRM
    - Billing

3. Data Integration

    This section describes the parameters that string the systems together, such as the account ID. It delineates which part of the overall customer data they've designed to be consolidated in a particular system so they make sure no one starts slopping around data that shouldn't be repeated between systems. For example, they make it clear that no other system besides the quiz application should need to know about individual students. Additionally, no application except billing needs to know about payment status. If you want to display that information in the CRM for customer care, you fetch it from billing. But you don't store the payment status in CRM. There's no need for that and the data will easily get out of sync, causing a big mess. Enable Quiz wants to hire experienced developers and give them a long leash to approach new development according to their judgement. But part of that is giving them clear guidelines and telling them that's where they can use their paintbrush.

4. Workflows

    The workflow section describes the most common scenarios, detailing what happens on each system at each step. The troubleshooting section is critical for the troubleshooters since it anchors their understanding of what is supposed to happen when something's going wrong.

5. Logging

    Troubleshooting an issue is impossible without logs of some kind. The logs provide a place for the application to say to the sysadmin what happened and why. This section describes how actions are logged in the various subsystems. Parenthetically, logging is another dull thing developers will neglect if they're not specifically motivated and monitored. Bad logging increases costs and diminishes customer satisfaction because it takes more time to identify and fix problems.

6. Troubleshooting

  Though the last two sections contribute to the troubleshooting process, this section specifically describes it. It specifies how you discover what the application should be doing (from the workflows) and how you determine what is happening (logging). It has a few case study examples Enable Quiz will add to as it completes post-mortems on problems that arise in production.

Documentation and Systems Administration

Enable Quiz's metrics for success in systems administration are the following four items:

1. The cost of the program.
2. Their ability to fail over transparently, without affecting customer experience if one or more of the servers goes down.
3. Their ability to scale up capacity quickly and cheaply against demand.
4. Latency—how fast the system responds when users click on the pages.

Joe, their sysadmin, will work with Mike to maintain four main items: the installation guide, the integration guide as well as the Puppet Master, and the Zenoss management system.

For the sysadmins, the integration guide describes the sysadmin essentials of how the system operates. For example, it describes the layout of the network. Figure 6.8 shows the first section of the integration guide.

Enable Quiz maintains its own servers, in the cases of their front end and the quiz application. The cloud items are SaaS applications where their providers (Salesforce.com and Zuora) maintain the infrastructure and Enable Quiz connects to their cloud.

The integration guide is where the sysadmin's maintain the firewalling rules.

They track the details of individual servers in their management system, Zenoss. The next item they have is database clustering. Joe has established profiles for hosts, which may be designated as a front-end server, application server, or database server with the database servers set up as read/write or read only. This is captured in the Installation Guide. They can set up a server to host a database for read/write activities or just host the application. Each of their servers is performing every function at the moment. However, as they scale

CUSTOMERS

WEB FRONT END
This includes the company website as well as the quiz application.

This subsystem operates in Enable Quiz's virtual data center.

QUIZ APPLICATION
This includes the quiz application core.

This subsystem also operates in Enable Quiz's data center.

CRM
This includes the customer relationship management function.

This subsystem operates in salesforce.com's 'cloud'

BILLING
This includes orders, invoicing, and payments.

This subsystem operates in Zuora's 'cloud'.

Figure 6.8   Integration Overview

All Services Run Over
HTTP/S (TCP 80, 443)

01

03

02

Figure 6.9   Service Flows

up, they'll break them apart into clusters according to function. This is part of making the system scalable. The database portion of the whole thing is one of the most intensive and will require them to use a few tricks. For example, once you start having a lot of reporting activity, one thing you can do is elect a subset of the database servers as read only. This helps performance because you can optimize a server for read operations as long as you know that's all it will do.

Puppet Master

From a systems administration point of view, you want to make your hardware resources as dumb as possible. This means that you want to be able to take a new server out of a box, push a button, and have it come up as a new application server. Establishing an OS plus application install can take a day if you do things by hand, though an experienced sysadmin can multi-task between several servers. However, that's expensive and it makes scaling up new capacity and recovering from a failure slow. Puppet allows you to create recipes for installing new servers. Enable Quiz will take the Installation Guide and set it up in Puppet, initiate a connection from the new server to Puppet, then walk away. They'll have a properly installed server when they come back, which will save them weeks of sysadmin time over the next year (Figure 6.10).

All this is maintained between QA and sysadmin, and it's where the rubber hits the road in terms of deploying and upgrading the software. When Enable Quiz finishes an iteration, development is responsible for updating the Installation Guide. QA updates the Puppet Master (the central brains behind the Puppet infrastructure) and tests the upgrade and installation processes. QA hands it to sysadmin as part of the new release. So, testing the upgrade and installation process is part of testing the software.

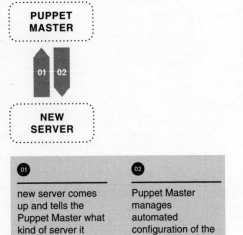

Figure 6.10

Puppet

01 new server comes up and tells the Puppet Master what kind of server it wants to be

02 Puppet Master manages automated configuration of the new server against the corresponding 'recipe'

Management System

The management system maintains an inventory of all active hosts and their profiles, meaning the job those servers were set up to do. Enable Quiz's sysadmin team (Joe) keeps all this in the management system instead of the integration guide because it's always changing and because they use the management system to watch the servers. Zenoss, the application they're using, has models for the subcomponents running on the various hosts, such as Apache and mySQL. It knows how to go into the hosts and discover their configuration and status.

You have two techniques available to you when you're managing servers. The first is a "push" technique involving "traps" or "alarms." You set up the server to push a message to the management system that indicates what's happening. The management system decides if it's serious and if it should notify someone—in the case of Enable Quiz, that's Raul and Mike. Though traps are great, you have to design them into the software, and you may not see them if things go wrong.

The other technique, which is usually used in conjunction with traps, is polling. In this case, you run a set of logical tests on the servers and report the results in the same fashion. The simplest are the most powerful. One simple poll Enable Quiz will run is to make sure they can log in to all the front-end servers. If the test succeeds, that means that all the basic subsystems are working.

Mike presented the diagram in Figure 6.11 to summarize how the management system reaches out to poll servers and listens for alarms the servers send back to the management system.

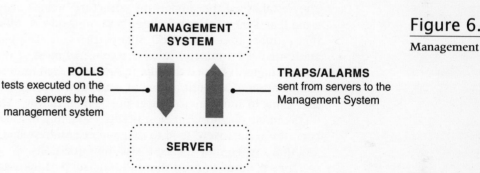

Figure 6.11

Management

Training and Self-Help

Andrew had been toiling over the user help files for Enable Quiz. He knew that good help would reduce calls to support and customer issues at large. Even though it was easy to use and the screen recording application allowed him to record his voice on top of actions he performed, he had grossly underestimated the number of hours it took to formulate the help and record it. He thought he could extemporize from a basic outline, but found himself tongue-tied and resigned himself to writing a script.

He'd been working with the Snoetrope members on interleaving what they called "aspirin help" with "vitamin help." The idea was that aspirin help appeared close to an individual screen. You were looking to answer a specific question or avoid a specific mistake before or immediately after it happened. For example, if users didn't fill out the sign-up form correctly, a few messages popped up, showing them where they needed to fix the form and providing an explanation of items that might be unclear. Getting an error or submitting their account information for sign up was a headache, and that help was the aspirin. Vitamin help was more of a big picture approach, introducing users to general system concepts. Most of what Andrew did in the Flash and multimedia help fell under the vitamin category, including introductions and tutorials on how to use the application.

Support

They established the support infrastructure by beta. Customers could submit tickets through the portal or by e-mail, and they had a help line that rang Andrew, Mike, and Marek's cell phones. However, they only gave that number to a few critical Beta participants. The plan was to provide support mainly through the portal and e-mail. Fortunately, Salesforce.com had most of what they needed in terms of built-in support and case management. It helped that the tickets were filed under the customers' accounts in case they called in about a combination of account, payment, and support issues. Cases were automatically matched to customers when they came in and went to a triage queue that Andrew, Mike, and Marek shared. The idea was that Marek would do the initial diagnosis on most tickets, escalating to Mike as needed. Though it had worked reasonably well for beta, the results were hard to extrapolate. Andrew had personal contact with over half the beta participants, and that's when they tended to ask their questions.

They planned to bring in a full-time support manager once the level of customers and tickets justified the hire.

Chapter 6 Summary

1. Development Methodologies

   Development methodologies exist on a spectrum from predictive to adaptive. Predictive methodologies involve detailed plans over long timeframes. Any change during those timeframes is highly disruptive. Adaptive methodologies break development into short cycles of two to four weeks, each of which has a period for defining the product features to be implemented. In practice, many companies balance their long-term planning with adaptive type development cycles that allow them to refine and change their applications' target functionality. Agile is a popular development methodology and on the adaptive end of the spectrum.

2. Iterations to Beta

   Understanding and managing the dependencies between parts of the system is critical at this stage.

3. Beta to Release

   Beta will probably flush out a flock of new feature requests. If your release timeframe is important, continue to defer these to subsequent iterations.

4. Post-Release Iterations

   Listen to customer feedback and make sure you're looking at the big picture of what the user is really requesting. In your product management role, write functional descriptions for each new feature. You'll probably find a number of details you need to articulate to your development team.

5. Documentation

   You'll probably want an integration guide if your system has multiple components. If your system requires installation, be sure to have an installation guide. Puppet is a popular tool for automating installations, which can be expensive and time consuming without automation. User Help is critical in any application.

6. System Monitoring

   Most monitoring programs have a push as well as a pull component. The push is when your application or server OS sends a message to the management system indicating trouble. Pull is when your management system goes out to the applications and checks to make sure they're functioning properly.

Checklist

1. Formulating your Minimum Viable Product

   Have you determined the minimal viable product for your initial release? Have you prioritized your story (feature) backlog accordingly?

2. Settling on a Development Methodology

   Have you reviewed the pros and cons and arrived at a development methodology with your team?

3. Kicking off Tools and Processes

   Have you put in place tools and processes to support the methodology?

4. Systems Administration

   Have you staffed and contracted the sysadmin function? You should avoid having your developers do this if possible. Does a well-understood process exist to bring up the software and get it online?

5. Management

   How will you know if your system goes offline or otherwise stops functioning?

Specialty Reading by Topic

If you want to know more about …	… then read
Agile Development	*Agile Excellent for Product Managers,* by Greg Cohen This is an excellent starting point for businesspeople to introduce themselves to agile. See also Alexandercowan.com/agilestuff
Systems Administration	See Alexandercowan.com/sysadmin
Puppet	See Alexandercowan.com/puppet
Monitoring	See Alexandercowan.com/mon

Beta!

Slaying the Hydra of Operational Readiness

7

Preparation is the key to slaying the Hydra of Operational Readiness. Without the right preparation, you'll keep slashing at the hydra and it will keep sprouting more heads. You're short on time, you're not sure what to prepare for, and the company is in a state of flux, uncertainty and intense learning. This chapter provides a few fundamental frameworks and habits you can put in place to make your operation more efficient, and more importantly, to set yourself up for rapid learning and evolution.

Process, Process, Process

Why Process?

Process isn't something you'd freely associate with a high-tech business. All the mythology around high-tech has wild-eyed engineers miraculously conceiving and creating the next great website in the wee hours of the night. A more fluid environment might be the right thing in your early days when you're exploring the frontiers of your business and running short-cycle experiments to see what works. Ultimately, however, this approach will exhaust your resources and prove incompatible with a large-scale system servicing paying customers. You may hear a choice posed between being an agile organization or a process-driven organization: reject this false choice. Having processes doesn't mean you're not agile. Agile development is a set of processes created from a set of principles and your internal processes should be as well. If you want less structure, design your processes at a higher level of abstraction. Ignoring the need for good process design is like denying gravity, because processes occur in any business. It's your job to design them to be focused and effective, instead of diffuse and wasteful. An explicit process design gives you a platform to accomplish that and work on continuous improvement.

In the same way that a well-organized financial plan keeps you from constantly worrying about cash, the right amount of process will free your key creative resources from the daily drudgery of trolling for information and fielding miscellaneous interruptions. Unfortunately, process turns people off, particularly those who have worked at large companies, because the process design is usually done poorly. Business process design should cohere to the reality of the operating environment, and companies should create it in close cooperation with its intended practitioners. Instead, it's often produced in a vacuum with excessive zeal around the process itself.

You can easily do better than this, and you'll probably find a little bit of the well designed process in the right areas goes a long way. Some key areas where you're likely to benefit from some basic process definition are the following:

Sales: How do you close new customers for billing (if applicable)?
Product Design: How are new features captured for engagement with product engineering?
Product Development: How do you create, test, and release new features?
Systems Operation: How do you handle critical system outages and put new releases into production?

What Process?

The goal of your process design shouldn't be to computerize people, or define every button people push to do their job. What you're looking to do is answer core questions around who does what, when they do it, and how you'll monitor the health of these processes.

The first step is to define job roles. Most people have multiple roles in a small operation, and that's okay. Just make sure you design the processes around roles and not individuals. While business process design involves a lot of interpretation and adaptation, there are established standards for how to organize them. A business process takes an input and, by way of a series of transformative sub-processes, produces an output.

You can use a few litmus tests to determine if you have an atomic process or just piece parts of something you do. First, you have the discrete input and output. Let's say you're making doorknobs: The input is metal and the output is a doorknob. Figure 7.1 lays out such a process: it has an input, a set of processes that transform the input, and an output. Next, the process should have three types of identifiable metrics:

1. Process Metric: This measures your rate of output. In the case of the doorknob factory, this is the number of doorknobs produced per hour.
2. Output Metric: This measures the conformance of your outputs to the target specification, meaning how many of the doorknobs have flaws.
3. Outcome Metric: This measures the output on the basis of how it affects end users. For example, do people like our doorknobs? This metric takes more thinking and doing to define and measure, but it is the most important for a tech startup. A lack of precedent and an abundance of uncertainty are what define a startup versus an established company. You don't yet know what's going to work well for you or how and why your customers will buy your product. You should link the key assumptions we covered in Chapter 1 and the metrics we discussed in Chapter 2 to your outcome metrics. There's an example of this for Enable Quiz in the section on process inventory.

All this is not to say that you're going to take great interest in metrics for every single process. However, an inability to at least describe the three metrics above for a process is a red flag that what you have is not a discrete process. One thing you want to consider as you examine what's driving the metrics is the categorization of employee time we discussed back in the section on development methodologies: Non Value-Added (NVA), Business Value-Added (BVA), and Real Value-Added (RVA). Though it's unlikely you'll have the time to do time studies, do your best to keep an eye on how time's being spent.

Figure 7.1 represents an input to the process with the ellipse on the far left, and the output with the

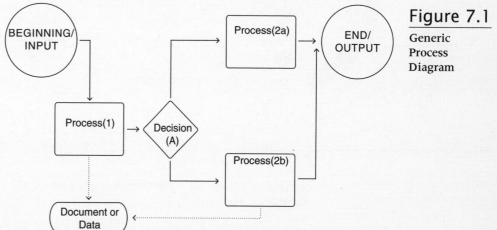

Figure 7.1

Generic
Process
Diagram

ellipse on the far right. The rectangles in between represent the various transformative processes. The diamonds stand for decision pivots and links to data or documents are indicated with the modified rectangle. Processes are organized in a process inventory (see further on) that you may want to diagram separately. For example, Process (1) in Figure 7.1 may be composed of several sub-processes.

Resist any temptation you have to build a single gigantic process map. The processes should be discrete and consumable by your target audience, the employees in all their various roles. As a consultant, I've seen lots of giant process maps hanging on a COO's wall, and that's where they stay and that's the only person who sees them.

Figure 7.2

Process
Design

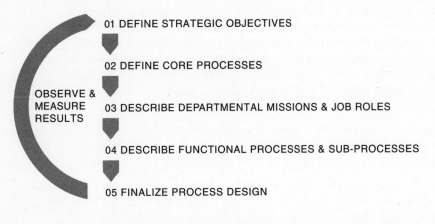

01 DEFINE STRATEGIC OBJECTIVES

02 DEFINE CORE PROCESSES

OBSERVE &
MEASURE
RESULTS

03 DESCRIBE DEPARTMENTAL MISSIONS & JOB ROLES

04 DESCRIBE FUNCTIONAL PROCESSES & SUB-PROCESSES

05 FINALIZE PROCESS DESIGN

The longest journey begins with a single step. How do we approach process design so we come out the other end a winner? Figure 7.2 describes the overall flow. Start by defining the company's strategic objectives, which should follow from the company's mission statement (which you should draft if you haven't). The strategic objectives for a startup are likely to change over time. Most commonly, they will transition from an objective of discovery (pre-chasm) to an objective of scaling and incremental learning (post-chasm). For example, during Enable Quiz's early days, their strategic objectives might look something like this:

Enable Quiz will build a technical quizzing platform that dramatically increases our customers' success in recruiting and employee skills development. This means working with our pioneer customers to discover what works and establishing a foothold in the mainstream market.

Once they are scaling within a market where they're emerging as a major player, they might transition to something like this:

Enable Quiz will build a .... Enable Quiz aims to be the leader in technical quizzing, growing sales by (x%) per year and receiving the highest customer satisfaction ratings in the e-learning segment.

The next step is to define the core processes that will allow the company to achieve their stated objectives. Is this starting to sound a little business school-like? Don't start skimming yet. Having a relevant and powerful mission is what allows you to start a company in the first place. Tying that mission to a set of core processes (explicitly or not) is what will enable you to achieve that mission. The core processes are the key business activities that will allow you to realize the company's mission. You should only have around four to six of them, otherwise you've probably skipped to defining the functional processes.

Next, you'll want to define your departments and their missions, followed by job roles in the various departments. If you're the founder, you may be running three to four one-person departments or, technically, fractional person departments. I still recommend taking the time to do this: It will help you make explicit what's important in the chaos of context switching between several topics on a daily basis. Having well-defined departmental missions frees you from worrying daily whether you're dropping the ball on marketing, sales, and so on. A departmental mission statement should answer the following questions:

1. What is the department's objective?
2. What specific activities does this include?
   - The goal is not to cover every little thing but to identify the major tasks which are particularly useful to other departments.
3. How do you define success in that objective?
   - This is likely to change from a learning-oriented definition to a quantitative definition as the company scales.

In the following section, we'll cover these for Enable Quiz's departments. Next, you should delineate the various job roles. Again, this is important even if you have a few founders doing many job roles. Creating an enduring company is about roles and institutions, not individuals. In their seminal work on building successful companies, *Built to Last* authors Collins and Porras refer to this as management being "clock builders" versus "time tellers." Enable Quiz is off to the races on job roles, since we covered them in Chapter 5.

Once we have our objectives, core processes, missions, and roles, we're ready to detail a process inventory. This is a hierarchical definition of all the company's processes. The hierarchy is as follows:

- Core Processes: What are the fundamental things the company must do to accomplish its objectives?
  - Functional Processes: What are the specific activities attached to each core process?
    - Sub-Processes: How does each of these things get done? What are the inputs and outputs? What are the transformative steps? Who completes them, and what IT systems are involved in each?

Enable Quiz's process inventory appears in the next section. If you're still early in your development, you may want less detail here. That said, even if you're getting started, I recommend creating a process inventory that goes down to functional processes. This will help you organize your time, staffing, and skill sets.

As simple as the fundamentals may seem, many business process designs go off the rails, producing stillborn deliverables that have no impact on the company. Typically, these focus too much on minutiae and do a poor job of linking back the company's objectives and core processes. Another common failure mode (and sadly it's not mutually exclusive with the first) is that someone in a vacuum who isn't familiar with any or some of the departmental domains creates the design. Of course, this is the last thing you want.

The following are a few tips for success:

- Start from the top and work down.
  - Define strategic objectives and core processes first. Then move on as shown previously.
- Provide easy-to-use templates to participants.
- Provide examples.
  - The full business process design for Enable Quiz is available in Microsoft Office format at Alexandercowan .com/process.
  - You can use both as a template and an example.
  - I recommend completing at least one core process for your particular company if you plan to delegate creation of the design.
- Review in an open forum and iterate.
- Don't bite off more than you can chew.
  - Even if everyone is working 70-hour weeks, you should still take the time to do this.
  - However, if you are still in the early stages, only down to the level of functional process.

Table 7.1 describes a few quick smoke tests that will help predict whether you're headed toward a process design that will focus and enhance your business, or one that will end up as an expensive wall poster.

What happens if employees deviate from the process? Nothing. It's fine if it's occasional. You're a startup, which means your core capability is learning and adaption. Employees should never be obliged to follow the

Item	Correlated with Success	Correlated with Failure
Involvement of Management	Senior management defines the objectives, core processes, and drafts at least one departmental mission and job role definition.	The task is delegated to an administrative employee or consultant.
Use of Consultants	Consultants organize a framework and coach senior and departmental management on its use.	Consultants go into a room for a week and hand you a huge poster and an invoice on their way out the door.
Delegation to Department Heads	Senior management defines objectives, core processes, examples, and instruction and delegates the balance of the work to department heads.	Senior management hands some general material off to department heads and asks them to do the design for their department.
Level of Detail	The design goes down to the sub-processes level but deals with inputs, outputs, transformative processes, and their roles. It might identify applicable IT systems but not their specific use.	The design is detailed, purporting to show in some cases every operation an employee must complete for a process.
Disruption	In the course of doing the process design, many troublesome questions arise about how the company does things.	No material questions arise about how the company operates and why.
Organization	The process design is organized into discrete, consumable but interrelated pieces.	There is one gigantic flow chart that (supposedly) describes how the company operates.
Review	The design is reviewed in an open forum. Employees understand that though the design is always subject to revision, this is how they're expected to do their jobs. Employees raise material questions and concerns.	The deliverable is reviewed by senior management and accepted.
Revision	The design is revised many times before finalized and, thereafter, at least once a year.	The initial deliverable isn't revised much and rarely revisited because it's irrelevant and almost immediately obscure.

Table 7.1

Litmus Tests for Process Design

process instead of doing what they think makes sense on a case-by-case basis. However, if you find your operation consistently deviating from the process design, you'll need to determine if the design needs revision or if parts of your team need to better adhere to it. For example, let's say an employee in operations, who manages your systems, sends an issue to engineering development without any diagnostic information and little context. Your process design explicitly requires they complete a checklist of diagnostics operations before sending an issue to engineering. So, is this good or bad? Well, it depends. If it's a bona fide emergency, it might be best to have your subject experts in engineering drop what they're doing to help put out the fire. However, if this happens routinely for all kinds of issues, the department head will need to review with the employee the importance of completing diagnostics (and attempting resolution) before sending issues to engineering.

Process doesn't equal bureaucracy or ossification. Processes exist and ensuring you've aligned them with the company's objectives is worthwhile. You want to avoid any slide into bureaucracy. As tech startups grow and achieve some success, management will frequently pantomime the bureaucratic behavior of larger companies, in the unconscious belief that acting out big company behaviors will somehow tame their operating environment and make them a big company. This sounds ridiculous but I've seen otherwise smart, even brilliant and talented, managers do it. If this is your first time as a senior manager, you will have few checks on your behavior and anything bad you do will probably be tolerated, though resented, and have geometric ramifications as it ripples through the organization. So, make the processes work for you and your staff. You'll reap terrific benefits even at the earliest stages. I guarantee you'll feel a little elation the first time an issue for which you would have had to intervene resolves itself as the result of a process.

If your tech business is an internal IT project, process design has special importance. Ideally, it's the blueprint for a lot of what you do on your project and helps you with your metrics for success.

Process Example: Enable Quiz

Strategy and Core Processes

Andrew starts out by defining the company's strategic objectives:

Enable Quiz will build a technical quizzing platform that dramatically increases our customers' success in recruiting and ongoing skills development. This means working with our pioneer customers to discover what works and establishing a foothold in the mainstream market.

As we discussed earlier, the second part of their mission is likely to morph into something more oriented toward measurable growth and scale.

Next, he outlines the four core processes to implement those objectives:

1. Acquire and Retain Customers

    This covers every action the company takes to get customers and keep them, including marketing, sales, on-boarding, and retention. In high-tech businesses, sales and post-sales are often divided up organizationally. However, Andrew wants these functions to be organized together since, in a SaaS business, revenue is as much about customer retention and average billings as it is about acquisition.

2. Provide Service

    This deals with everything the company does to keep the service running and performing well per the customers' expectations.

3. Develop Product

    This deals with everything the company does to deliver the product, all the way from the point of conceiving new features to releasing them in a nice, tidy, consumable package.

4. Bill

    This last process deals with making sure customers are billed, done so in the correct amount, and that Enable Quiz collects its billings.

You'll notice there's nothing here about standard administrative items like accounting, legal, and HR. That doesn't mean Enable Quiz doesn't do them; it means they're not core to the business and that's why Andrew's outsourced most of them.

Departmental Missions and Job Roles

Andrew tackles the departmental mission for marketing, sales, and product management and hands the examples to Mike Fedor to tackle engineering and operations (Table 7.2).

Table 7.2

Departmental Missions

Department	Mission
Marketing	Marketing's mission is to position Enable Quiz as a valuable solution to the problems of new-hire evaluation and employee skills management in technical disciplines. This means driving organic traffic to the site through promotion and making productive investments in targeted advertising. Our success is measured in unique visitors, percent conversions, cost per acquisition (CAC), average revenue per customer (ARPU), and average customer lifetime.
Sales	Sales' mission is to acquire and retain customers in Enable Quiz's early market and establish a beachhead with more conservative customers that marketing identifies in the early majority segment. This means following up on leads that don't close online, assisting customers with the on-boarding process, acting on low usage indicators to increase involvement, and acquiring renewals. Our success is measured in percent conversions, ARPU, and average customer lifetime. We're also measured by our ability to close referenceable strategic customers in the early majority segment.
Operations	Operations' mission is to make the experience of using the Enable Quiz product a world-class one. This means keeping adequate system capacity online, securing the system, and ensuring good performance. It means ensuring our content managers consistently update the banks of technical quiz questions that are part of our customers' service. When customers run into trouble, it's our job to resolve those troubles. Our success is measured in our customers' perception of stability and performance, quiz quality, and customer support, which we gauge by using surveys and post-mortems as well as net promoter score.
Product Management	Product Management's mission is to improve product quality and marketability, making astute investments in development engineering. This means knowing our users like the back of our hand, designing new features, guiding engineering in the effective implementation of those features, and producing documentation that allows our customers to have a fantastic, touchless experience. Our success is measured in unique visitors, percent conversions, CAC, ARPU, average customer lifetime, and net promoter score (NPS).

Table 7.2
(*continued*)

Department	Mission
Business Development	Business Development's mission is to identify, close, and cultivate partnerships identified by product management to enhance the sales of Enable Quiz and whole product required by our customers. This means calling on prospective partners, determining what a successful partnership means to them, closing contracts, and managing the relationship to make it a success for both parties. Our success is measured in new sales, ARPU, and average customer lifetime for partner-driven sales.
Engineering and Quality Assurance (QA)	Engineering and QA's mission is to execute new features that are manageable and supportable in the field. This means applying best of breed system components, software development techniques, and QA practices. Our success is measured in story points/month, cost/story point, the count and severity of field bugs, and NPS.

At this point, Andrew and Mike refresh the job roles we described in Chapter 5. Andrew sees the need to define two new roles, both of which he'll take for now: sales consultant and business development. The sales consultant's job is to spend additional time with the customers helping them understand how to best make use of Enable Quiz in their organization. This might be as simple as helping less proficient users get started to helping HR liaison with a busy technical manager to choose the right quiz banks. Andrew's in the role currently and focuses on Enable Quiz's largest and most strategic customers, particularly those he thinks will serve as a beachhead in the crucial early majority segment. He instituted the business development position, recognizing he is seeing a lot of important sales come from or through a few strategic customers who are using Enable Quiz to augment their business.

Table 7.3 summarizes all the job roles at Enable Quiz, including icons we'll use in the process flows that follow.

While we don't specifically deal with them in this section, the customer role shown in Table 7.4 bears mentioning since they'll appear later in the process definitions.

Table 7.3

Roles at Enable Quiz

(icon)	User	Description
	Marketing Manager	Tasks • Front Page site design • Site analytics • Organic promotion • Paid advertising Skills • Marketing management • Knowledge of target market • Site design and analytics
	Salesperson	Tasks • Closing leads • Customer on-boarding • Customer retention Skills • Successful sales track record • Knowledge of target market
	Sales Consultant	Tasks • Application consultation • Customer on-boarding • Training • Retention and upsell Skills • Knowledge of target market • Experience with training and consultation
	Business Development Manager	Tasks • Partner identification • Close new partnerships • Manage partnerships to success Skills • Track record of successful partner management • Knowledge of target market

Table 7.3

(*continued*)

(icon)	User	Description
	Operations Director	**Tasks** • Recruitment and management of talent • Continuous improvement of functional processes • Resolution of critical or sensitive issues **Skills** • Background in technical operations
	Systems Administrator (Operations)	**Tasks** • IP networking • Server maintenance • Application maintenance **Skills** • Background in related systems and applications
	Tech Support	**Tasks** • Resolution of product-related issues • Classification and post-mortems on customer issues • Supplementary resource for documentation and QA **Skills** • Deep experience with product • Experience with support of online applications
	Customer Service Representative	**Tasks** • Resolution of customer issues • Classification and post-mortems on customer issues **Skills** • Experience with support of online applications • Fluency with company's application, customer relationship management (CRM), and billing systems

(*continued*)

Table 7.3

(*continued*)

(icon)	User	Description
	Product Management Director	**Tasks** • Responsible for a particular product—to the extent possible, a ''mini CEO'' for their product • Assess market needs and formulate product design to fulfil them **Skills** • Ability to handle singular responsibility of making a product successful • Customer-facing experience in relevant market • Understanding of development process and drivers of efficiency • Competency in design thinking to pull together approach on product
	Engineering Director	**Tasks** • Software delivery per specifications • Developer recruitment, management, retention • Participant in overall product improvement process **Skills** • Interdisciplinary perspective • Experience with relevant development methodologies • Planning and project management • General management
	Developer	**Tasks** • Implementation of discrete portion of product implementation **Skills** • Genuine professional interest and enthusiasm • Track record/portfolio in area of interest • Good communications skills • Team orientation

(icon)	User	Description
	Quality Assurance	**Tasks** • Review output from developers and evaluate its conformance with the specification and intent • Design and maintain test plans • Create and maintain automated test regression systems **Skills** • General interest and understanding in customer experience with the product • Attention to detail and organization • Experience with test automation tools
	Finance and Billing	**Tasks** • General accounting management (general ledger, accounts receivable, accounts payable) • Customer billing management **Skills** • Accounting experience (CPA, ideally) • Experience in financial management of high-tech businesses • Experience in SaaS billing operations • Attention to detail and organization

Table 7.3

(*continued*)

(icon)	User	Description
	Customer	These are end users of the service. They receive various phone and service configurations on the network.

Table 7.4

The Customer Roll

Process Inventory

Figure 7.3 shows a sample of Enable Quiz's process inventory for one core process, Acquire and Retain Customers.

This sample of the process inventory table goes down to the level of functional process (sub-process is the next level). The first column, called Owner, describes who owns the process. However, this doesn't mean others aren't involved. You can see an appraisal of the level of involvement by other roles in the last set of columns with the heading of Involvement by Job Role. The Tools column describes the systems involved in the functional processes. The columns in the Metrics section describe the three key types of metrics we identified above. Table 7.5 describes each of the functional processes in brief.

Figure 7.3

Core Process: Acquire and Retain Customers

Enable Quiz Core Processes

Acquire & Retain Customers

	Owner	Tools	Metrics Process	Output	Outcome	Mkting	Sales	Sales Cons.	Bus. Dev.	Ops	Prod.	Dev.	Fin.
1.1 Define and Position Product	Marketing	(various)	mostly n/a	mostly n/a	CAC = marketing spend/ sign-up's , ACL	high	med	med	med	low	med	med	none
1.2 Develop Website	Marketing	Joomla!	story points/ month	bugs/ month	visitors, sign-up's/visitors, gen. revenue	high	med	med	low	low	high	high	none
1.3 Generate Visits	Marketing	Google AdWords, Analytics	visits/ month	pages/visit	ad + promo. spend/visits	high	low	none	med	none	med	none	none
1.4 Generate Leads	Marketing, Bus. Dev.	CRM	leads/ month	unqualified leads/ leads	sign-up's/ total leads	high	med	none	high	none	low	none	none
1.5 Close Leads	Sales	CRM	pitches/ month	sign-up's/ total leads	average customer life (ACL), ARPU	low	high	med	none	none	low	none	none
1.6 Onboard Customers	Sales	Online Training	onboards/ month	cancellations/on boards	ACL, ARPU, NPS	low	high	high	none	none	low	none	none
1.7 Drive Usage	Sales	CRM, internal analytics	interventions/ month	av. usage increase/ intervention	ACL, ARPU, NPS	med	high	high	low	none	med	none	none
1.8 Obtain Renewals	Sales	CRM	pitches/ month	renewals/ pitches	ACL, ARPU, NPS	high	high	low	none	low	med	none	none
1.9 Drive Partner Infrastructure	Bus. Dev.	CRM	partner sales/month	partner churn	ACL, ARPU, NPS for partner sales	med	med	low	high	low	med	none	none

Functional Process	Notes
Define and Position Product	This covers everything marketing does to promote Enable Quiz such as customer research, usage studies, search engine optimization, site analytics, application analytics (looking at who's using the product and how), writing white papers and posts, e-mail campaigns, direct mail, and paid advertising. Though some tech marketing departments organize their projects on the agile model using story points, most tasks here are not repetitive in a systematic way. Therefore, the process and output metrics are inapplicable because there's no good way to measure them (remember, this is measurement of the work that the marketing team is doing, not the results of it, like site views). The only metrics that matter are the outcome metrics: CAC, and average customer life (abbreviated here as ACL). Since we want to look at the aggregate outcomes of everything marketing does, we'll measure CAC as the total dollars spent on marketing (including staff) divided by signups per period.
	Everyone's a critic when it comes to marketing. Since most of the activities don't require a specific technical skill set to execute, all people consider themselves experts and they may be. However, none of this means that it's easy to do marketing well. Marketing's job is to learn as much as it can from customers and the rest of the organization and then make decisions on behalf of the company. Committees usually produce bad marketing. So, though the table shows medium involvement by many job roles, that doesn't make marketing a collective activity.
	In the early stages, determining which sources drive traffic to the site is crucial. Using A/B testing (that is, testing different version of the landing pages), will be pivotal to discerning whether the Enable Quiz proposition is on the right track or needs to materially adjust its strategy.
Develop Website	This refers to the non-quiz part of the website, the part that deals with describing the offer, the company, and managing the sign-up process. Marketing owns this part of the site and interfaces with Product Management when changes to the sign-up procedure are required, since that touches the back-office application infrastructure. Marketing has access to the content management system Joomla!, which allows its members to make changes directly to the website. Here Marketing does organize new initiatives around story points, which it measures per month, along with any defects that arise. The outcome metrics are visits to the site, the portion of visitors that convert, and general revenue since the site is Enable Quiz's primary sales platform.

Table 7.5

Functional Process Under Core Process: "Acquire and Retain Customers"

(continued)

Table 7.5

(continued)

Functional Process	Notes
	Product Management and Development have a high degree of involvement since aspects of the site require development.
	In the early phases, Enable Quiz will be aggressively testing different landing pages and sign-up funnels.
Generate Visits	Even though it's tightly related to the previous two functional processes, generating visits to the site warrants its own functional process since it involves specific activities around search engine optimization, AdWords-based advertising, and related analytics.
	Marketing uses Google AdWords to buy search engine advertising and Google Analytics to analyze traffic to the site. The process metric, visits per month, measures raw traffic, and pages per month measures the quality of the visit and whether engagement with the visitor was successful. The outcome metric is the percentage of sign-ups versus raw visits.
	Early on, detailed analysis of the visitor traffic will be pivotal to evaluating whether Enable Quiz is on the right track.
Generate Leads	This process, unusually, has two owners since it's two distinct processes. Marketing deals with all direct-to-customer lead generation, visits to the site, and outbound e-mail. Business Development deals with generating leads through partners. Both use the CRM system (Salesforce.com). The process metric is the volume of leads, and the output metric is the portion of leads that are fundamentally not qualified (flawed leads). The outcome metrics is the portion of leads that sign up.
	Involvement from Marketing and Business Development is high. Sales and Product Management contribute ideas from their contact with the market.
Close Leads	This specifically refers to Sales closing leads that don't close online. Leads that close online are measured as good outcomes against the previous functional process, Generate Leads. The process metric considers the number of pitches: Since the desired output is a lead who registers, the portion of signups is the output metric. This speaks to how well the customer engagement is working.
	Early on, the critical question will be the extent to which customers can onboard themselves and can purchase and use the product with the resources on the site. If they cannot do so easily, Enable Quiz might have to make a material change in approach.

Table 7.5
(*continued*)

Functional Process	Notes
Onboard Customers	On-boarding refers to the process of getting customers operating and engaged on your service. The Sales department handles this, with heavy involvement from the Sales Consultants. The product's objective is that the "average" customer has a touchless experience—paying with a credit card, using the product, and consulting the online help where needed. However, larger and more strategic customers (like beachhead customers in the early majority segment) will warrant concierge services, especially in the early days when Enable Quiz is learning about the product and customer experience. Even if things are going perfectly, Sales Consultants and Product Management will always want to hand on-board a few customers to ensure the company understands the customer experience. The process metric speaks to the amount of on-boarding. The output metric speaks to customers that cancel, in other words, failed on-boards. The relevant outcome metrics deal with the customer experience: ACL, ARPU, and NPS.
	Early on, everyone, including management, is likely to take part in on-boarding customers since this will be a key indicator of which customers bought the product, why, and how they intend to use it. Micromanaging these data is crucial to determine whether Enable Quiz needs to accelerate down the path it's on or detour to a new strategy. For example, which quiz banks are selling will show where the business lies.
Drive Usage	Since salespeople are compensated on the recurring revenue of customers (just like the company itself), they are inclined to keep an eye on usage since it drives retention (and it's easier to keep a customer than get a new one) and ARPU (since increasing billings is an easy way to increase revenue). Sales will gravitate toward larger customers. This is fine, since the company can't afford to provide concierge service to everyone. Salespeople and Sales Consultants have the CRM system and automated reporting on usage to use in executing this activity. The process metric is usage interventions per month since this measures activity. The average increase in usage after an intervention measures the conformance of this activity with its purpose, but that will take a little reporting magic though it is highly doable as long as Sales records the intervention in CRM.

(*continued*)

Table 7.5

(*continued*)

Functional Process	Notes
	Involvement from the Sales functions is high. The medium involvement for Marketing and Product Management is for cases where the company wants to examine customers who are not on Sales' A-list for revenue reasons. These might be customers in a new segment or small customers in a beachhead segment. It is unfair and ill-fated to ask a commissioned salesperson to perform market research on behalf of the company. Sales' comments are one of the best and most focal conduits to the market: but departments whose core mission is product and customer developments should be the ones to execute strategic customer investigation.
Obtain Renewals	This refers to retaining customers who have cancelled or not renewed a fixed contract. Since it's easier to renew customers who understand the service than to acquire new ones, this activity is important. Additionally, nonrenewals and cancellations are red flags and the company needs as much data as possible on them. The process metric is the number of renewal pitches, and the output is their rate of success. The outcome metric deals with everything related to long-term customer value.
	Again, Marketing and Product Management should pick up renewals of interest for those that Sales does not pursue.
Driver Partner Infrastructure	Product Management and Marketing set the agenda for Business Development. Business Development will likely fail if it processes whichever partners come in the door. Marketing should be responsible for identifying at least the type of sales (channel) partners that business development should pursue. Product Management should determine the type of partners needed to fill gaps in the whole product. This is not to say that business development should be mindless foot soldiers. In a small company, successful collaboration is a huge determinant of success versus failure.
	The process metric is the number of partnerships created, and the output metric is the number of failed partnerships, which are ones that churn out through cancellation or inactivity. The outcome metric is all key customer lifetime value metrics related to channel sales and sales augmented by partner resources.
	The fundamental question of whether or not customers will buy and on-board directly via the web will be highly pivotal in this area. If not, Enable Quiz will need to aggressively pursue partners to sell and service/augment the offer.

The full business process design describes the balance of the core processes (Provide Service, Develop Product, and Bill) and is available on Alexandercowan.com/process.

The following subsections show the actual process diagrams for some of the sub-processes.

Process Example: Plan an Iteration

Figure 7.4 shows a sub-process, called "Plan an Iteration" that would fall under the functional process, Develop Features, which is part of the core process, Develop Product.

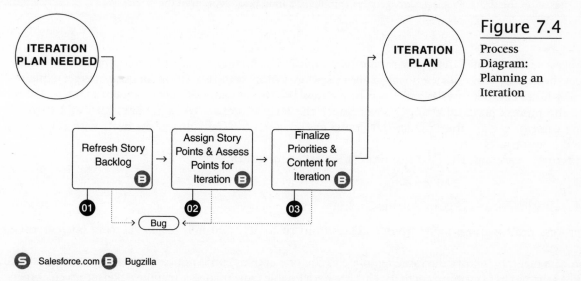

Figure 7.4

Process Diagram: Planning an Iteration

Enable Quiz augmented the rectangles showing the transformative processes with icons that denote the systems concerned. For example, the "B" in the first process (1) represents the Bugzilla bug/feature tracking system. The ellipse (Bug) stands for a system item modified in the process, in this case a bug record, which is what Enable Quiz uses to represent new features as well as product defects. Table 7.6 describes the process.

Table 7.6

Notes on
Planning
an Iteration

Note	Description
1	The Engineering Director notifies the Product Management (PM) Director that a new iteration is starting. The PM Director then goes through Bugzilla to make sure the items (bugs) with the highest priority reflect his or her current view of priorities and adds any new product enhancements since the last time he or she visited the system.
2	The Engineering Director works with his or her team to assign story points (size) to each of the Bugs at or above priority six. Bugs below this level are considered to be in the backlog for a subsequent iteration. The Engineering Director posts the number of story points available for the next iteration.
3	Based on the sizing, Product Management completes a final prioritization of the stories.

This process seems simple, and many people might question whether it's worth describing in this fashion. But consider the details: How does the business about a priority of six being the cutoff for estimates get explained to everyone who needs to know? What if you hire a new product manager or development manager? What if you find the process needs to change? Also, notice the level of detail. We don't say, "... and then the Engineering Director e-mails the Product Development Director...." The sub-process deals with the inputs, outputs, and transformative steps.

That was just a warm up. The next sub-process is a little more intricate.

Process Example: Resolving a Trouble Ticket

This sub-process deals with resolving trouble tickets from customers and falls under the core process, called Provide Service.

This process diagram follows the same template as the one above. You'll notice that Salesforce.com is used frequently. As the nexus of customer activity, this is where Enable Quiz manages trouble tickets from customers. This process has a lot of steps and is close to being to the point where it should be further decomposed. That said, it's a useful contract in how the process framework accommodates more complex processes.

Table 7.7 describes the process in more detail.

The full process design for Enable Quiz is available on Alexandercowan.com/process.

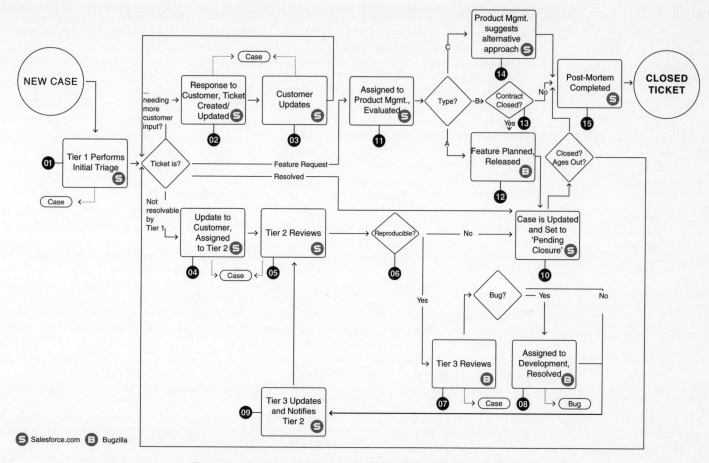

Figure 7.5 Process Diagram: Resolving a Trouble Ticket

Table 7.7

Notes on
Resolving a
Ticket

Note	Description
1	Support is divided into three tiers. Tier 1 is part of Operations within the job role of Tech Support. Tier 2 Tech Support is in Operations. It has some basic job roles and more senior, more technical staff. Tier 3 support is part of Engineering. When a trouble ticket arrives, whether by phone, e-mail, or portal, it's first assigned to Tier 1 for initial diagnosis or triage. If support has a solution for the customer, we go directly to step 10.
2	If the ticket is valid but requires more specifics from the customer or appears invalid (not related to Enable Quiz), then Tier 1 updates the ticket and reassigns it to the customer. This generates an e-mail to the customer so they know action is required on their part.
3	After the customer updates the ticket, we're back to step 1 where Tier 1 will diagnose the issue.
4	If Tier 1 can't resolve the issue, it's escalated to Tier 2.
5	If Tier 2 can resolve this issue, it goes to step 10.
6	If not, Tier 2 reproduces the issue and assigns to Tier 3, engineering.
7	Tier 3 reviews the issue.
8	If the issue is a bug (defect), Tier 3 resolves it and reassigns the issue for Tier 2 (providing updates along the way if the resolution will take more than a few hours).
9	Once Tier 3 has resolved the issue, at least to their understanding, they reassign it to Tier 2 for next steps.
10	At this point, Tech Support considers the issue resolved and reassigns it to the customer for closure. The customer may close it, in which case we go to step 15. The customer often won't respond on a resolve issue, so the issue automatically closes after a set amount of days (five in the case of Enable Quiz).
11	If Tech Support determines the issue is a feature request, it assigns it to Product Management (PM). PM then determines if the issues falls into the A (good feature), B (OK feature but not compelling), or C (bad idea) bucket and proceeds to the next steps accordingly.
12	If the feature is an A bucket, the feature is placed in the backlog and the Customer is notified that the company will likely implement the request and thanked for their feedback, and we go to step 15.
13	If the feature is a B bucket, and the customer is large, Product works with Sales to offer the customer a fee for accelerating the feature.
14	If the feature is a C bucket, Product suggests an alternative approach and assigns back to the Customer for closure.
15	A post-mortem is completed once the issue is closed. This is often as simple as choosing the post-mortem category, but it is always required.

You Are My Beta

The Importance of Observation

Most of what you need to be successful in your Beta and launch period you'll need to find out from prospective customers and users. This can be a challenge since meetings, even virtual ones, can be difficult to set up. You have a lot going on the office that needs your attention. At least one member of the founding team should be spending a large chunk of his or her time with customers, watching and learning. Even though this is critical during your initial product validation, it will continue to be a vital part of the company's success. Your primary purpose is to observe. This is your chance to see what's likely to be happening with the 99 percent of users you'll likely never meet in person. Though you're probably there to help out as well, avoid assuming, judging, instructing, or selling early in the process. These customers and/or users are in their natural state, and you want to understand that state since your job is to figure out how your company can effect a wholesale change or accommodation of that state to your advantage without user-by-user intervention.

Instrumenting the Chaos

You're likely to be operationally swamped during Beta. If not, you will be during launch. It's important to instrument some structure in your CRM (and other systems) prior to going live. You should consider your assumptions about the areas in which you assume you're likely to see issues and make sure you make items like those in Table 7.8 mandatory in every trouble report from the field or customer contact (trouble ticket).

Enable Quiz's Beta

The purpose of Beta is to have a set of friendly users outside the company using the product as a means of conducting a final test of its proper functioning. Betas are generally short in adaptive methodologies since you've been building and testing in small increments. In the case of Enable Quiz, Andrew has pulled together 50 beta participants, mostly contacts from his initial market research and reality testing. Many are friends of friends, though a few signed up for notices on the pre-launch landing pages and later agreed to participate. In addition to validating functionality, this marks the first time, aside from a few demos and user tests, that Enable Quiz will have a chance to observe the on-boarding process and how users interact with the system. Most beta participants want to use the system to quiz their existing staff. Though a few are actively interviewing to fill positions, the notion of Enable Quiz as a valuable service for evaluating new hires won't get a whole lot of exercise in Beta. The participants are early adopters and only somewhat representative of the market at large,

Table 7.8

Parameters for
Trouble-
Tickets

Item	Description
Queue	There are lots of ways to do it, but most issue tracking systems are organized around the idea of queues or something similar. The queue is basically a topic. For example, Enable Quiz might have the following queues and secondary queues: Sales (new inquiry, upgrade, downgrade, renewal, cancellation, other) Trouble Ticket (access issue, bug, other) Service (banks, quizzes, students, reporting, other) Billing (question, dispute, refund) Depending on the system, you can use these queues to drive where the issue is assigned and how it is escalated.
Secondary Queue	This is a secondary queue for use with the above, providing additional definition (shown above in parenthesis).
Post-Mortem (type)	This covers the final disposition of the issue—was the issue solved? Was it an issue with the system? The users' setup?
Post-Mortem (notes)	This is a free text field for users to make notes. It's good to have these, but you'll want to enforce structured lists on the above items, otherwise you won't be able to report on the issues and review trends.

so easy on-boarding and lots of usage doesn't necessarily indicate smooth sailing in the general market. That said, if this audience can't use the product, it's definitely time to take a step back and see why before launch.

Andrew decides to assist in the on-boarding process with 30 of the customers and have 20 onboard themselves, sending them a login by e-mail. This will give him hands-on intuition about how customers will interact with the systems as well as seeing how the process of touchless on-boarding works in practice.

Andrew does a few of the on-boards in person and the rest over a screen share, with the screen sharing software Gotomeeting. The customers make their way through the system well except for two points where many of the users got stuck and Andrew had to intervene. The first sticking point was that creating quizzes from question banks didn't immediately click for most users. By default, the system has no quizzes. The users are expected to select from the banks of technical topics (such as Linux OS and IP networking) they've purchased to create their own custom quizzes. Andrew sees a relatively straightforward solution to this by creating a set of default quizzes for customers to use as a starting point while making sure they know they can create their own.

Another shortcoming is that the process of loading students and inviting them to take the quiz was rocky for most users. Andrew sees a high rate of abandonment around the process of creating quizzes looking at the site analytics for the 20 users who on-boarded by themselves. He follows up with a few of the self on-boarders and they confirm what he found with the assisted users.

Andrew follows up by writing a detailed redesign for the relevant areas of the site though he feels less confident as he gets into the details. He phones Mike (development lead), who suggests he upload screen recordings of the on-boarding sessions to their web designers at Snoetrope. Andrew wonders whether using Snoetrope to solve the problem is the best approach; Mike explains that even a great designer rarely nails it the first time and useability issues like this are part of the reason Betas exist.

Andrew and Mike work with their web designers to formulate a series of interface updates, workflow updates (automatically creating a set of starter quizzes for each customer), and enhancements to the online help media. A few of these Snoetrope prototypes and tests are used with the Beta users, and the results are promising.

Chapter 7 Summary

1. Process

    Getting your functional process in place will help you avoid waste and put you in a position to scale. Don't fear explicit process but ensure you do a thoughtful job and account for the reality of how things can work at your organization. After you have it in place, you'll probably find it's a big relief.

2. Obsess about the On-boarding Process

    If your solution is a web-delivered application, customers can end up in an easy come-easy go pattern that will lose you money. Many customers are lost in these cases during the initial on-boarding process, the process where they need to learn about the product and incorporate it into how they do things. Make sure you think through and monitor this process obsessively.

3. Rigidly Classify Customer Complaints

    At NASA, every piece of the Space Shuttle was instrumented to detect problems. Likewise, you should have a fixed classification scheme wherever you track customer calls and complaints so you collect quantitative data about where your customer issues originate and how they're resolved.

Checklist

1. Process
   Have you completed a basic process design?
2. On-Boarding
   Do you have a strategy to monitor on-boarding and bounce the results off your key assumptions?

Specialty Reading by Topic

If you want to know more about . . .	. . . then read
Process Design	*Process Redesign*, by Arthur Tenner and Irving J. DeToro This readable book will take you through all the key ideas behind process design and its application.

Scaling the Business

Riding the Whale of Scale

Starting a tech business is fundamentally about identifying a model where you can leverage technology, learning how to perfect it, and then scaling it. Your technology and model of choice should give you returns to scale, which is why so many technology franchises have huge multiples on earnings and sales. This last chapter looks at how to perfect your customer acquisition and retention model, focus your development, and strategically develop your customer base to position yourself for hockey stick growth.

The Launch: Is It Working?

In Chapter 1, we reviewed a few lightweight methods for reality testing your key assumptions, such as search term analysis, customer interviews, Google AdWords, and prototyping. In the case of Enable Quiz, Andrew learned the following:

- Technical quizzes don't look like an existing product category, at least by that name.
- There was a surprising amount of interest in Windows Server quizzes.
- Firms that do technical staffing and contracting look like a good early market.

You confirmed the product functions as designed during Beta and hopefully had a chance to do some validation of useability and the on-boarding process. Enable Quiz found a few issues at that point and had to revise its schedule, which was worth it. You put a basic process infrastructure in place. It didn't need to be elaborate, but it's key to avoiding waste and burnout, and it puts you in a great position to scale.

Now you're at launch, which means you're offering your product to the general public. In the dot-com period, this usually meant you were spending huge amounts of cash in hopes of being an early winner in your category. It doesn't anymore. If you're in a new market, you should shepherd your resources as you perfect your model and develop your customer base. The newer your market, the more careful and deliberate you have to be. New markets can take years to develop: Overstaffing and overspending before your market goes mainstream is a classic failure mode for tech startups. The money and the founders' credibility often run out just at the point where the market is ready to go mainstream. The sections that follow will describe how to monitor and tune your operating model, creating a bridge to the mainstream market.

Customer Funnel

The idea of the customer funnel is that you start with raw leads, site visitors in the case of an online business, and you lose a portion of those raw leads at each step along the way to closing a sale. With all these new buzzwords, it may be comforting to know that one of the most powerful frameworks for customer acquisition is over 100 years old.[1] The Attention, Interest, Desire, Action (AIDA) framework does a great job of organizing the customer acquisition process. Many tech businesses are based on subscriptions or some other continued use of the product, so thinking the funnel through all the way to On-boarding and Retention is important (AIDA**OR**, if you will). AIDA's inventor missed this part, but it was 1898 and telephones were just catching on, so you can hardly blame him for the omission.

Understanding what drives intake and success rates through your funnel is crucial to arriving at a scalable model. Having your numbers increase is encouraging, but what's important is to ensure your performance all the way through the funnel is at least steady or, ideally, improving. Figure 8.1 shows a general funnel.

Once you have some experience with the buyer, it's a good idea to organize your key assumptions and metrics around this funnel. After all, it's the life of your buyer that determines your own. We apply this to Enable Quiz's customer funnel in the next section.

---

[1]It is credited to marketing pioneer E. St. Elmo Lewis, released in 1898.

Step

1 Attention: you've got someone looking at the product.

2 Interest: they've taken interest in its benefits.

3 Desire: you're convincing them or they're convincing themselves they want it.

4 Action: they're undertaking the steps to purchase.

5 On-Boarding: whatever is required to get them using the product, mission accomplished.

6 Retention: they're repeat buying, renewing their contract if applicable.

all prospects

interested prospects

motivated prospects

buyers

users

success stories

Key Questions

1 Is the proposition relevant? Is it reaching your target buyer in the volume you expect? If not, why? If someone else, who? If you're paying, how much is it costing?

2 Is the proposition relevant to the buyer? How are you getting them interested?

3 Is the proposition compelling enough to bridge the emotional and/or financial threshold to getting the sale and/or usage?

4 What are the final barriers to purchase? Use? Have you adequately simplified the buying process?

5 Are customers getting up and running on the product? Are they able to use it out of the box? If not, is the necessary "whole product" there for them to get going?

6 Are customers renewing? Repeat buying? How are up-sells?

Figure 8.1

Customer Funnel

Funnel: Enable Quiz

Figure 8.2 shows Enable Quiz's customer funnel, which we'll use as a specific example.

Figure 8.2

Customer
Funnel at
Enable Quiz

What we assume will happen.

1 Our proposition(s) and promotions will get the **attention** of prospective buyers, and they'll visit our site.

2 The landing page will **interest** prospects and they'll continue to browse for more information.

3 We've created enough **desire** with the prospect for them to view the online demo and questionnaire.

4 We've created enough **desire** with the prospect for them to take **action** and request a callback or online chat.

5 We've created enough **desire** with the prospect for them to take **action** and sign up online.

6 The customer on-boards successfully.

7 The customer uses the service at expected levels.

8 The customer renews and supplements their order.

prospect visits the site

prospect views at least 3 pages/items

prospect views demo and/ or fills out survey

prospect requests contact

prospect signs up

customer on-boards

customer becomes regular user

customer renews and upgrades

How we'll see if it does.

1 Analysis by landing pages and Google Ad Word reporting and general site analytics (Google Analytics).

2 We'll look at progress through the site by visitor by source (landing pages and ad's).

3 We'll look at progress to the demo and interaction with the integrated questionnaire.

4 We'll look at progress to the callback and chat controls through the funnel.

5 We'll look at progress to sign up.

6 We'll look at configuration and initial usage by customer.

7 We'll look at reporting from the quiz engine.

8 We'll set up reminders for all renewals and treat them as sales calls.

Attention: Site Visits (1)

The key assumptions here are that Enable Quiz has a relevant product and an economical, scalable means to promote it. It's a new category, so even though the Google AdWords around technical quizzes aren't overly expensive, it also doesn't yield a lot of visits. AdWords, related to hiring on technical topics that were trending well (Windows Admin, PHP, Ruby, and .NET), has worked reasonably well driving traffic to the site. Andrew has created a number of informational items on the Enable Quiz site and elsewhere, using small white papers and blog posts about the value of technical quizzing, and those appear to be driving some traffic. He's been using promotional codes or special landing page URLs to ensure he has measureable follow-on traffic across these various sources and the propositions he's presented. Additionally, it seems as if some of the customers who do technical staffing are referring their customers. Andrew recognizes a few of the customer names from mentions by these other partners.

   Andrew's assumptions about the proposition look fundamentally solid. A few things need tweaking, but traffic is growing and visitors are coming for the reasons Andrew expected when he laid out the company's key assumptions. It looks like intake through the current sources will allow Enable Quiz to hit some respectable revenue numbers.

Interest: Browsing (2)

Think about the Enable Quiz site like a physical store. If customers walk in the door, do a 180, and walk back out, you somehow managed to get their attention but not their interest. Site analytics can tell you the same thing: If users are hitting the home page or a landing page and going no further, it's the virtual equivalent of that 180. Fortunately for Enable Quiz, no particular group appears to be doing a 180 other than those tied to a few experimental AdWords. Users who click fewer than three pages on Enablequiz.com are 20 to 30 percent, which isn't out of the ordinary. However, the number of prospects that have enough desire to go to the following steps and view a demo or ask for a callback varies widely by source. Andrew will do some tweaking to cultivate the productive sources and trim the less productive ones.

Desire: Demo and/or Callback (3, 4)

Enable Quiz created an online multimedia demo interleaved with a questionnaire about how the prospects might want to use Enable Quiz. The results of the questionnaire are available for analysis, and are of particular interest if the customer doesn't take action to convert (placing an order or requesting a call back). If the customer wants to go to the next step, the pages at the end of the demo either inform a salesperson to initiate a call back and generates suggestions for purchase in case the customer wants to buy online.

Andrew has found some material differences between prospects coming through the funnel to this point. Those who come in via AdWords make it to this point less frequently. Prospects who discover Enable Quiz through search or linking in from a posting elsewhere are more likely to get to this point.

Action: Sign Up! (5)

This is the key step. Andrew's worked with Snoetrope (their front-end designers) extensively to simplify the buying process. Prospects from the previous step convert at an even rate across sources and areas.

On-Boarding, Usage, and Retention (6, 7, 8)

Though signups are thrilling, the value of customers is a function of their longevity. Therefore, successful on-boarding and retention are critical to Enable Quiz's success. Since Enable Quiz is a SaaS service for which customers pay monthly, the cost of entry for a customer is low, reducing the perceived and actual barrier to cancelling. This sudden death zone between when a customer buys and when they incorporate the product into their business is almost as important as acquisition. The first key is on-boarding. Enable Quiz has found that if a customer doesn't have a quiz put together and sent out to students within three weeks, they're 80 percent likely never to use the service in a meaningful way and cancel within a few months. For that reason, customers that haven't set up after three weeks get a call on the 22nd day from a Sales Consultant to see what's going on. Since customers with this profile have purchased the product without a huge commitment, they take the implementation lightly, neglecting to substantially use the system. Completing the implementation ends up at the end of applicable manager's to-do list, and they cancel their subscription a few months later from lack of use. Winning them back is difficult once the account gets to that point. Getting customers involved with the product is part of any good post-sales execution, but it's especially critical with a SaaS sales model and it's a change of paradigm for many software account managers. In traditionally deployed

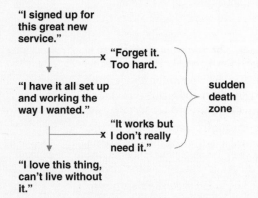

Figure 8.3

Sudden Death

software models, a firm implementation plan and organizational commitment is more likely if customer pays substantially up-front for the software.

The second key is monitoring usage on an ongoing basis and deciding when to intervene. This may be based on the customer's size or segment, or it might be something you do all the time. Enable Quiz intervenes quite often in the early days. They frequently find that when companies used Enable Quiz for a skills audit, they haven't had much cause to use it since the audit. Enable Quiz's pricing is set up so low utilization customers don't pay much, reducing cancellation. Unless they opt out, these customers get regular e-mails with suggestions on how to use the system, for instance reminding them that it's a great tool for new hires, updating them on new question banks, and more. A salesperson will check in on the larger accounts. The reward for diligence in this area is retention and up-sells.

Enable Quiz: Post-Launch Conclusions

With the online formula working, Andrew wants to pursue partnerships with firms that do technical training and learning management system for referral agreements or other promotional programs to further promote growth, expansion, and learning at Enable Quiz. After looking at the trends in visitors and on-boarding, Andrew has concluded that one of the most promising investments of the company's available time and money is to pursue partners for referral sales and OEM/powered-by solutions where partners can use the Enable Quiz system but label it as their own product. Enable Quiz will continue direct promotion. The assumptions that customers want the product and that they can self-purchase and most can on-board by themselves has been proved correct. That said, partner sales look like a more promising avenue than increasing the budget for direct sales or advertising. In the next section, we review partnerships.

Note on Analytics

If you're using Google Analytics or something similar to track users who don't have an account, you should organize your analysis by cohort. This means that you'll want to analyze any users who visited the site and did a little browsing in March, then came back in May along with all other users who did their initial visit in March. Do not lump them in with those who first visited in May. This is important because you may be changing the site over time, so different messages may be reaching different segments. Good analytics are about isolating the partial effect of a single variable and cohort analysis helps you do that. Notes on how to set this up are at Alexandercowan.com/webanalytics.

Partnerships

To Be or Not to Be

The successful high-tech business is increasingly a pack animal, so running with the right pack can increasingly make or break your business. Partnerships are hard. Actually, that's not true. Partnerships are easy to form yet hard to make successful. A classic failure mode is two CEOs meet at a trade show, hit it off, and tell their overworked managers to form a partnership. The partnership lacks a clear objective, definition of success, and wastes time for each company until it dies on the vine.

A necessary precursor to successful partnerships are for both parties to define a clear objective, the value they ascribe to it, what they'll have to invest to make it successful, and how they'll measure success on a progress basis. Table 8.1 provides a set of good and bad signal traits you should consider in a prospective partnership.

Partnerships at Enable Quiz

With daily operations at Enable Quiz progressing nicely, Andrew embarked on his discovery process with partners. Enable Quiz's goal was to find partners to enhance sales and on-boarding. It had several candidates already using the system—firms that did temporary technical staffing and training, learning management system vendors, and technical trainers. After talking to some potential partners, Andrew obtained a few important facts, most of them promising:

- There was a material level of interest among partners to sell the solution.
- The partners felt Enable Quiz's pricing was on the low side, which led Andrew to assume they would not require large discounts.
- The partners' customer base resembled the profile of firms Andrew was acquiring as direct customers.
- The partners would want to be able to sell their own quiz banks, which would require development at Enable Quiz.
- Some partners would prefer an OEM model where Enable Quiz re-brands a site to look like the partners' site; others would prefer to refer customers to Enable Quiz and be able to sell their own question banks.
- The partners had a lot of good—and many similar—ideas on how to improve the system.

Trait	Good	Bad	
Market and Sales Channel	Nothing drives a partnership like quick, incremental sales, all the better if the new sales partner serves a new or underserved market. One of the most successful partnerships we have at Leonid Systems is with a company called SIPhon Networks that sells our products in Europe to the same type of customer we have in the North America.	A less attractive partnership is one for an unproven market or a market you or one of your partners already serve.	**Table 8.1** **Good and Bad Partnership Traits**
Pricing	You only need to offer the partner minimal discounts.	You need to offer deep discounts. This, coupled with a "bad" on one of the other items, could push the partnership into negative territory for you.	
Customer Base	An existing, substantial population of joint customers is evidence there's a customer-driven relevance to the partnership.	If not, you should ask yourself why not and whether the new customers are strategic to the partner in question.	
Development	The partnership requires no new development or merely front-end customizations. This is something to consider in your design phase. If you think private-label partnerships are likely (where another company sells your product with its label), you'll want to build in simple, supportable front-end customizations as a key use case.	The partnership requires substantial additional development, and the partner is unwilling to make arrangements to defray the cost.	
Support	The partner takes responsibility for technical support as well as sales.	You're taking on the burden of product support for the partner. A classic sore point for high-tech partnerships is that the new partner underinvests in quality sales and operational expertise, and you end up supporting a lot of unhappy customers who have the wrong expectations about your product.	
Domain Expertise	The partner has strong domain expertise in your area. This will reduce your cost to support the partner in areas, like sales, technical operations, and general operations.	The customer has no knowledge of your domain. This will drive your costs in support.	
Working-Level Contacts	Once you start engaging, the working level contacts are productive and require little prodding to make progress.	The working-level contacts don't breathe their own air. The work takes constant prodding from management.	

Concerning the improvements to the system, the chief recommendations from partners were better online help and how-to instructions. Andrew knew his neglect of more extensive help and how-to instructions had been hurting them. With the general availability (GA) release, he considered the help to be the bare minimum acceptable. It included a solid overview and description of all the application's functions. He knew the system needed more material on how and why to create and use quizzes. Teaching customers how and why to use the product constituted the essence of his core discipline, marketing, and the principle applied to everything from Legos to lumber. The irony irked him, though not as much as the fact that he didn't have enough time to sit down and solve the problem. No one else at Enable Quiz had the background for such a task either. He could use an outside firm to formulate the how-to instructions, but finding a firm that understood skills management and the process would be expensive and too slow.

Andrew needed a partner that could help improve the site's online help and individual on-boarding capabilities, serve as a guinea pig for the partner sales/OEM program, and hopefully act as a reference for a successful sales and content partnership. The solution hit him as he was thumbing through stats for some smaller customers: Customers set up by Minucci Brothers had outstanding usage levels. The Minucci Brothers had spent the past 20 years in the discipline of corporate skills management. It helped companies define the skills their employees needed, assess that skill level at the employee level, and then (verifiably) close the skills gap with training. The company had shown Andrew its methodology before, but he'd been in a hurry and had not paid much attention. It seemed like a good candidate for partnership, but before Andrew went further, he wanted to get a sense of how much work they were looking at to allow partners to sell their own quiz banks.

Andrew put together a few thoughts for Mike in the form of a brief functional description (FD) for the initial rollout of the quiz store. They worked out a plan to roll out a minimum viable definition of the quiz store to see how it did, with Minucci Brothers acting as the primary guinea pigs. It was a good partnership for both parties since the Minuccis had been asking about a platform to sell their own quiz banks. The initial version would not allow partners to create their own quiz banks: they would have to submit them to Enable Quiz, and all the billing and payments for the partners would be manual. It was basic but it worked fine as a way to try things out on a limited scale. The key questions Andrew wanted to be able to answer about the question bank feature before investing further were the following:

- Are there partners out there who want to create and market these banks? Will they do it on Enable Quiz?
  - He knew of Minucci Brothers, a few other similar firms, and HAL, a large consulting firm his team had met through Ray, the Enable Quiz chairman. That was a good start. At first, Andrew figured his team

members would need to wait to launch the store until they got out of Alpha with Minucci Brothers. Mike suggested they could put a link up on the page, soliciting partners to fill out a sign-up form if they wanted to market their own quiz banks. Once Enable Quiz was ready, they could bring these new partners online right away and have additional data on who was interested in the meantime.

- What is the support and operational cost of doing this right?
  - Andrew figured they'd get a good sense of this supporting Minucci Brothers.
- Beyond the obvious basics, what do the partners want from the new feature?
  - They'd be getting feedback from Minucci Brothers that they could use here. Andrew would demo a prototype to a few other customers.

Mike explained that the ''quiz store'' feature would take some rework and new plumbing. However, their ability to roll with that was a feature of the adaptive processes they had adopted. When Andrew apologized for the rework, Mike told him about his trip to Tibet. Tibetan monks create these fantastic sand paintings on the ground, which are detailed and beautiful, and any one of them could go in a museum. Once they complete the sand paintings, the monks stand up, grab a broom, and sweep it all away. Mike's point is that you have to take that kind of attitude about rework. It's not to say you should tear up what you have and make changes on a whim, but when you look at successful products that falter, a resistance to fundamental change is often the culprit.

Enable Quiz and Minucci Brothers

Andrew got Richard Minucci on the phone that afternoon. To audit their on-boarding process and update the user help, he offered Minucci Brothers cash compensation at their usual rates and a preferred position on the partners' page they were going to create on Enablequiz.com for nine months. Richard had a few small reservations about splashing their secret sauce all over the Enable Quiz website but agreed that the mastery was in the doing and the opportunity for exposure outweighed any downside.

Andrew mentioned that, though direct solicitation would be inappropriate, he'd gladly introduce Richard Minucci to some of Enable Quiz's largest customers with a clear description of what Minucci Brothers offered. This excited Richard since his company had hired some new personnel to expand outside its current base.

They agreed that the engagement would consist of the following:

- Interviews with a dozen sample customers to assess the on-boarding process.
  - Minucci Brothers would investigate the following:
    - Why the customer bought the product.
    - What skills management program the customer had in place.
    - Who was involved in rolling out the system.
    - How they planned to roll out the product.
    - The status of their rollout.
- A series of write-ups and videos describing best practices in employee skills management.
  - How to use technical quizzes in a job interview settings.
  - How to define specific skills requirements by job role.
  - How to formulate quizzes to measure how employees stack up against the skill requirements for their jobs.
    - How to communicate a company-wide skills management program as a professional development opportunity for employees (and not a pass/fail exam that puts their employment at risk).
  - How to formulate training to close skills gaps.
  - How to follow up with assessments to close the loop and ensure the per employee skills targets were reached.
- Sample project plans for a skills management program.
- Case studies with three successful customers.

Minucci Brothers dove into the project with gusto as soon as the ink dried on the agreement. It had completed its assessments within three weeks. The results reflected their mutual hunches on the situation but provided important detail on its resolution: at most of the inactive customers, Human Resource (HR) managers had been signing up for the system, doing some initial setup (usually not well), and then passing the system along to functional managers who were to use the system to quiz their staff against their required skill set. The functional managers agreed that the whole thing was a good idea in principle. However, the HR department and/or superiors hadn't explained the system and its capabilities well to them. Consequently, doing the quizzes got put on the functional managers' B list and eventually dropped into the void where projects that aren't important enough to get done go to die.

The results thrilled Andrew. Minucci Brothers had done an outstanding job with its forensic analysis of customer on-boarding. All the customers who had participated in the interviews called Andrew to catch up and thank him for his following up on their account. To top it all off, most had ordered additional quiz banks. The interviews showed that since most companies' HR departments generally weren't familiar enough with their firms' technical disciplines, they often ordered too few or not the right number of quiz banks. On seeing this less-than-optimal set of quiz banks, the functional managers had assumed they had to write up most of the questions themselves, further delaying (indefinitely it seemed in many cases) their getting the quizzes to their staff. Once the functional managers realized they could order formulated quiz banks for most of what they needed, they upped their subscriptions and accelerated their plans to roll out use of the system.

The new online help was online three weeks following the interviews, and the results were visible six weeks after that. Minucci Brothers was happily selling its own quiz banks. Andrew was ready to approach other partners with a success story and a system he knew worked.

Focus, Focus, Focus

Prospective customers and partners will start to bring you proposals once you get on the map and many of these will be outside your core strategy. It's easy to say yes, especially when money is attached. So, how do you decide when to sign and when to pass? It's easy to say, "I'm sticking to my knitting." In other words, don't dilute your core strategy. But you might need the money and this might be the market speaking to you about what you should be doing.

Here are a few minimum qualifying questions you should make sure to answer explicitly:

- How do the numbers look?

  What is the initial and ongoing expense of the project versus the revenue attached? Roughly, how do these shake out over time? Work with your technical team to determine a way to make a coarse estimate without taking up a lot of their time. The engineer's inclination will usually be to make a detailed analysis. However, this can absorb huge amounts of key engineering time and will probably be more than you need for the first-order decision making. Don't underestimate the expense of maintaining what you build.
- How far off the path are you going?

  In other words, does the technical and operational infrastructure you have to execute for this deal diverge substantially from your core strategy? Is it 100 percent different than your current plan? Does some of the new infrastructure serve your current strategy?

- What is the extended opportunity?

  What other opportunities would building new infrastructure create? Are those good opportunities for your firm?

- What is the effect on soft resources?

  You'll estimate the big, direct items like engineering time and product support infrastructure. A lot of new partnerships and ventures fail because of management attention. Is key management talent available to watch this new undertaking develop, make sure it's bearing out as planned, and pivot as needed?

- How deep is the feedback loop?

  How much do you have to put in to validate your key assumptions on why this new item is a good idea? This question may be one of the most important. When you're operating in an uncertain environment, you must gather some empirical validation of your key assumptions before you bet the farm.

Figure 8.4

IP Phone

One area where we regularly encounter this kind of question at Leonid Systems is with our visual phone management portal. It works in a simple way: If you have an office phone on your desk, you can go to an online portal to change the function of the various buttons on your phone, something like Figure 8.4. A few dominant manufacturers of these office phones exist, so we rolled out support for these models first. However, we regularly get requests for other manufacturers and models. We understand how much it will cost us to support a new model since we've done it a few times. On the revenue side, we see how many of our customers are using the phones in question and whether they're interested in buying a new plug-in for the phone. If the revenue isn't attractive enough, we ask the customers or manufacturers if they're interested in paying a nonrecurring fee to offset our development costs. Depending on the circumstances, we may offer to rebate them this cost against a percentage of our directly related sales. This doesn't take us too far off our core product development strategy since we have a plug-in framework for supporting new devices and a new device is one more plug-in to support. This is a tactical item so there isn't an extended opportunity. We support this new phone, which helps us sell a few add-ons to our software and maybe bring in a few accounts that wouldn't have purchased the core software without the new device. The effect on soft resources is small, in that someone in management needs to work with the manufacturer to get test devices for our lab. Other than joint selling (which is a bonus for us), there isn't much other management attention required beyond the core product implementation and support required. On the feedback loop, we always roll out a new device with the minimum capabilities to see how things go in the field. Do end users like it? What do they use most? What do they ask for? What unexpressed needs can we uncover by talking to them? Only after having the new device out in the field for three to six months do we roll in extended support.

Let's look at an example with Enable Quiz. Andrew gets an exciting new opportunity from one of his old mentors to build a new certification program for a company in the medical industry, called Acme Hospitals. Few sectors are growing as quickly and reliably as the medical one. It's like being handed the keys to the oil fields in Saudi Arabia. It's not 90 degrees off from Enable Quiz's core strategy, but it's at least 45 degrees off. Enable Quiz is focused on quick, casual skills assessment quizzes, and this would require a more formal exam format, including possible compliance with stringent regulations the health care industry has to observe. This gives Mike pause. The project will require a fair amount of work at a time when the team members are struggling to keep on updates to their core product. After some consideration, they settle on the following proposal to Andrew's mentor:

- Enable Quiz is interested.
- Enable Quiz will initially support Acme Hospitals with its standard product and will work with Acme Hospitals to prototype the product it wants.
    - In addition to product functions, this includes processes and support Acme Hospital will need to create.
- This process is estimated at three to six months.
- During this time, Andrew will work with Acme Hospital on the specific product modifications it requires.
- Acme Hospital will consider a prepayment of roughly $70,000 to defray initial development at Enable Quiz.

The goal is to retain the opportunity, and get it started in a constructive way, but avoid biting into Enable Quiz's core engineering and operations resources, which are currently stretched to the max.

The Chasm and the Hockey Stick

Your early sales are the most thrilling, yet it's important they don't lull you into falsely presuming you're on a reliable sales trend. Many promising tech companies have ended up as a flash in the pan after a few early successes. In a traditional business, if you set up a better lemonade stand, so to speak, than the guy next door, you'll do well, increasing your sales on a linear basis.

Technology has quirks. Depending on your product's novelty, you're likely to see your customer development progress across something like the functions in Figure 8.5. Most importantly, these functions involve a crucial (and perilous) crossover from the early market to the mainstream market, with a related spike in sales.

Sociologist and writer Everett Rogers (along with a few others) came up with the idea of a technology adoption lifecycle. Author Geoff Moore enhanced this theory's application to technology by identifying a chasm between early adopter and early majority segments. The basic idea is that you have two segments that will buy a useful product early on when it's still high risk: the innovators and the early adopters. The next segment, and the first big one, is the early majority and it's more averse to risk. This is where the chasm comes into play, transitioning from the early adopters to the early majority. You need a way to establish a beachhead in the early majority, or you'll exhaust the early market and fizzle, without having achieved mainstream success.

The hockey stick is a classic portrait of revenue growth at a successful tech startup. The blade (relatively flat) is where you're in the early market perfecting your product and customer development strategies. The shaft is the sales spike that starts once you've crossed Moore's "chasm" and are successful with the mainstream segments. Figure 8.5 summarizes these two functions and their relationship.

The two key questions you should ask yourself to prepare are the following:

1. How big is your chasm?
2. How do you cross it?

Chasm size is a function of three things: market type, novelty, and the need for a whole product. Crossing it requires a highly focused plan to establish a beachhead in the mainstream market and assiduous execution.

Market Type

Market type isn't like blood type, and you can't administer a test and get a definitive result. Two primary types exist: new and existing. In a new market, you're introducing something your customer doesn't have today. You could say that televisions were an innovation in the existing market for home entertainment, but most marketers would classify the initial market for TV sets as a new one. Flat screen televisions are a new segment within the existing market for televisions.

If you're entering a new market, the good news is you have lots of upside and you may make history. The bad news is that it will probably take a fair amount of time and money to create and grow your new market.

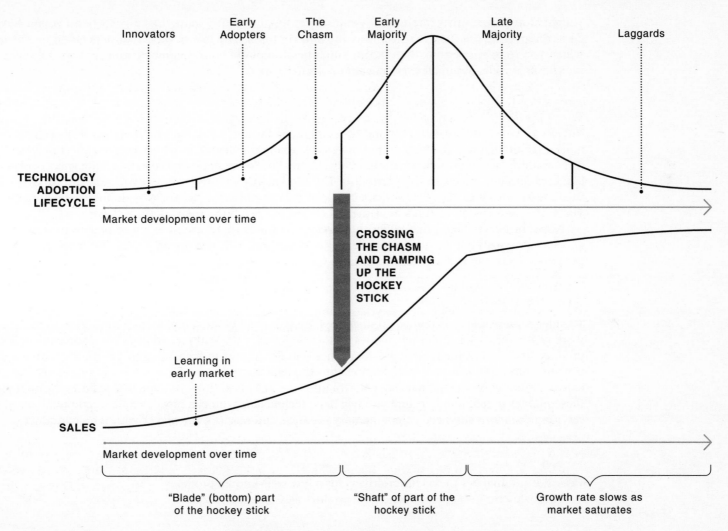

Innovators   Early Adopters   The Chasm   Early Majority   Late Majority   Laggards

TECHNOLOGY ADOPTION LIFECYCLE

Market development over time

CROSSING THE CHASM AND RAMPING UP THE HOCKEY STICK

Learning in early market

SALES

Market development over time

"Blade" (bottom) part of the hockey stick

"Shaft" of part of the hockey stick

Growth rate slows as market saturates

Figure 8.5   The Chasm and the Hockey Stick

Shepherd your resources carefully. If you're entering an existing market, the good news is you have less to do in discovering the market's size, viability, and contours. The bad news is that depending on the degree to which you're re-segmenting the market, you'll need to outdo your incumbent competitors. In a new market, the chasm is wide, but in an existing market, it's narrower.

Novelty and Network Effects

Novelty comes into play with new and re-segmented markets. By definition, there's little novelty to a product in an existing market. The basic test of novelty is asking the degree to which you're expecting your buyers to do something new versus do something they already do. For example, social networking was novel before sites like LinkedIn and Facebook popularized it. The Walkman was novel when it was introduced, Many cynics at the time asked things like, "People have music in the car and at the house. Why do they need portable music?" The more your success requires fundamental changes in behavior, the wider the chasm.

Network effects take place when the product becomes more useful as more people have it. Telephones and social networking are good examples—not much fun with just one of them. The more your product has network effects, the wider your chasm, since it increases the stakes for your reticent early majority segment.

Need for Whole Product

The idea for a whole or extended product is where you need other complimentary products to make a product work well for the user. Office telephones that use voice over IP (VoIP) technology are a good example of such a product. The phones themselves are great since you don't have to have separate telephony wiring and service in your office. You can plug VoIP phones into the data network you have for your computers and ride your existing Internet services, cancelling your traditional voice lines. However, you will need application servers for these phones to talk to others and you will need technicians who can install, explain, and maintain these new services. The more you need complimentary products and services, the bigger your whole product.

Examples

Table 8.2 summarizes these chasm-drivers for a few well-known products.

These descriptions apply to when the product was first introduced.

Item	Market Type	Novelty and Network Effects	Need for Whole Product	Chasm Size
Skype: PC calling service	New: PC calling was small to nonexistent in 2003.	Novelty was high since little to no PC-to-PC calling existed at the time. Network effects were high since it was a closed network.	Low: download and go	Large
Office VoIP Phones	Existing: These phones resegmented the existing enterprise telephony market.	The novelty to the user was low but high to those providing the whole product (service providers, installers) since the technologies were so different. The network effects were low since these phones always connect to the existing phone system through gateways.	Very high: Beyond the new phones, a whole new marketplace of service providers, equipment providers, and field technicians was required.	Medium to large
Angry Birds mobile game	Existing: Other mobile games existed.	Novelty was moderate: Though it helped popularize mobile gaming, many apps and games existed in the market. The network effects were very low since the game is a single player.	No whole product was required at the time. The existing development, deployment, and online sales infrastructure were all that people required.	Small
Original Palm Pilot: A personal digital assistant	New: Few such devices existed at the time.	The novelty was high: People wondered, "Why do I need a PDA?" The network effects were relatively low since these were mostly non-networked devices at the time.	Moderate: PC software for synchronization, applications were required.	Large
Enable Quiz	Existing: Though the use of lightweight quizzes is infrequent, there is a large existing market in online testing and e-learning.	The novelty for the target market is relatively high. Most employers don't do a lot with structured quizzing of new employees or internal skills audits. The network effects are low.	TBD: Assuming Enable Quiz remains happy with the amount of customers it can get through touchless online sales, it's low. However, it needs to test this assumption as it moves into the mainstream market. It's possible someone will need to be out in the field introducing the product, possibly a partner.	Medium

Table 8.2

Chasm Examples

Crossing the Chasm

On the one hand, I would say chasms have tended to narrow some over the last few years. For example, in enterprise software stakes were higher for customers when they had to buy a server, install your application, and more. The cloud and its corollary developments, like application stores, have lowered the cost of acquiring new technology products and, in the same vein, the cost of switching between technology products. However, The chasm remains, is very real, and is pivotal to the success of any tech business. Your sales won't keep rising and moving to the right unless you embed your product with the mainstream market, and to do that, you must cross the chasm. The key is determining how you'll pry open a big enough beachhead in the early majority to spur growth in the segment (and those that follow it). The most natural thing to do is to find early majority customers who resemble your early adopters as closely as possible. Obviously, these people don't wear buttons classifying themselves or their companies. One clue that you have an early majority customer is when you're subject to a standardized selling process, versus getting special, expedited treatment from an interested party. If you need to sweeten the deal for these customers, better to focus on extra, free service than lowering your product prices. If you're selling enterprise software, for instance, you can offer extra consulting to help make the applicable project a success.

One key point is frequently made about crossing the chasm: You need to be prepared for massive scaling. Before you cross the chasm, you have to carefully shepherd your resources. It can easily take two to five or more years to develop a new market and see major sales growth on the other side of the chasm. Before crossing the chasm, you should be a lean, learning organization, working to perfect your model and establish a beachhead in the mainstream market. After you cross the chasm, you need to be ready to scale. But scaling before you cross the chasm is a mistake.

Managing Feedback at Enable Quiz

Customer complaints and the trouble tickets they rode in on dropped with the GA release. Snoetrope's useability fixes had worked essentially as planned. The flow of tickets was above where Andrew and Mike wanted them to be, but they had identified more areas they could improve.

Getting to GA had been hectic, messy, and exhausting, but Andrew felt good about where they were. They got the cows out of the ditch, figured out why they stampeded the ditch, and the initial data post-GA got them on the right track.

They needed to make sure they were attuned to the early warning signs of any similar issues. By way of comparison, whenever NASA does anything to the Space Shuttle, it looks at how it might break and then instruments it, meaning it figures out how to detect flaws in the component, be it hardware or software. Building software has similarities: You instrument what the software is doing in logs so you know if something's screwy. Business processes are another abstraction away, but they have similarities, too.

Specifically, in a mass-market product like Enable Quiz, you need to have a clear view of why you're receiving tickets and how you're resolving them. Andrew noticed the form they were using for tickets didn't have much structure. This hit home when Andrew was going through the tickets to determine the patterns on the initial outbreak of customer issues: The process proved to be more manual than they expected. To provide better early warning of issues and quick analysis, they fixed on a two-tier classification system and a mandatory post-mortem field on the tickets. All these fields have drop-down menus with a specific list of issues, issue classes, and post-mortem resolutions.

Having an "other" class is okay, but if you let users fill in any information, you'll continue to have data you have to sift through by hand. For example, a tier 1 classification might be "Quiz Management," and a tier 2 classification might be "Trouble Sending Quiz." A post-mortem might be "Education Issue," "Documentation Gap," or "Bug." Ideally, the team members want to be able to pull up a report on tickets over time and immediately see the reasons behind tickets and how they're fixing them. That will make the job of continuous improvement easier. They were accepting tickets from customers over e-mail, but since the lack of structure in an e-mail doesn't allow for enforcing this kind of structure on submissions, they decide to remove that as an option for submitting tickets. Now any customer submitting a ticket over e-mail receives an auto-responder directing them to file it on the Enable Quiz customer portal.

Learning When (and How) to Say No

It's as important to learn to say no to features that aren't a good fit as it is to recognize ones that you want to include. Adding a feature is like getting a dog: You have to consider the cost of buying it, but the real cost is in the maintenance (ongoing documentation, testing, and support in the case of software).

Enable Quiz just got a big customer opportunity from a temporary staffing firm called GoTemps, which wants them to be able to query their internal Learning Management System (LMS) for their list of students. Other than that, they love the product and are ready to sign up for what Andrew thinks will be Enable Quiz's largest subscription. Mike and Andrew discuss the details.

Mike believes that having to build an interface to GoTemps system versus having them query the Enable Quiz system represents much more work. If Enable Quiz is the client and the customer has the server, that means Enable Quiz will have to build a new custom client interface to talk to the customer system, and it will have to build a custom interface for any future customers who want the same thing. Mike recommends they instead expose the Enable Quiz API to the customer, who can pull down whatever they want. Enable Quiz can't offer that at the moment, but the API is there. Mike just has to set it up to allow individual customers to authenticate to it directly.

Mike knows that this might sounds like an engineer's quibble, but it does have significant implications for their development program. Being able to integrate with customers' systems is a great way to deepen the relationship and increase retention of those prize customers. But pulling from their systems would make Enable Quiz the client and the customer system the server. That means Enable Quiz will have to do custom development and maintain that development on a go-forward basis for every new customer of that type. Mike can organize it around a plug-in framework to the quiz application, but it will be a lot of work. He'll have to test each of those custom clients on each new release, as an example, which will probably end up to be a dozen hours per new release per custom client. If the customers change their system, Enable Quiz will have to update its software and retest. On the other hand, if Enable Quiz publishes its API and sets up the customer to pull or push what they want from/to Enable Quiz, then Enable Quiz can build, document, maintain and support a single API for GoTemps and everyone else that comes along.

Andrew is concerned: He did mention the idea to the customer's IT Director, but he didn't sound too keen. Mike suggests that it is more work for GoTemps, which is probably why they didn't like it. If they're smart, they'll realize they're the guinea pig and will be resistant. Mike suggests they volunteer to do the extra work the customer would have to do on a custom client to pull from their system and instead help them pull from the Enable Quiz system. Then Enable Quiz will have a precedent, a success story for other customers and the documentation and systems to help others build interfaces to talk to their system.

Andrew hated saying "no" to such a large customer. But his response was more, "How about this?" The IT Director wasn't enthusiastic at first and asked if Enable Quiz really wanted the business. After Andrew confidently explained their direction on the product and their willingness to help with development in exchange for their being a new customer on the API, the IT Director warmed to the idea, and Enable Quiz won the business.

Henceforth, Enable Quiz puts every feature request in one of three buckets with clear direction for their customer facing teams on how to handle the requests based on their buckets (see Table 8.3).

The previous example was in the "C" bucket, a case where the development wasn't a good option for Enable Quiz. Hence, they worked toward an alternative with the customer.

This is not to say that you should do your product development based just on requests from customers. Part of your job is to think of things your customers will like that haven't occurred to them. But you need to

Bucket	Notes
A	This feature is a good idea and marketable to our base at large. It will go into scheduling, and we'll have a date for you in due time.
B	This isn't a bad feature, but it isn't marketable to our base at large. It's in the queue, but our B class items rarely make it into implementation. We have a rough estimate of the time needed and if it's important enough you can pay to accelerate the feature.
C	We think there's a better way to approach this. Your point of contact will be in touch to make sure we understand your objectives and suggest possible alternatives.

Table 8.3

Feature
Requests

have a clear process for responding when the request comes in. If your product is in the consumer space, you won't be able to respond to all these requests individually, and you will be less likely to get structured requests like this. Remember, adding a new feature is like getting a dog: The purchase price is one thing, but the real cost lies in the cost of maintaining the animal (feature) over time. If you do a feature on a paid basis and it's a stand-alone for the customer, make sure you consider the ongoing cost of maintaining (testing, documentation) and supporting the feature.

Post-Mortems

The objective of post-mortems is to avoid repeating the same mistakes and, more generally, consider how to do things better. Don't push too hard for perfection on these exercises. The most important thing is to do them and exit with specific recommendations for next time. The post-mortem should conclude with a basic write up that has at least the following elements:

a. Description of what's considered
b. What went well
    a. Why?
c. What went badly
    a. Why?
d. Specific recommendations

Table 8.4

Item	Results	Recommendations	Other Notes
Communication of Designs for New Features	Many hours were spent on nonaligned implementation of some features.	1. Development manager will complete daily demos and reviews with each developer. 2. Development and Product Management will review design documentation at least weekly to see if additional detail is required.	

Table 8.4 is an example of such a recommendation.

Over the course of the post-mortem, you will want to involve as many of the relevant parties as possible and dig as deeply as possible. The goal is to look as far inward as possible at the root causes of why things happened. For example, let's say someone tripped over a cable, unplugged a server, and caused an outage of the service. You're not looking to understand why someone was clumsy and tripped. You're looking to understand whether the server room is a mess and it's easy to trip on things, why there wasn't more redundancy in place, and how quickly the organization was able to detect and fix the issue.

Some organizations find that getting everyone together works well. Some find that smaller discussions work well. The important thing is to avoid having the exercise devolve into a blame game. Post-mortems should be about looking at how the organization is performing and what it can do to perform better. Save the personal discussions for between managers and staff.

Scaling

Fast forward a year and a half, and Enable Quiz is a huge success. The numbers are off the charts. Andrew wakes up at night in a thrall of exhilaration and fear. What does he do now? It's not just a matter of cashing bigger checks. A lot of things happen with the business to keep moving forward. A lot of things could go wrong. Here are a few things he should consider:

- A big plane flies a lot like a small one.

  Running a company that's going through a large increase in scale is difficult and it does require change. One key facet is to remember that you're still in the same business, and you need to keep doing the same basic things that made you successful in the first place. You'll need to operate at a higher level of abstraction since more people will be involved, but that doesn't mean having stifling bureaucracy and process. You're still a learning machine.

- It's not your company anymore.

  If you're the founder, you'll have a strong feeling of ownership over the whole company, as well you should. That said, it's not your company anymore. You're responsible for commitments you've made to customers, employees and their paychecks, and probably shareholders as well. It's your responsibility to do what's right for the company. Think of the company as its own entity rather than an extension of yourself.

- Things have to happen without you.

  We reviewed department missions, job roles, and process in Chapter 7. If you have too many e-mails, if the whole company's waiting on you for critical items, look at your infrastructure to figure out why. Think about it this way if it makes you feel better: If on any given Tuesday, you decide to stay home and watch Animal Planet, the company should be able to function fine without you.

- Bring in talent.

  If you've never run a company (or company division) before, you may want to bring in a professional manager. Management requires a particular kind of talent that only sometimes coincides with what it takes to be a successful tech entrepreneur. Companies have fizzled because they failed to bring in professional management or they fizzled because the founders left. No silver bullet exists, but it's important to keep an open mind to the possibility.

What Now?

Starting a tech business is ultimately a creative endeavor. Though the tools here will give you a big leg up, the most important thing you'll do is dedicate yourself to your users. Most enduring technology franchises have a singular focus on their users. The reverse is also true. Tinker relentlessly and you'll find what works. Make sure you've set out explicit assumptions about the business and the means to determine whether the business is meeting those or needs a revision to its strategy.

Make sure you're enjoying the endeavor, and others will too.

I hope you enjoyed the book, and I wish you good luck. If the spirit moves you, please share your experiences and ideas on the book's website, Alexandercowan.com, or by e-mailing me at alex@alexandercowan.com.

—Alex Cowan

Chapter 8 Summary

1. Funnel

   Use AIDA**OR** to build an explicit, measurable funnel that's linked to your key assumptions.

2. The Power of Partnerships

   Look to expand the business through partnerships. Since partnerships can be a distraction as well, make sure they're tied to revenue in a timeframe you can live with.

3. Mind the Chasm

   Don't assume you can extrapolate your sales growth. Tech startups undergo a critical transition from early markets to mainstream markets, and many don't cross that gap. After your early sales, your focus needs to be on establishing a beachhead in the mainstream market.

4. Rigidly Classify Customer Complaints

   At NASA, every little piece of the Space Shuttle was instrumented to detect problems. Likewise, wherever you track customer calls and complaints, you should have a fixed classification scheme so you collect quantitative data about where your customer issues originate and how you resolved them.

5. Know When to Say No

   Particularly if you sell to businesses, you'll end up with a lot of specialized requests that you have to decline. In addition to considering how much you can do how soon for your core market, in accepting requests for new features, you should place them in one of three buckets:

   Bucket A: The feature is a good idea and relevant to your base at large; prioritize it with the rest of the requests you have.

   Bucket B: The feature isn't detrimental to the product but is not relevant to your base at large; only implement if you receive compensating payment from your customer or that customer is critical.

   Bucket C: The feature is detrimental to the product; decline the request, suggesting alternative approaches to meet the customer's needs.

6. The Post-Mortem: Just Do It

Above all, get the post-mortems done. Make sure the output is specific, with actionable recommendations for next time. Peel back the onion as much as you can on root cause, but avoid the blame game at all costs.

7. Scaling

You're the same company you were, but you need to get bigger. Don't forget the things that made you successful, but prepare to operate at a larger scale. That means you should treat the company as its own entity and ensure the organization is strong enough to function without you, at least for small periods of time. Go on vacation. Consider bringing in professional management talent if you feel growing the business is outside your comfort zone.

Checklist

1. Funnel

Do you have an explicit funnel concept? Are all the stages measurable and linked to your key assumptions?

2. Partnerships

Are partnerships important? If so, have you gone through and identified what you want from them?

3. The Chasm

Have you identified a strategy for establishing a beachhead in the early majority segment?

4. Feedback Loop

However customer issues reach you, is there a structure to classifying them where you can easily look at where they're coming from to figure out what's driving issues?

5. Feature Requests

Do you have a process for explicitly classifying requests?

Specialty Reading by Topic

If you want to know more about ...	... then read
Funnels	Analytics around the Enable Quiz funnel are available on Alexandercowan.com/funnel.
Marketing Online	*The New Rules of Marketing & PR*, by David Meerman Scott
	David Scott was an early leader taking corporate marketing efforts online, and this book provides many practical examples of how to promote a product and/or company online.
Crossing the Chasm	*Crossing the Chasm*, by Geoffrey Moore
	This is a high-tech classic, putting a modern take on the technology adoption lifecycle.
Building Enduring Companies	*Built to Last*, by Jim Collins and Jerry I. Porras
	This business classic addresses key features of enduring companies.

Index